Stand Down

STAND DOWN

*How Social Justice Warriors
Are Sabotaging America's Military*

JAMES HASSON

REGNERY GATEWAY

Regnery Gateway™ is a trademark of Salem Communications Holding Corporation;
Regnery® is a registered trademark of Salem Communications Holding Corporation

Cataloging-in-Publication data on file with the Library of Congress

ISBN 978-1-62157-918-2
ebook ISBN 978-1-62157-919-9

Published in the United States by
Regnery Gateway, an imprint of
Regnery Publishing
A Division of Salem Media Group
300 New Jersey Ave NW
Washington, DC 20001
www.Regnery.com

Manufactured in the United States of America

10 9 8 7 6 5 4 3 2 1

Books are available in quantity for promotional or premium use. For information on discounts and terms, please visit our website: www.Regnery.com.

To Lieutenant Colonel Ed Doyle, US Army,
who inspired me to join the Army; and to my grandfather,
Lieutenant Colonel Charles E. Rice, USMC

CONTENTS

PREFACE

The Army that I entered as a second lieutenant during President Obama's initial years in office was nothing like the Army I left in late 2015. It was smaller, less-equipped, and struggled to maintain its vehicles and aircraft. Sequestration—the deep and broad cuts in defense spending imposed by the Budget Control Act of 2011—and the massive personnel cuts ordered by President Obama provoked a readiness crisis that received, fortunately, a great deal of attention. I lived through it myself. For several months in 2013, at the height of sequestration, my unit was told not to use our vehicles during training because we lacked the funds to repair them if they broke down. We deployed to Afghanistan the following year well aware that we could never recover those lost training hours.

But the lasting readiness crisis is not the disrepair into which our planes, ships, and armored vehicles have fallen. Those problems, as real and grave as they are, can be remedied by a series of appropriations bills that prioritize necessary programs over congressional pet projects and pork-barrel spending. No, the lasting readiness crisis is the priority that has been given to progressive hobbyhorses over the needs of ground soldiers, and it is the continuing result of the Obama administration's eight-year social engineering campaign against our armed forces. The effects of this campaign are often hidden from the public, partly because they are harder to quantify than troop levels or combat-ready brigades and partly because only a narrow sliver of society experiences them directly. But the progressive policies of the Obama era, if unreversed, (and halfway through the Trump era, they have not been fully reversed), pose a greater long-term threat to the readiness of our armed forces than any budget cut. They will continue to undermine readiness long after we rebuild the manpower of our hollowed-out force and return to a pre-2009 training tempo.

The troubling policies discussed in this book reach the very core of our military. They invert the traditional military ethos, placing the affirmation of individual identity above the needs of the unit. They shift the military's resources and focus away from the central task of preparing for and winning wars. And because they continue to receive support in spite of their damage to combat readiness, they suggest that the military has a new purpose. These policies were not imposed overnight or unintentionally. Throughout his two terms of office, President Obama appointed hard-left ideologues to some of the most influential national security positions. Some of these figures are well known, others less so. But all of them played a role in shaping the military as it now stands. This book tells that story.

To be sure, veterans—and for that matter, most active service members more than six months removed from boot camp—are notorious for lamenting the "softness" of the current force and recalling the harder standards of the "old days." I pray that this book—and the service members it quotes—will not be viewed in that light. This is not a rant about the glory days. I offer a comprehensive discussion of purposeful, monumental changes to the military's culture. I examine policies set by persons who had no business setting military policy and had no idea what damage they were inflicting.

Certainly, progressive social policies are not the only contributors to the readiness crisis. A broken acquisition system and rigid promotion timelines, for instance, play a role. So do cultural and demographical changes: how do you maintain performance standards when 71 percent of millennials are not even eligible to join the military because they are obese, have criminal records, or lack a high school diploma or GED?[1] But some of those problems have been around for decades and are categorically distinct from the problems I write about; the others are the products of broader societal trends that are outside the scope of this book. It is important, however, to keep these other issues in mind as you read those discussed in this book, as they are the backdrop against which changes to the military's culture and policies are being made.

The issues I discuss in this book, moreover, are the subjects of some of the most contentious debates of our era, though they are among the least understood by the general public. It is all the more difficult to discuss these changes openly and honestly because the military is now manned by a tiny fraction of American society and military bases are often far from population centers, keeping much of the country in the dark about the damage these policy changes are doing at the ground level.

The changes I write about in this book took place during my military service, including my preparation for and deployment to eastern Afghanistan, so I am keenly aware of their effects. But this book is not a memoir. It is a cautionary work of journalism, a warning about the state of our armed forces, and an appeal to the American people to demand changes. The stakes are too high to leave these policies unchallenged.

Some of these topics are sensitive and complex. They are not easy to discuss in polite company, so many people shy away from them. Believe me, they are no easier to write about. But the well-being of our military affects the safety of every member of our society—to say nothing of the safety of the twenty-year-old soldiers we send to the battlefield—and this conversation is therefore necessary. I am not staking out a position in America's culture war. I am simply making an assertion about the fundamental purpose of our military and forcefully arguing against any policies that are incompatible with that purpose—whatever the merits of those policies might be in other contexts. And as you will see in the chapters to come, the social engineering of the hard left is incompatible with the military's sole mission of winning wars.

No one should think that these problems ended when Barack Obama left the White House. The disastrous effects of his policies on military readiness continue to the present day, and the longer those policies are left in place, the more damaging they become. That's why this conversation is so necessary.

I am not arguing that the military should follow "conservative" policies and shun "liberal" policies. The men and women of our armed forces hold views that span the political spectrum. I know infantrymen who were Bernie Bros in 2016 and Apache pilots who were early Trump supporters. No, the problem with left-wing identity politics in the military is not the distinction between the "right" politics and the "wrong" politics. As former Secretary of Defense and Marine General James Mattis has pointed out, the military is "conservative" in the most traditional sense of the word—it embraces "organizational conservatism" as a fundamental principle, with an eye towards mission accomplishment above all, versus a social or fiscal conservatism.[2] The problem is imposing on the military political goals *of any sort* instead of letting it pursue its apolitical mission.

The National Defense Authorization Act of 2017 directed the bipartisan National Defense Strategy Commission to assess the military's ability to execute the National Defense Strategy and "examine and make recommendations with respect to the national defense strategy of the United States."[3] The commission, composed of national security experts selected by the House Armed Services Committee—half by the Democrats and half by the Republicans—issued its report in 2018.

Thomas Spoehr, a retired Army lieutenant general who directs national defense studies at the Heritage Foundation, summarizes the key conclusions of the report:

> Numerous defense experts, both inside and outside of government, have been telling us the same thing for years.... The

Air Force says it needs 386 squadrons; they have 312. And the Army states it needs 500,000 active soldiers; it has only 476,000.[4]

The report finished with a dire warning: "America has reached the state of a full-blown national security crisis."[5] As you read about the priorities of the Obama appointees in the Department of Defense, keep that final sentence in mind: "America has reached the state of a full-blown national security crisis."

Public discussion of these issues is critical. The men and women of the military have no voice in this process. They are prohibited from speaking publicly about politics, have little to no money to donate, and wield precious little lobbying power. And while the draft once ensured that politicians' treatment of the military affected the broader society (even those politicians' own children), today's all-volunteer forces are at the mercy of government actors who are isolated from the political consequences of their decisions. As General Mattis warned in 2016, "Having so small a military that only one half of one percent of the public will be directly affected [by changes driven by progressive social engineering] and so inattentive a public ensures that political leaders pay no real price for diminishing combat effectiveness."[6] These social justice "demands," he added, "impose a burden the public and political leaders refuse to acknowledge and will only be evident in the aftermath of military failure."[7]

I am immensely proud to have been part of the military. I can say without reservation that it was the greatest endeavor of my life so far, and I would never take it back. I loved the men and women I served with—and I still do—and I care deeply about the welfare of those still serving (who include many members of my family). The US military has always comprised the very best our country has to offer, and it still does.

We owe it to the men and women we are sending overseas on our behalf to have this conversation.

James Hasson
Houston, Texas

FUNDAMENTAL TRANSFORMATION

"Our military has the power to lead the way—just as it has done before, driving change not only within the armed forces, but within American society as a whole.... So we are meeting frequently with the Pentagon's senior civilian and military leaders to generate bold initiatives that will make a real difference."[1]
—*Valerie Jarrett, senior advisor to President Obama*

"Do you think Russia and China and our other geopolitical enemies are spending their time on these types of social engineering polices? The answer is a deafening 'no.'"
—*A decorated Army infantry officer who recently resigned from active duty*

On a breezy night in Missouri just before the election of 2008, Senator Barack Obama stepped up to a microphone and promised an adoring crowd that "we are five days away from fundamentally transforming the United States of America."[2] And for one very distinct segment of American society over which he would exercise nearly complete control, he kept his promise: In many ways, today's military is almost unrecognizable from that of January 20, 2009.

This is the story of what will be President Obama's enduring legacy: the sacrifice of the combat readiness of our armed forces to the golden calves of identity politics and progressive ideology. The chapters to come will survey the damage, including a scandalous cover-up at Army Ranger School, an Army study discussing the need to remove "hyper-masculine traits" and "paternalism" from combat-arms units, "Safe Space" stickers on professors' doors at the Naval Academy, Air Force Academy leadership apologizing to cadets for a "microaggression" committed by a first sergeant who addressed grooming standards in an Academy-wide email, senior political appointees overruling the Chairman of the Joint Chiefs and ignoring extensive evidence provided by the Marine Corps that a policy change would make Marines less effective in combat, and much more. Those chapters draw from more than forty sources ranging from generals who held senior command positions and served at the highest levels of the Pentagon to infantry company commanders at the ground level, internal documents obtained through leaks and FOIA requests, contemporaneous correspondence between key stakeholders, and open sources.

Before examining the policies the Obama administration implemented, it's important to show just how unfamiliar most of its members were with the workings and culture of the military. It's even more important to emphasize the sharp differences in priorities between the administration and the senior military leaders who had to answer to it. Understanding these differences is essential to understanding what happened to the military from 2009 to 2017.

We must start at the very top. I will avoid broader political controversies and focus on what led President Obama to implement some of the most destructive military policies in recent history and the lessons we must learn if we hope to avoid similar problems in the future. Barack Obama's relations with the military were uneasy from the beginning of his presidency,[3] and they never much improved. One retired general complained that the commander in chief had "no interest in getting to know the military."[4]

In fact, all available evidence indicates that the president's preconceived notions about the military were similar to what one might hear at an anti-war conference in Berkeley. During his first presidential campaign, Obama told his supporters that the military needed to have enough resources because otherwise it would just be "air-raiding villages and killing civilians."[5] In a 2008 college commencement speech encouraging graduates to "serve abroad," Obama cited several laudable ways of serving overseas—the Peace Corps, community organizing, the United Way, "teaching folks about conservation," and working on renewable energy, among others—but he never mentioned serving in the military.[6]

Unsurprisingly, the inexperienced commander in chief appointed equally inexperienced politicos to oversee the military. As in any change of administrations, differences between the incoming Obama team and the outgoing Bush administration surfaced quickly. But these differences ran much deeper than tax policies or attitudes towards labor unions. The new Obama administration was packed with far-left ideologues who neither understood nor cared to understand the military now under their control. In their minds, it was a blunt-force tool for driving broader change within society as a whole.

Obama's choice of advisors, even those with no formal role in setting military policy, reveals much about his views of the military. Valerie Jarrett, for example, the most influential aide in the West Wing, a woman described as "ground zero in the Obama operation, the first couple's friend and consigliere,"[7] couldn't recognize a military officer if she bumped into one. Literally. More than two years into Obama's first term, Jarrett tapped General Peter Chiarelli on the shoulder at a reception and asked him to refill her glass of wine, mistaking the vice chief of staff of the United States Army for a waiter.[8] Indeed, Jarrett generally viewed men and women in uniform as personal staff. She demanded that a military chauffeur transport her to and from the White House, even though military escorts were historically reserved for top national security advisors.[9] Jarrett was so detached from the lives and concerns of service members that she posted a gaudy selfie with the actress Julia Louis-Dreyfus only a few hours after a terrorist killed four Marines and a sailor at a recruiting station in Chattanooga, Tennessee, in 2015.[10]

Obama's Defense Appointees Were Politicians First and Military Officials Only When Necessary

For the most part, senior military officers and the political appointees placed in charge of them by President Obama may as well have been from different planets. The appointees were almost all either civilians from top graduate schools who had worked in the private sector but had little or no military experience or former politicians who placed a premium on political considerations. Obama's branch secretaries—the secretary of the Army, secretary of the Navy, secretary of the Air Force—were especially political. A branch secretary is the "CEO" of a particular military branch, and his undersecretary is comparable to a chief operating officer. Generals, by contrast, have spent nearly thirty years or more in service to the country. Often commissioned from one of the military academies, they have come of age in an environment of strict discipline. Those differences in outlook and priorities extended down the chain of command as well. "There are a lot of people like me who are really pissed about how the last eight years managed to turn the military into—you know," one officer who served throughout the entire Obama era and recently left active duty told me, "you know" being shorthand for a laboratory for progressive social engineering. I was surprised by the number of service members of all ranks who were eager to share their experiences with me for this book, and I was even more surprised by how many of them had—for years—kept records of their experiences on the off chance that one day someone might want to know the truth.

In a Department of Defense packed with progressive ideologues, Ray Mabus, the secretary of the Navy, was the worst. After a brief stint in the Navy (1970–1972), he spent three and a half decades in politics, including a single (and disastrous) term as governor of Mississippi. He was the youngest governor in his state's history, but his tenure was anything but successful. The *New York Times* called him a "Porsche politician in a Chevy pickup state," and the disconnected relationship he had with the people of Mississippi was a foreshadowing of the disconnected relationship he would have with the sailors under his charge.[11] Before he finished his first gubernatorial term, Mabus was challenged by fellow Democrats, who described him as "arrogant and out of touch" and distributed "Save Us from Mabus" bumper stickers.[12] Mabus survived the primary but lost to his Republican challenger, making him the first Democrat to lose a governor's race in Mississippi in more than one hundred years. (When Mabus became secretary of the Navy, he brought one of his top aides from his term in the governor's mansion, Thomas Oppel, with him to serve as his chief of staff.[13])

Mabus was an early supporter of President Obama's campaign during the 2008 primaries, campaigning "extensively" on the future president's behalf, and he was rewarded with a nomination after the new commander in chief was elected.[14] After Obama announced his nomination, Mabus briefly drew scrutiny due to court documents revealing that he'd surreptitiously recorded a conversation he and his wife had with their family priest and subsequently used statements his wife made during the conversation to obtain custody of the couple's children in divorce proceedings.[15]

After his career in elected office ended, Mabus turned himself into a progressive's progressive, a persona he brought to the Navy, which he relentlessly politicized. Departing from the tradition of naming ships after American presidents and war heroes, he instead named vessels after left-wing activists like Cesar Chavez and Harvey Milk. During his eight years as secretary of the Navy, Mabus tweeted about diversity, climate change, and gender-neutral combat-arms units more than thirty-six times. In contrast, he tweeted about Naval "readiness" a grand total of five times—once to praise the South Korean military, once to express admiration for Australia's and Timor-Leste's naval engineers, once about the US Navy's "Citadel Pacific" exercises, and twice about the congressional budget process of 2013.[16] Mabus's tweets reflect his real priorities as secretary of the Navy. "I worked for the guy for years and not one time did he ever mention the word 'readiness,'" a senior Navy official who served in the Obama-era Pentagon told me.

Mabus played a role in virtually every controversial military policy of the Obama era. When the president tapped him to replace Navy

Secretary Donald C. Winter, a career national security professional, Mabus's official White House biography noted his National Wildlife Federation Conservation Achievement Award but made no mention of his time in the Navy.[17] His eight years in office made Mabus the longest-serving secretary of the Navy since World War I, but he ought to be remembered as the most political secretary as well as the most widely disliked by the Navy rank and file. He boasted about his ignorance: "I think one of the great strengths I brought to the Navy was that I had no idea what the issues were when I came in."[18] The sailors who served under him would certainly agree with him about one thing—he was clueless.

"He was a pure political animal, and he really enjoyed the trappings of the office," a three-star admiral who regularly interacted with Mabus told me. (One of Mabus's favorite perks was arranging to throw out the first pitch at baseball games when he visited cities with Major League teams, and he became the first person to throw the first pitch in all 30 MLB stadiums. Mabus said that the purpose of his first-pitch circuit was to "put a face on the Navy" for the American people and to raise awareness about the Navy and Marine Corps, but it is unclear why that goal would not have been better achieved by arranging for local sailors or Marines who served under him to throw out the first pitch instead.[19]) When I asked the admiral if Mabus was receptive to his and his peers' professional judgment, he laughed and replied, "No. He had no use for us, unless we just said 'yessir, yessir, three bags full.'"

But as Mabus focused on his own agenda, the Navy he led was falling apart. Aside from pushing progressive pet projects and prohibitively expensive environmentalist projects, Mabus's other fixation was on securing his legacy. To do so, he focused on building the most durable representations of his tenure: ships. Mabus was consumed with building ships. Admittedly, it seems counterintuitive to say that it's problematic when a Navy secretary's legacy is an increase in ships. But nevertheless, it was a problem. The Navy's senior admirals—from the beginning of Mabus's tenure to the bitter end—did not want more ships, at least not while under the constraints of the Obama-era budgets; they wanted to use the Navy's money to properly maintain and enhance the capabilities of the ships they already had and to provide enough sailors to man them effectively, among other priorities. While Mabus was overseeing personnel cuts downsizing the Navy by thousands of sailors, he was increasing the Navy's operations tempo and the number of ships the remaining sailors had to operate at the same time. The outcome: undertrained but overworked crews manning a fleet that was rapidly falling into disrepair.

Speaking at the Surface Navy Association Symposium in 2013, Vice Admiral Thomas Copeman III, whose primary role from 2012 to 2014 was to ensure "the fitness of the Navy's ships for combat,"[20] warned that Naval readiness was in a "downward spiral."[21] The situation was so bleak, Copeman said, that "[I]t's getting harder and harder, I think, for us to look the troops in the eye."[22] But Copeman's warnings made for bad publicity for Mabus and his agenda. A few months after he gave the speech, Copeman was asked to retire early, more than a year before his assignment was slated to end.[23] Copeman told public-interest investigative journalism outlet *ProPublica* that despite being forced into early retirement, he didn't regret his decision to speak out: "If you're an admiral in the Navy, you may have to make that decision to send people into combat, and you better not have blood on your hands the rest of your life because you didn't do everything you could" to make sure they're ready.[24]

In February 2019, *ProPublica* published a damning investigation revealing that senior admirals commanding the Navy's surface warfare fleets had repeatedly warned Mabus and his staff that if the Navy didn't correct course from Mabus's obsessive ship-building to the exclusion of nearly all else, it faced severe risks of deadly accidents.[25] In fact, "alarms had been sounded up and down the chain of command, by young, overmatched sailors, by veteran captains and commanders, and by some of the most respected Navy officials in Washington."[26] Those warnings were not exactly presented at the twelfth hour, either: the *ProPublica* investigation found that a 2010 report "all but predicted the accidents."[27] Almost immediately after taking office in March 2016, Undersecretary of the Navy Janine Davidson told Mabus "that the Navy was devoting too many resources to buying new ships and weapons systems and dangerously neglecting readiness," but Mabus's chief of staff Tom Oppel reportedly told her to stop raising the issue.[28] The admirals' worst fears came true shortly after the Obama administration left office, when multiple collisions between Navy surface vessels and commercial ships left seventeen sailors dead. Before the accidents, a sailor on one of the ships involved—The U.S.S. John S. McCain—told his chain of command, "It's only a matter of time before a major incident occurs."[29]

When asked why the Navy secretary was so adamant about continuing to use the Navy's budget to contract for more ships, one of the senior Navy officials involved in those efforts to persuade Mabus and his staff to focus on the massive readiness issues afflicting the fleet as it was and to stop building additional ships told me that Mabus was more concerned with "leaving a legacy." Mabus's priorities were "building ships, green energy, and getting social justice things taken care of—that's all he cared about," he added.

Indeed, it is difficult to read a speech by Mabus without coming across boasts about the number of ships built or put under contract during his tenure. (Mabus has also been vigilant about ensuring that the ship-building legacy belongs to him and him alone. Commenting on a headline about the Navy's projected ship count in 2020, Mabus tweeted "The reason" the Navy will hit 300 ships "is [because] of ships I built in @Barackobama Admin. Trump Admin had nothing to do with it.[30]) Well, if Mabus wanted a legacy, he got one: despite periodic lip service to maintaining the Navy's strategic advantage, he will be remembered as a Navy secretary who devoted himself above all to his own vanity projects and enacting a progressive cultural agenda. When you read about Mabus's priorities in the chapters to come, keep the *ProPublica* report in mind.

The vast disparity in philosophies, experience, and priorities between senior military leaders and Obama administration appointees produced rocky, if not downright hostile, relations from the beginning. A former Marine general who held multiple positions during the Obama years recalls that he and his peers were "always disappointed, [but] never surprised" about administration policies. A former Army general was only slightly more circumspect, describing senior military leaders' relationship with the administration as "lukewarm or tepid, but respectful." Obama's officials "were willing to listen, but only to a certain degree," he added. "Readiness wasn't [their] number one priority. It was something else," a third general remarked. "The military in general was used as a political tool.... But this wasn't a national security kind of political power. It was [a] social-engineering kind," he added. A fourth said that he was "struck by how the Obama administration cared about a lot of things in the military, but none of them had anything to do with military readiness or war fighting."

Each of these officers served in senior command positions or in senior Pentagon assignments during Obama's presidency. One of them refused a promotion to a third star and retired instead because, in his own words, he could no longer in good conscience command soldiers in a military that did not prioritize their safety in combat (emphasis added):

> I turned down a promotion and left the Army early, because I was just fed up with a lot of this foolishness.... I promoted a guy to lieutenant colonel when I was a two-star. And he wanted to re-swear his oath of office, so we did that. **And when I got to the point where he had to repeat back to me 'that I take this obligation freely, without mental reservation or purpose of evasion,' I realized that I could not swear this oath anymore myself.** Because I do have serious reservations about what we're doing. So I left, because...**I don't want to be responsible for the people who are going to die in future combat because we are not the force that we need to be and that we could be,** if we hadn't have done the—you know, hadn't fallen prey to these serious, ridiculous policy changes.

One of the officials who most inflamed tensions between the administration and the brass was Brad Carson, a former Democratic congressman from Oklahoma who became the acting undersecretary of defense for personnel and readiness in 2015. Obama and Carson met in 2004 when they were campaigning for open Senate seats in their respective states. After Carson lost his race to Tom Coburn by nearly twelve percentage points, he penned an op-ed in *The New Republic* blaming his loss on socially-conservative voters who were fighting a "culture war" about "modernity itself" and believed that "cultural concerns are more important than universal health care or raising the minimum wage."[31]

Military personnel who regularly interacted with him say Carson was as condescending during his stint at the Pentagon as when he was a politician. He put on "the most arrogant and pompous display of leadership I have ever experienced," recalls one general, an assessment confirmed by other senior military officials who served in the Pentagon during Carson's tenure. Carson, those sources said, simply would not listen to them and presumed that he knew all of the answers already.

Carson's intentions were no secret. "He was certainly pushing the [progressive] agenda on a timeline," I was told by one senior Pentagon source. Proudly acknowledging his influence, Carson wrote in a national security journal that he was "closely involved in every recent controversy at the Pentagon: [including] women in combat [and] transgender service."[32] Carson told NPR's Mary Louise Kelly that the policies he pushed were "all part of this ambition to make the Department of Defense the nation's most progressive employer."[33] The quote unintentionally highlighted a fundamental tension that arose repeatedly during the many battles over the Obama administration's preferred policies—many of the President's appointees could not understand or refused to acknowledge that the military is not simply a government employer like any other.

The conflicts between mission-focused generals and the Obama administration were not limited to personnel policies and budget cuts. In response to pressure from non-governmental organizations (NGOs), the administration sent 100 special operations troops to Uganda in 2011 to hunt for the warlord Joseph Kony and his tiny band of guerillas.[34] Troop levels and resources for the mission were "sharp[ly] increase[d]"— the administration sent another 150 special forces troops and four CV-22 Osprey attack aircraft—in the years after the Internet video *Kony 2012*, produced by the NGO Invisible Children, went viral and provoked an outcry on social media.[35] At that point, the number of elite American troops on the ground outnumbered the entire size of Kony's ragtag militia scattered around the jungles of Uganda and its neighbors.[36]

Invisible Children admitted that *Kony 2012* and its accompanying social media campaign were designed to pressure Obama into increasing America's investment in the mission and, although the video was later found to be highly misleading,[37] the plan worked. Invisible Children's website boasts, "On April 24, 2012, we achieved the primary goal of the *Kony 2012* campaign when President Obama publicly announced that he would reauthorize the US mission."[38] Even as the defense sequester was squeezing the military, Obama ramped up the Kony campaign. A source described National Security Advisor Susan Rice and Grant Harris, a Special Assistant to the President and Senior Director for African Affairs on the National Security Council, as the principle forces behind the administration's Kony obsession. (Harris served as Rice's counselor and Deputy Chief of Staff during Rice's role as Ambassador to the UN in Obama's first term.[39]) "We spent a huge amount of time hunting the guy," a general with firsthand knowledge told me. "We were wasting time, money, and resources hunting someone who was zero threat to the US, and no amount of rational thought could drag them off of that."

And an admiral who worked in the operations section of the Office of the Joint Chiefs at one point fumed about the mission during a high level meeting about allocating resources for the Kony mission, telling his peers, "We are diverting resources at a time when I don't have anything to give to anyone, for any reason, to go hunt some guy that *isn't even a threat to the country next door*, much less the United States," according to a source with firsthand knowledge who requested anonymity to discuss sensitive Pentagon meetings. (Keep in mind, while the administration was sending additional and precious special operations resources to hunt for Kony in March 2014, ISIS was already well into its reign of terror and was crucifying Christians and enslaving Yazidi women on a near-daily basis in Iraq and Syria.) But for the Obama administration, the Kony campaign was a PR win, and that's what mattered. A *Washington Post* story about the mission noted in passing that, in the face of criticism that Obama's Syria policy was weak, "the Uganda action is a relatively inexpensive way to show resolve in a popular cause."[40]

The Kony mission was finally terminated in 2017, a few months after Donald Trump took office.[41] The official reason for ending the mission was that Kony was no longer considered a threat. The real reason was that Kony had *never* been a threat to the United States. In fact, the Ugandan government itself dedicated only 1,500 troops (part of an African Union mission, no less) to hunting Kony, who was supposedly a critical threat to its own existence.[42]

Evaluating the administration's decision to allocate four CV-22 Osprey aircraft to the Kony mission puts the Pentagon's frustration in context. The Osprey can take off vertically like a helicopter but rotates its engines to fly like an airplane. It was described in 2013 as a "favored platform for special operations strikes" in Afghanistan.[43] At the time the administration sent four of these special operations aircraft to track down Joseph Kony, the Air Force was still waiting to receive its full order of the first fifty aircraft to be delivered. (The order was completed in 2016.[44]) Worse, by the end of the Obama administration, 50 percent of the Marine Corps' MV-22 variation of the Osprey were grounded by a lack of parts.[45] The United States had no Ospreys to spare when the Obama administration sent four of them to Uganda, leaving fewer attack helicopters for missions that directly affected national security.

A similar clash of priorities (and viewpoints) occurred when members of the Obama national security team sought to divert intelligence, surveillance, and reconnaissance assets—better known as drones—from active missions to South Sudan to detect old mass graves that could be used as evidence of prior crimes (dating before the creation of South Sudan as an independent country) against the people of Darfur. Once again, the diversion did not sit well with the Pentagon, which naturally viewed such archival work as of lesser importance than fighting America's enemies. That time, the Pentagon was able to nix the request.

Several generals independently raised the point with me that the administration's pet projects—such as the Kony mission—and its relentless focus on identity politics not only were harmful in and of themselves but also consumed the brass's time and diverted their attention from more important matters. One general offered the example of the Obama State Department's fixation on "transparency" in special operations. He described repeated meetings in which officials vacillated over disclosing the number of operators in a certain country before finally deciding to maintain the status quo. He thought the incompatibility of "clandestine operations" and "public disclosure" should have been self-evident. But to the Obama administration, apparently, it was not.

One general who served in the Pentagon in the Obama era told me that the White House's social-engineering agenda "is what consumed the time of the senior leadership inside the Pentagon every single day" to the near exclusion of actual military priorities such as training and readiness.

One of this general's peers expressed the same frustration almost verbatim: "You could read the guidance that the White House would send over, and it would talk about elements of a progressive agenda [or] it would talk about increasing research on topics not directly concerned with the military.... You'd read this guidance and you'd find nothing about 'I want you to get x number of brigades or fighter squadrons ready' or something like that."

To be clear, not all of President Obama's initial national security appointees were naïve ideologues. One of his best national security decisions was keeping Robert Gates, President George W. Bush's secretary of defense, in the same position. A serious man, intent on doing the right thing and motivated by a deep love for the men and women under his command, Gates kept in his desk in the Pentagon a prayer that

Abraham Lincoln's secretary of war, Edwin Stanton, had uttered, sobbing, his head in his hands, after choosing a course of action that would cause a Union soldier to die: "God, help me to do my duty. God, help me to do my duty."[46]

But Gates was the exception to the rule. Even he had his fair share of problems with his politically minded peers in the administration. Years later, Gates recalled a meeting in which President Obama had overruled the military's preferred strategy in Afghanistan. Vice President Biden, jumping into the conversation, explained to the generals that they "should consider the President's decision as an order." Obama quickly concurred, saying, "I am giving an order."[47] Gates was stunned. He called the exchange "unnecessary and insulting," and wrote that the "order demonstrated... the complete unfamiliarity of both men with the American military culture." Biden's interjection was "proof positive of the depth of the Obama White House's distrust of the nation's military leadership."[48]

Gates was not overreacting. Every service member knows that orders are orders simply because they are given by the person in charge. Saying a magic phrase at the end of a directive does not have an "abracadabra" effect on a robotic listener. Soldiers are not free to disobey a simple command from a superior but duty-bound to comply once the speaker specifies that the command was "an order."

The vice president's views about the military fueled mistrust between the White House and the Pentagon during the early years of the administration. Gates thought "Biden was subjecting Obama to Chinese water torture, every day saying 'the military can't be trusted.'"

The strained relations between the White House and the military were aggravated by the ideologues whom the White House appointed within the Department of Defense and as the secretaries of the various branches. The politicized tenure of Ray Mabus was the norm rather than the exception. A high-ranking officer in the Obama-era Pentagon told me that while "you expect" political appointees to have "different priorities," the Obama administration took that to an extreme.

Eric Fanning was in President Obama's first wave of nominations and served in the administration for all eight years. He held political-appointee positions in all three major branches of the military, ultimately becoming secretary of the Army. He was tapped for deputy undersecretary of the Navy in 2009 and promoted to undersecretary of the Air Force in 2013 (and later acting secretary), despite having no military experience whatsoever. None.

Fanning publicly advocated changes to the longstanding transgender service member policy early in Obama's second term.[49] Indeed, accepting an award at a gala shortly after he was nominated to be secretary of the Army, Fanning hinted that a reversal of the military's transgender policy was forthcoming.[50] After Trump defeated Hillary Clinton in the 2016 election, Fanning remained confident that the changes would be irreversible. "It's hard to undo these things," he bragged to an audience at the left-wing Victory Institute.[51]

The Air Force's civilian leadership was no less politicized. Deborah Lee James became secretary of the Air Force in 2013 and immediately set out to leave her mark. A former Democratic congressional staffer and a political appointee in the Clinton Defense Department, she was no stranger to politicized military policy. Like the other service secretaries of the Obama era, James featured prominently in many of the administration's most contentious—and damaging—policy decisions. Asked how she balanced competing priorities as secretary of the Air Force, she answered that her guiding principle was "people first."[52] That sounds nice, but it has never been the first principle of the military. Quite the opposite. The principle has always been "Accomplish the mission; take care of your troops"—*in that order.* Any other approach is simply nonsensical. Under a "people first" policy, how does a Marine sergeant tell a lance corporal to run toward gunfire to accomplish the mission, even though he knows his order puts the young man's life at risk? Indeed, "people first" is the opposite of Stanton's prayer—"God, help me to do my duty."

This inversion of priorities was evident at all levels of the force. In 2014, a correspondent for the Air Force Sergeants Association posed a decidedly pointed question to James:

> A perception exists among the rank and file of our 110,000 members that there is a growing frustration within the current force that senior DoD leaders are not speaking out on behalf of service members in their discussions with Congress and the Administration.... What do you plan to do to improve transparency in communications regarding force shaping [and] proposed changes in personnel policies...?[53]

The question clearly implies that the Obama administration's policies did not enjoy broad support among the rank-and-file. The reason they did not is because they were geared not towards the mission that service members had signed up for but for the ideological goals of the administration.

Toxic Leaders Generating Toxic Policies: How the Social Engineering of the Obama Era Transformed the Military's Culture and Policies

"There will be mixed genitalia in military bathrooms, showers, and billeting," announced Anthony Kurta, the deputy assistant secretary of defense for military personnel policy, in 2016. On a conference call with Army Colonel Ron Crews and others, Kurta explained that the new policy allowing transgender soldiers to serve according to their "gender identities" rather than their biological sex meant that a person whose gender identity and biological sex did not match would be allowed to use the barracks of the opposite sex. It also meant that transgender soldiers would be evaluated not according to the physical standards appropriate for their own sex but according to the standards for the *opposite* sex. In practice, then, a biologically male soldier who "identified" as female would be treated as if he had the body of a young woman and, for instance, be allowed to pass Army fitness tests at a lower level or pass body composition standards designed for a member of the opposite sex. In an institution that is concerned exclusively with physical realities and physical outcomes, that is no small thing.

Crews, a former chaplain, was concerned about the privacy of female soldiers under the new policy and the effect it might have on recruiting and retention:

> *Crews*: A larger proportion [of the force] comes from the Southeast US than from any other region of the country—the so-called Bible Belt.... Don't you think that moms and dads will have some second thoughts about encouraging particularly their daughters to join a military where their daughters may be exposed? If we have an eighteen-year-old female coming from an evangelical Christian home, and she's in a two-person billet [and receives a transgender roommate who is biologically male], this young lady will have no recourse, correct? If she complains, she's the one in the wrong—is that correct?
>
> *Kurta*: That's correct.
>
> *Crews*: Don't you think that's going to raise concerns for recruiting?
>
> *Kurta*: I believe Americans will be proud that our military is leading the way in this social transformation.[54]

A Marine chaplain with a decade and a half of service had a nearly-identical, albeit slightly more personal experience with Kurta. After Kurta made similar statements in a meeting with a collection of chaplains at the Pentagon, this particular chaplain approached him and asked if he was serious. He said Kurta "looked me right in the eye and said, 'Hey look, there will be mixed-genitalia in our berthing areas, in our barracks, and it's good for America.'" The chaplain cut to what should have been the heart of the issue, asking Kurta, "Wow sir, do you really believe that? This is going to make us better at warfighting?" Kurta simply replied, "Well, that's just the way it is."[55]

Kurta's separate interactions with those two chaplains perfectly capture the chasm that separated the Obama administration's priorities from those of the senior military leaders in the Pentagon.

Kurta, by the way, was one of the few appointees in the Obama DoD to stay in the Pentagon after the Trump administration took over. He served as the acting under secretary of defense for personnel and readiness—essentially a promotion from the position he held during the exchanges described above—for most of 2017. Kurta was also tapped to be the principal deputy undersecretary of defense for personnel and readiness, something that multiple sources who served under him during the Obama era called surprising and concerning. His nomination stalled in the Senate, however, and was ultimately withdrawn in September 2018.[56]

In early 2016, retired Marine General James Mattis co-edited a book titled *Warriors and Citizens: American Views of Our Military* about the risks and consequences of the civil-military divide in America, amidst our long-running wars from which much of the public and the media have long since disengaged.[57] Hailed as a mission-focused warrior undistracted by political considerations, the future secretary of defense expressed his concern that "an uninformed public is permitting political leaders to impose an accretion of social conventions that are diminishing the combat power of our military, disregarding our warfighting practitioners' advice."[58] Mattis observed: "There remains an underlying deference by the public to allow the military to operate by its own rules, an interesting factor since our political leadership has not advocated for such a difference. In recent years political leaders have instead often used the military as a vehicle to lead social change in the broader society."[59]

Like other flashpoints in the culture wars, a very vocal minority is the driving force behind political leaders' efforts to use the military as a tool for social change. Because politicians are "naturally responsive to activism, we could be moving toward a military that is more responsive to the values of the 5 percent of very liberal Americans than those of the vast majority of our fellow citizens, liberal and conservative," Mattis warned. Allowing these ideologues to set military policy would "force the military to sacrifice practices it perpetuates not for reasons of social conservatism but for reasons of military practicality and battlefield success."[60]

President Obama apparently did not welcome General Mattis's opinions. As CENTCOM commander, Mattis had forcefully advocated a more muscular approach to Iran when the administration was seeking a nuclear deal at all costs. In January 2013, the renowned general was fired without the courtesy of a phone call.[61] A report by the House Intelligence Committee later concluded that removing Mattis, whose vaunted military career spanned four decades of impressive service, had itself reduced CENTCOM's effectiveness.[62]

The unabashed political activism of Obama's service secretaries *after* the transition to the Trump administration confirms Mattis's assessment of their motives. Four days after President Trump announced that he would reverse Obama's ill-conceived transgender policy, Obama administration appointee Eric Fanning appeared in a Human Rights Campaign video promising to "fight" the Trump administration.[63]

Fanning, Mabus, and James all participated in lawsuits filed to block the *current* commander in chief's reversal of the *former* commander in chief's policy. (Of course, President Obama had himself reversed the transgender policies of his predecessors).[64] This political maneuvering appeared to mark the first time in American history that former service secretaries had resorted to the courts to force the *current* commander in chief, by order of a single federal district judge, to implement *their* preferred policies instead of his own. The court did not disappoint them, citing many of their arguments in its unprecedented nationwide injunction blocking the commander in chief's military policies. An Army general who served under the Obama administration was astonished that the courts would substitute "their judgment for who should be in the military and who should not" over that of the commander in chief, as if the military were "like a bank" or another standard employer.

The former service secretaries have not confined their partisan sniping to the courts. Fanning has retweeted posts calling President Trump a "traitor" guilty of "high crimes and misdemeanors"[65] and telling him to resign.[66] He has frequently tweeted about the Trump administration using the hashtag #DrainTheWhiteHouse.[67]

Mabus, for his part, has retweeted posts promoting the anti-Trump website PutinsPuppet.net.[68] Six weeks after Trump took office, Mabus attacked the new president for the supposedly wasteful way in which the new aircraft carrier *Gerald Ford* was built. "They were designing the *Ford* while they were building it—[that is] not a good way to build a ship," he wrote. Doubling down, he added, "This is just a dumb way to build any type of ship, particularly something as big and complicated as a carrier."[69] The flaw in Mabus's criticism was that the *Ford* was built almost entirely during his own tenure and according to his own decisions. One is hard-pressed to decide which is worse, Mabus's partisanship or his ignorance.

The Obama Administration Stifled Dissent from the Military

The administration's heavy-handed approach combined with its unfamiliarity with military culture left military leaders with the impression that those who publicly opposed the administration's politically driven priorities would suffer unpleasant consequences. "My impression is that everybody [understood] what happened if you spoke out...so there was not going to be anybody that spoke out," an Army lieutenant general who served during the early years of the Obama era told me. I asked another general officer, who retired just as the Obama administration came to power but remained close with many of his peers, whether he thought the administration's heavy-handed approach to dissent in its first few years was intended to intimidate senior military leaders. His reply: "absolutely."

After the Obama administration made it clear that it would brook no dissent, the military leadership adapted, apparently on the assumption that if the administration was going to do whatever it wanted, the best thing the brass could do for the military was to try to mitigate the damage instead of directly opposing the administration in battles they could not win. In other words, "They are going to do *x* anyway, so we need to figure out how to stay combat-effective with *x* in place." I repeatedly encountered variations on that theme in my interviews with officers for this book. As one general said, "Most of these culture changes are viewed by...those that are in the military as a done deal, and it's the military mentality, as you know, that once a decision is made, we make it work." A navy admiral from the Obama era echoed the sentiment, saying "Once a decision had been made, whether it's a good decision or not, we typically just give a cheery 'aye-aye' and execute it to the best of our ability."

In at least one instance, the administration explicitly relied on that attitude. A general recounted an interaction with Pentagon civilian appointees that took place when he was in a senior command position:

> [They asked] us what we thought the impact [of the new transgender policy] would be. And we completely—all the leadership said it's a major readiness issue in our mind and it's going to detract from readiness.... And they told us in closed-door sessions, "Hey, look. This is going to happen. You guys have got to figure out how to make it have the least impact you possibly can, but this is going to happen. We can't stop it. You can't stop it."

Even those leaders who did not receive that message explicitly seemed to have internalized it by the time the decision was made. The long-established tradition was that military leaders could disagree with the administration—but only to a point—and if their opinions conflicted with political priorities, politics took precedence. The *New York*

Post reported in 2015 that "[m]ilitary officials [were] reluctant to publicly discuss their opposition" to the new transgender policy.[70] Several senior military leaders from the Obama era told me the same thing: "You could have predicted that from the very beginning. Nobody was going to speak up."

The obvious result of this intimidation campaign was that senior officers who were willing to "play the game" were promoted ahead of those who weren't. "Many of those that actually got to the top were there because they were known to be willing to accept the Obama agenda," an Army general remarked. A senior officer in the Air Force concurred: "I think more and more the deck was stacked with people that were probably a little more to Obama's line of thinking." The system "self-selects people that are going to play the game," he added. Navy admirals offered similar assessments. Of course, neither they nor I mean that every senior general or admiral who moved up the ranks got there by simply accepting the administration's agenda, or that most of them are not highly competent and deserving. But it appeared to be the case in some instances.

The Military Has a Single Purpose, Which the Obama Ideologues Didn't Grasp

On May 12, 1962, General Douglas MacArthur delivered a valedictory to the Corps of Cadets at West Point. At eighty-two, he knew firsthand the evil that human beings are capable of inflicting upon one another and sought to impart his hard-earned lessons of two world wars and a life lived in his nation's service:

> [T]hrough all this welter of change and development, your mission remains fixed, determined, inviolable. It is to win our wars. Everything else in your professional career is but corollary to this vital dedication. All other public purposes, all other public projects, all other public needs, great or small,

will find others for their accomplishment; but you are the ones who are trained to fight. Yours is the profession of arms, the will to win, the sure knowledge that in war there is no substitute for victory, that if you lose, the Nation will be destroyed, that the very obsession of your public service must be Duty, Honor, Country.

More than a half-century after MacArthur uttered those famous words, there is still no better summary of the single, all-encompassing mission of the United States armed forces.

MacArthur's speech was a cultural reference point for many of my peers who graduated from the US Military Academy. The purpose of our military is fixed, determined, and inviolable: "to win our wars." In a sign of how embedded MacArthur's speech is within the psyche of the Army's senior officer corps, multiple sources independently referred to it during my interviews with them. One now-retired three-star general who spent much of his career in the special operations community heatedly reminded me that MacArthur told the cadets that their mission was to win their nation's wars, period, nothing more or less. "So everything in the military should be focused on that mission statement: to win the nation's wars." The "enemy does not care about your concept of equality or fairness," he added, his voice rising. "That is not something that ever crosses their minds." To those who have served, especially those who served in war zones, this purpose is not an abstract principle; it's personal.

Over and over, the service members I spoke with—a group of more than forty men and women that spanned every branch of the military and included division commanders, senior physicians, intelligence officers, operators who served in units across the entire spectrum of special operations, and light infantry company commanders, to mention only a few—emphasized that combat effectiveness is the only context in which military policies should be evaluated. The reason for their single-minded focus is apparent upon a moment's reflection: The overarching purpose of their profession is to prevail in combat, and their lives, and those of their comrades, are at stake. Winning in combat means they live; losing means they die. All else flows from this inescapable reality. To military professionals, then, the worthiness of every policy proposal boils down to a single question: "Will this make us more effective in combat?"

But, one of the generals quoted earlier in this chapter said, the sad thing was, "the Obama administration never asked that question."

CHAPTER

THE ACADEMIES

One of many "Safe Space" placards now outside the doors of uniformed and civilian professors at the Naval Academy

To understand the corrosive impact of the social-justice orthodoxy on military culture and effectiveness, a natural place to begin is where many of America's greatest military leaders began their careers: the service academies. I am not an academy graduate and cannot claim firsthand experience about the institutional health of our service academies. I've served with many academy graduates; some of them are the best leaders I ever met, and I hold their alma maters in the highest esteem. The academies remain among the most selective educational institutions in the country—a service academy ring is something to be proud of in 2019 every bit as much as it was in 1919. In fact, it is precisely because the academies are critically important to the vitality of America's military that the academies' strength is so crucial to the future of our national defense. "If you want to see what the Army is going to look like in ten years, just go to West Point and see what the Corps of Cadets are like, what they think, how they think, and that's the way it'll be like," an officer who graduated from West Point within the past decade and recently left active duty told me.

But I interviewed academy graduates of all ranks who raised serious concerns about the cultural changes imposed upon the academies from above. In this chapter, I relay their insights and shine a light on the growing evidence that these changes undermine the mission of the academies. Every graduate I talked with is worried that America's future military leaders are being deprived of the preparation they need because of the insidious politically correct culture seeping into the service academies.

In October 2017, Robert Heffington, a retired Army lieutenant colonel, an outgoing West Point professor and an academy alumnus, published a scathing public letter about leadership failures at his alma mater. "I firmly believe West Point is a national treasure and that it can and should remain a vitally important source of well trained, highly educated Army officers and civilian leaders. However, during my time on the West Point faculty...I personally witnessed a series of fundamental changes at West Point that have eroded it to the point where I question whether the institution should even remain open," Heffington wrote.[1]

"[S]tandards at West Point are nonexistent," he continued. "They exist on paper and nowhere else." Heffington took aim at the academy's failure to enforce the honor code and its lax enforcement of conduct and disciplinary standards. Perhaps most telling, however, are the changes Heffington identified in West Point's curriculum:

> The plebe American History course has been revamped to
> focus solely on race and on the narrative that America is

founded solely on a history of racial oppression. Cadets derisively call it the "I Hate America Course." Simultaneously, the plebe International History course now focuses on gender to the exclusion of many other important themes. On the other hand, an entire semester of military history was recently deleted from the curriculum...the curriculum at *West Point*!

If Heffington's letter was one warning sign, the case of cadet Spenser Rapone was another. Rapone is the now infamous "Commie Cadet" who was kicked out of the Army shortly after he graduated from West Point. Photos emerged of him wearing a Che Guevara shirt under his dress uniform and having the slogan "communism will win" pasted into his uniform cap. Rapone's social media accounts revealed tweets disparaging then-Defense Secretary James Mattis as "the most vile, evil fuck in the [Trump] administration" and bragging that he would "happily dance on" John McCain's grave.[2] He posted a picture on Instagram in 2016 of an Antifa flag in his bedroom with the caption: "New room décor...until it's flying proudly in the streets. #Antifa."[3] As many social media users pointed out when the story broke, this former member of the 75th Ranger Regiment apparently became radicalized *while attending West Point*.

Why Are Politically-Minded Civilians Teaching Cadets How to Be Soldiers?

The Rapone saga highlighted a disturbing issue—the influence that (often left-wing) civilian professors have on the education and development of future generations of America's military leaders. One of Rapone's mentors was his Western Civilization and Middle Eastern History professor, Rasheed Hosein, who began teaching at the Academy in 2011.[4] Hosein, Rapone's advisor in the History department, struck up a friendship with the cadet. Rapone's social media postings in 2012 and 2013 were mostly about music and punk counterculture. They took a sharp left turn in 2014, when he began extolling the virtues of communism and embracing radical left-wing causes.[5] Rapone and Hosein traveled to India together in March 2014. Hosein posted pictures of the trip on his Facebook page with the caption, "The brothers are gonna work it out."[6] Reporter Kristina Wong noted that "A review of Rapone's Facebook page shows that over time, since 2014, his posts became increasingly [leftist and focused on]…pro-Communist, anti-military, and anti-police [themes]. On January 5, 2015, he posted a Slate.com article calling for the abolishment of West Point. As a Facebook friend since 2014, Hosein would have been aware of Rapone's Facebook postings between 2014 and when he graduated in 2016."[7] Although various pundits speculated that Hosein had a role in fostering Rapone's Marxist radicalization—or that he was aware of it and said nothing, or that at the very least he should have been aware of it—there has been no firm connection between Rapone's transformation and his relationship with Hosein, until now.

Heffington told me (and other sources agreed) that while Rapone was responsible for his own radical conclusions, "he certainly had help and encouragement from Rasheed Hosein…[who] seemed to believe that he was 'helping' Rapone on his intellectual journey." Heffington said Hosein once proudly informed him that Rapone was "experimenting with Marxism."

Alarmed by cadet Rapone's increasing radicalism and Hosein's apparent role in fostering it, Heffington repeatedly reported his concerns to the History Department chain of command but was ignored. "Like so many other civilian faculty members," Heffington said, "Rasheed was not at all concerned with the fact that Rapone was destined to become a US Army officer—he was only interested in Rapone's 'intellectualism,' and I guess befriending him and helping him along his journey toward radical Marxism was a part of that."

"Rasheed's main problem," Heffington added, "was that he desperately wanted to cultivate a much-too-close, much-too-friendly relationship with his cadets. It was completely inappropriate and bizarre." Hosein's office became "basically a cadet hangout where 'his' group of cadets were allowed to congregate during all hours of the day and evening, even when Rasheed was not there."[8]

When news broke of Rapone's relationship with Hosein, West Point spokesmen told the media that Hosein had already been placed on administrative leave for reasons unrelated to the Rapone scandal.[9] In a response to an inquiry for this book, a West Point spokesman told me that Hosein "is definitely no longer here" and was no longer employed by the Academy. The spokesman refused to provide details about the causes or circumstances of Hosein's departure, however, describing the information as an administrative matter that was non-releasable.

It might surprise the average American taxpayer to learn that civilian professors at the service academies are as leftist as any other group of professors, but that appears to be largely the case in certain departments. Higher education appeals to progressives—liberal professors outnumber conservative professors by a ratio of twelve to one[10]—and the culture of the academies is changing as they add more civilian instructors. In the early 1990s, only 4 percent of West Point's faculty and between 2 and 3 percent of the Air Force Academy's faculty were civilian academics. Today, those numbers are roughly 25 percent and 37 percent, respectively.[11] (The Naval Academy has long had a 50-50 split between military and civilian instructors because of the technical necessities of its curriculum. But while engineers tend to be less prone to progressivism than those teaching liberal arts, the Naval Academy is far from immune to the leftist, politically correct trend, as we'll see.)

In the wake of the Rapone scandal and Heffington's letter, defense reporter Patrick Granger published an article citing several current and former West Point faculty members who agreed with Heffington's assessment.[12] One now-retired senior faculty member explicitly tied the "significant increase in the number of civilian faculty" to a deterioration in disciplinary standards and an inappropriately permissive culture.[13] "With no understanding or first-hand experience of cadet life, these individuals are not tied to tradition; nor are they imbued with a commitment to the institution. Instead, at best it is a good assignment—and at worst, it is a 'good gig,'" he said.[14]

Heffington told me that "The sad and simple truth is that the civilian faculty have never spent a day in their lives in uniform, and therefore they have zero loyalty or respect for the academies and their ultimate mission." He added that "The vast majority of civilian faculty members simply ignore the fact that cadets are going to become military officers after graduation. Standards and discipline are not even in the equation for them. Naturally, many cadets gravitate toward their civilian professors because they are 'cooler' than the majority of the military faculty. Rasheed Hosein took this to an extreme, but he is by no means the only one. In my experience, most civilian faculty members revel in 'bucking the system' and refusing to have anything to do with the military aspect of the Military Academy."

To be sure, there are talented, professional, and patriotic civilian professors at the service academies. Their contributions to the academic and cultural life at the academies speak for themselves, and their dedication is unquestioned. But unfortunately, a not-insignificant percentage of their civilian peers apparently do not share the military faculty members' passion for the mission and possess little understanding of military life and culture—and even less interest in remedying their ignorance.

Indeed, not only do many civilian professors seem to discount military standards of punctuality, appearance, and discipline, but their "scholarship" is often indistinguishable from what might be found at the most progressive, leftist university. A case in point is an academic article titled "Dinner and a Conversation: Transgender Integration at West Point and Beyond" published by West Point sociology professor Morton G. Ender and four coauthors in the journal *Social Sciences* in March 2017.[15]

For their research, the authors conducted eighteen focus groups with cadets and three with active duty instructors at the academy. The purpose of the focus groups was to explore "(1) cadet and military faculty and staff education and experience with transgender people; (2) personal perceptions about the impact of transgender people on good order and discipline in the Corps of Cadets at the United States Military Academy and the U.S. Army; and, finally, (3) perceived perceptions of respondents about how fellow cadets and soldiers might think transgender people will impact good order and discipline generally at both West Point and the U.S. Army."[16]

The article's disdain for anyone outside of the urban, secular progressive bubble is impossible to miss. "[W]e anticipated that familiarity with transgender notions would be sparse or narrow at best, and indeed this is the case for the typically inexperienced; the younger, first-year, rural-oriented, and military inexperienced subjects in our study," one of the very first paragraphs sniffed. The inexperience of the simpletons from flyover country and their need for an education in trans issues was a repeated theme. "A majority of these respondents [those lacking experience with transgender people] qualified that they grew-up in more rural or suburban parts of the United States and attended high schools in these regions before coming to West Point or heading off to college.... These included cadets and military members from rural areas, Christian-affiliated single-sex schools, and most home schooled individuals."

The authors' proposed solution to the presumed lack of sophistication and evident parochialism of cadets was "gender cosmopolitanism." According to the article, "Transgender cosmopolitans are cadets and officers that have experience and knowledge about the transgender community, are curious about it, and are comfortable with entering and engaging members of the community. They seem to be sub-culturally competent and possess cultural capital to bond with transgender comrades-in-arms and civilians. Further, cosmopolitans are empathetic about transgender people being tokens in the military community."

The focus group comments—and the authors' dismissive response to them—are telling. The article reported that cadets were concerned about the privacy issues raised by sharing open-bay showers and bathrooms with cadets of the opposite sex.

> Cadets anticipated that community or shared showers could be problematic. One cadet simply said, 'Where do they shower? I don't know.' An officer replied somewhat

sarcastically: 'Are we going to have 'Starship Trooper' showers?,' referring to the shower scene in the 1997 film of the same name depicting a future military academy where male and female cadets shower together with no sexual intimacy associated with the scene. Showers are seen as especially problematic if they are open showers.[17]

Cadets raised similar concerns about "living arrangements":

West Point currently houses straight and gay, lesbian, and bisexual cadets together. The vast majority of cadets reported being "fine" with the arrangement. They do see anatomy, not sexual orientation, as a distinguishing feature. However, they do not perceive the same logic with transgender cadets and soldiers, and some struggle with making sense of the arrangement. In the focus groups, participants often came back to anatomy, i.e., genitalia should room with like-genitalia. They likewise extrapolated to soldiers in the broader Army as well, who they perceived would have difficulty with similar living arrangements.[18]

Other cadets noted the problem of holding cadets to the physical fitness standards associated with their "gender identity" rather than their sex. One female cadet summarized the issue perfectly:

When you think, why are men held to higher PT standards than women? It is just like, their physical capacity, they are able to do more, so just because you change from a man into a woman, do you still not have that physical capacity to do more? So then, are you now held to the women's standard where you will be able to do more than the women because, still physically, you have the strength a man would have. Vice versa, as a woman transitions, she will not have that physical capacity naturally that a man would have.[19]

These were, by far, the most common responses in Professor Ender's focus groups. But one sub-section of cadets had no qualms about changing the Army's policies. Ender reported that third-year cadets (all sociology majors) "who had completed a number of sociology courses including 'Introductory Sociology; Social Inequality; or Marriage and Family,' where the topic is broached objectively and systematically, indicated a more nuanced understanding" of the issue.[20] The course website for the "Social Inequality" class reveals the typical progressive focus on the "intersectionality" of race, class, and "gender":

> The course focuses on the state of social inequality in the U.S. with respect to the distribution of wealth, power, occupational status, and social opportunity. Cadets will explore both past and present forces which contribute to social inequality and class structure in this country. In addition, cadets will learn concepts, theories and perspectives which contribute to their ability to evaluate contemporary social issues, policies, and programs which affect social inequality. Throughout the course, race, class, gender, and ethnicity will be discussed as critical categories of personal and social experience that affect all Americans.[21]

Inevitably, Professor Ender and his team concluded that more "education is needed for most cisgender service members,"[22] dismissing their valid military concerns as something that could be—and should be—cured by further "education." Gender ideology is not Ender's only interest. In 2015, Ender and a fellow civilian West Point psychology professor co-authored an article that purported to "support the concept of intersectionality" in a military context."[23] Intersectionality is the theory that interlocking societal systems of power marginalize certain classes of society. To correct that systemic injustice, society should defer to the "lived experiences" (that is, the demands) of individuals who belong to "marginalized communities." Intersectionality ranks categories of people based on their perceived "privilege," (white males at the very top, of course) and seeks to reallocate power to those at the bottom. Intersectionality asserts that those who identify with the greatest number of underprivileged categories deserve the most deference. Thus, white males should defer to the lived experiences of women of color, who in turn should defer to the lived experiences of transgender women of color. (In 2016, for example, a group of Black Lives Matter protestors disrupted a Toronto LGBT Pride parade and refused "to budge unless pride organizers acquiesced to a list of demands, which included... 'prioritizing black trans women' in hiring."[24])

To say the obvious, the credo of intersectionality is entirely incompatible with traditional military culture, with its hierarchy of command, its focus on duties rather than rights, and its emphasis on the merit, disciplined conduct, and professional competence of its members rather than their assumed victimhood. Intersectionality is all the rage in higher education, but it has no place in the service academies, which exist for the express purpose of training future military officers.

The lack of military understanding or experience among civilian academy instructors is embarrassing and borderline scandalous. A civilian economics professor at West Point, for instance, wrote an op-ed for the *New York Times* in which she compared the military academy to Hogwarts (the magical boarding school in *Harry Potter*). "Cadets wield sabers instead of wands," she wrote, "but students are students." Actually, they aren't. The glaring distinction—that most "students" are not preparing to lead soldiers into combat after graduation—was apparently lost on her. It's not hard to see why:

> My very first day teaching in historic Washington Hall I realized how out of place I was. Upon reaching for what I presumed was a dusty eraser to disappear my calculations, I found an M16 rifle magazine on the dusty chalkboard ledge. Though my instinct was to recoil in horror, I feared my cadets viewing me as anything but a collected professional.... [I]n

the classroom I met cadets excited to teach me of their world: "survival swimming" terror, inspection anxiety, class ring excitement and more.[25]

How can a professor who recoils in horror at the sight of a weapon magazine prepare cadets to be future military leaders? Cadets are supposed to learn about military life from their instructors, not teach their mentors. West Point is not a Hogwarts fantasyland but an institution ennobled by the service and sacrifice of its graduates. It is also worth noting that this professor, a former Clinton White House staffer, signed an open letter opposing the election of Donald Trump in 2016, which is inconsistent with the nonpartisan nature of the military.[26] One has to ask the question: why can't the military academies make a point of hiring professors who support—and understand—their mission?

Cultural Changes Are Contagious

Unfortunately, by their very nature, once indulged, intersectionality and identity politics demand compliance from everyone. For example, at the United States Naval Academy—that prestigious institution that molded heroes of generations past—"safe space" placards now proliferate outside the offices of civilian and military instructors alike. If the signs were stripped of identifying features, you would be hard pressed to distinguish them from those marking the offices of Yale gender studies professors. The front door of the Academy's Department of Leadership, Ethics, and Law (LEL), for example, contains two separate placards that read: "I Am A Safe Space." The first lectures readers that an "ally" will "support all midshipmen...maintain your confidentiality at all times, [and] stand up against discriminatory language and actions." The signatures of the Academy's "Safe Spaces Faculty Rep" (a civilian economics professor) and the officer in charge of the LEL department are at the bottom of the sign. The second—which prominently features the "whichever" gender symbol—announces that the officers within "participated in Trans 101—Dec. 9, 2016." The sign also informs entrants that the officers within will "support all midshipmen" and "stand up against discriminatory language and action." Identical placards appear outside the offices of professors teaching physics, naval architecture, ocean engineering, and other subjects.

Midshipmen also reported that their civilian professors routinely reminded them during the Obama years that they were serving in the "new Navy." But "that went away after Trump was elected," one said. The implication is that the Obama administration's open social-engineering campaign emboldened the civilian professors' ideological agendas. The tenure protections at the Naval Academy (a policy the other two academies have not adopted) complicate any efforts to fix this problem. The Air Force Academy has its own problems. A former Air Force Academy professor (who now teaches at James Madison University) complained bitterly in a 2012 article that the Academy's primary focus was—*gasp*—to prepare cadets for military service.[27] "Academics, it seemed to me took a back seat to military training, athletics, religiosity, and other ethereal constructs such as 'character building,'" he sniffed. "Even the president of the [Air Force Academy] (called the 'superintendent,' a three-star general) rarely has a university conferred master's degree, let alone a doctorate." The professor lamented "a multiplicity of requirements that would look foreign, even dreadful, to most academics," such as a rule requiring "all faculty, civilian or military...to be in their offices every day by 7:30 a.m. even if they have no morning classes." Worse yet, "If an instructor is traveling to a conference or if he is sick, he will need to find a substitute teacher. Classes are not to be canceled." The worst offense in the mind of this professor nominally tasked with preparing cadets for service in the Air Force, however, was that USAFA leadership *"seemed to actually believe that any research should directly benefit the Air Force"* (emphasis my own). Imagine that.

Writing individually about every progressive ideologue teaching our cadets and midshipmen could fill a book of its own, but it is worth looking at one final example before moving on to other issues. In 2013, the

Air Force Academy hired Chris Kilmartin from the University of Mary Washington as a visiting professor to teach classes on "Interdisciplinary Perspectives on Men and Masculinity."[28] Kilmartin is a psychology professor who describes himself as a feminist and once wrote an article saying, "I challenge you to tell me one way in which the sexes are opposite." (Apparently no second-graders with a basic awareness of human anatomy were available for comment.) Christina Hoff Sommers, a resident scholar at the American Enterprise Institute, called news of Kilmartin's hire "so troubling." Kilmartin "is an expert in gender ideology—not masculinity," she added.[29] Articles about the academy's announcement reported that Kilmartin's stated goal was to "help cadets 'understand how masculinity and sexism operate' and challenge them to apply gender studies to their roles as leaders."[30]

In a 2013 interview with the *New York Times*, conducted while he was at the Air Force Academy, Kilmartin declared that playground insults like telling a "boy in sports that he throws 'like a girl'" were "the cultural undercurrent of rape." According to Kilmartin, the phrase conditions boys to "disrespect the feminine and disrespect women."[31] In the same interview, he also advocated integrating ground combat units. He argued that the change would, as paraphrased by columnist Frank Bruni, result in "bolstering women's standing and altering a climate of inequality." Bruni and Kilmartin did not, of course, discuss whether it would make our military more effective in combat. Nor did the Air Force explain how hiring a professor worried about "the cult of hyper masculinity" will improve the ability of America's next Air Force officers to fight future wars.

Hiring roughly a third of professors from the general pool of PhDs in civilian academia closely yokes the culture of the academies—and the type and tone of the material taught at them—to the trends and developments in academia that manifest themselves at the average university. After all, "students are students." And anyone with a passing knowledge of developments on college campuses in the U.S. over the past few decades understands why that symbiosis is problematic in the military context.

How We Got Here

The question of who should teach at America's service academies has been a subject of debate for decades. Military leaders, generally speaking, have vehemently opposed reducing the percentage of military faculty members and argued that removing military officers from the classroom would reduce mentorship opportunities for cadets, weaken enforcement of military customs and courtesies, and potentially undermine good order and discipline. Proponents of reducing the number of military faculty members say that the military professors at service academies lag behind their civilian peers in terms of professional degrees. They also argue that constant rotations of military faculty prevent instructors from gaining expertise and "stay[ing] abreast of current scholarship and developments in their fields."[32] The lower cost of hiring civilian professors instead of sending military officers to obtain graduate degrees is another justification for the policy.[33]

The sea change began in 1992 when Congress passed legislation authorizing the academies to begin hiring greater numbers of civilian professors.[34] After the bill passed, then-Superintendent of West Point Lieutenant General Howard Graves pointedly noted that the bill did not *require* the academies to hire civilian professors but merely *authorized* the secretary of the Army to do so if he felt it was necessary.[35] But change the academies did.

That change was not necessarily for the best. A 2013 RAND study commissioned by the Air Force found that an increase in military faculty members would have a positive effect on cadets' development and on military order within the academies. The researchers concluded that they "were not able to find conclusive evidence of differences in [classroom] teaching effectiveness across faculty types."[36] They also determined that the Air Force had no difficulties finding qualified instructors to teach math, the sciences, and other technical classes that align with Air Force career fields, but that the academy was forced to rely on civilian faculty to teach classes like English and Philosophy because they did not have enough Air Force officers with PhDs in those fields. But one might ask whether such credentialing in the liberal arts is necessary at a military academy. Requiring cadets to read great books of philosophy and literature is one thing—and something that an officer with an undergraduate or master's degree in the humanities could do (and did do in the past)—but requiring them to be lectured on literary theory and intersectionality is another. America's service academies are sacrificing their military culture in order to hire liberal arts professors acceptable to academia, and that's a bad trade-off for taxpayers and cadets and midshipmen.

Senior academy leaders were under immense and constant pressure from external forces to bend the knee to the dictates of progressive ideology. Some academy leaders actively resisted those influences at great personal and professional cost. One of them was West Point Superintendent Lieutenant General Robert Caslen. Every West Point graduate and cadet I spoke with who attended the academy during Caslen's tenure expressed their appreciation for "The Supe." LTG Caslen himself was no stranger to pressure from the progressive left. He was castigated by a number of advocacy groups during his first stint at West Point for the alleged "offense" of telling cadets that he respected every one of them because they were all "God's children."[37] Many of the issues described in this chapter are structural or institutional and are outside the scope of any single leader. In some cases, high-quality and dedicated leaders like LTG Caslen can only do their best to mitigate the effects of those issues during their tenures.

But many of Caslen's peers did not seem to seem to share his commitment to the mission in the face of significant pressure from activist groups and Capitol Hill. The service academies are also adopting some of the worst aspects of civilian higher education, including, incredibly, a concern about "microaggressions." As reported by journalist Ryan Pickrell in February 2018, First Sergeant Zachary Parish emailed the Air Force Academy corps of cadets to address the steady decline in cadet grooming standards that he and other instructors had observed over several months. "Observations made by USAFA [United States Air Force Academy] permanent party members regarding cadet grooming standards have become increasingly unfavorable," Parish wrote.[38] "Going forward, I expect you all to do your part in reversing negative perceptions about cadet personal appearance that circulates USAFA and diminishes your credibility as a member in the profession of arms."

"Before Michael Jordan became a clothing brand mogul, he was actually a pretty good professional basketball player," Parish continued.[39] "In the later years of his career, and before the NBA's dress code existed, he would consistently appear at press conferences in a suit and tie. He was never seen with a gaudy chain around his neck, his pants below his waistline, or with a backwards baseball hat on during public appearances."[40]

Somehow, these encouragements to professionalism and improved appearance (which I received repeatedly in my own military career, in words that were far more provocative) were seen as crossing a line. Someone complained that his remarks amounted to a *microaggression*.

Instead of supporting First Sergeant Parish's admonishment to uphold standards, the academy's senior leaders publicly apologized to the entire corps of cadets for this "microaggression." Colonel Julian Stephens wrote an email stating, "On behalf of all [Cadet Wing Senior] Leadership and permanent party members, let me apologize for the email sent earlier today by our First Sergeant." Colonel Stephens went on: "These comments were very disrespectful, derogatory and unprofessional and in no way reflective of [cadet wing leadership] views. Microaggressions such as these are often blindspots/unintentional biases that are not often recognized, and if they are recognized they are not always addressed."[41]

After the emails were leaked to the press, the academy's subsequent official statements were entirely in the tone of a politically correct civilian university. "The comments were inappropriate. We have a responsibility for how we communicate and if anyone feels disrespected by someone's words, we take that very seriously. We need to take responsibility immediately and learn from it as we move forward," an academy spokesperson said. A reporter noted that the "commandant is making dignity and respect a priority for her staff."[42] Perhaps a better priority would be focusing on how to deal with enemy aggressions on a battlefield rather than the presumed verbal "microaggressions" of noncommissioned officers.

The "microaggression" incident was part of a larger trend. Consistent with the diversity emphasis in non-military universities (the University of Michigan, for example, spends $10.6 million annually to keep 82 diversity officers on payroll[43]), the Air Force Academy created the position of Chief Officer of Culture, Climate, and Diversity in 2010.[44] Indeed, the academy's dean of faculty told *The Atlantic* in May 2016 that an emphasis on diversity was "embedded in many of the courses we teach."[45] The *Atlantic* article also noted (approvingly) that "During the year, faculty gather occasionally at lunch to talk about books on belonging," such as Columbia University Provost "Claude Steele's *Whistling Vivaldi: How Stereotypes Affect Us and What We Can Do.*"

While "diversity" is on the rise at the Air Force Academy, religious liberty has taken a nose dive. Air Force regulations adopted in 2012 severely restricted cadet leaders' freedom to discuss even their personal religious convictions, let alone religion as a philosophical topic.[46] The same year, the Academy removed the phrase "so help me God" from the oath of enlistment in its cadet handbook, allegedly by mistake, but the following year, an academy poster displaying the cadet Honor Oath was removed because it contained the phrase.[47] In 2014, a cadet commander was forced to erase a Bible verse from his personal whiteboard outside the entrance to his barracks room.[48] Three years earlier, five faculty members sued the Air Force (unsuccessfully) to block a voluntary prayer luncheon at the academy chapel featuring a keynote speech by Marine veteran Clebe McClary, a Vietnam War hero who lost an arm and an eye in the service of his country. The faculty members complained that McClary's visit was inappropriate because he described himself as a "U.S. Marine for Christ" in his bio.[49]

These sorts of changes go beyond altering the service academies' traditional culture. They go directly to academy curricula as well. At the

Air Force Academy, cadets can now take "Gender, Sexuality, and Society," a class exploring how gender is "shaped by social processes, including social interactions, institutions, ideologies, and culture—and how these beliefs create and enforce a system of inequality."[50] West Point now offers a Diversity and Inclusion Studies minor, created by Professor Ender and two other civilian professors and funded by the Superintendent's Diversity and Inclusion Endowment.[51] The Academy's sociology department describes the minor this way:

> The content of the minor is similar to several other diversity minors offered at other universities. Though there are numerous diversity programs throughout the country, there are very few schools that offer minors in this field of study. None of our aspirant or peer institutions offer such a minor. Most universities including our aspirant and peer schools have gone significant steps beyond simply the diversity minor and now have departments and/or centers that specialize in race/ethnic/gender studies such as Black Studies, Native American Studies, LGBTQ Studies, or Women's Studies offering a major.[52]

Of course, the purpose of the service academies is not to emulate other colleges or universities but to train officers to lead soldiers, sailors, airmen, and Marines. Perhaps, then, politicized "diversity" studies should be less important at West Point, the Naval Academy, and the Air Force Academy than courses on military history or any other subject with concrete, real-world applications. But, as Lieutenant Colonel Heffington told me, "There was an enormous push to make diversity, inclusion, women's/feminist studies, etc., more important parts of the curriculum" at West Point, and, he noted, that push is only going to get worse as civilian professors are now pushing for senior academic leadership positions, which, traditionally, have been reserved for military officers.

To be accepted to a military academy is an honor that comes with a service commitment. The officers in charge of these institutions should remind themselves of their primary duty and mission. It is not to win plaudits from progressive ideologues or to accommodate the interests of leftist faculty. It is to prepare the next generation of military leadership. It is well past time that some of these officers showed more leadership themselves.

CHAPTER
3
THE TRANSGENDER MANDATE

"A soldier has completed Army gender transition from female to male. The soldier did not have sex reassignment surgery and recently stopped taking male hormones in order to start a family. Today, the soldier approached his commanding officer to discuss his newly-confirmed pregnancy."
—*Vignette from a Department of the Army training presentation teaching commanding officers how to deal with "male pregnancy"*

I do not and will not question the motives of the transgender persons who wish to serve in the US armed forces. I have no doubt they are every bit as patriotic and service-oriented as any other recruits. But a noble desire to serve does not, on its own, qualify one for service, and certainly not under any conditions other than those the military believes will enhance its mission of winning wars and protecting the country. The military is an institution with a singular purpose whose success ultimately depends on physical outcomes—and thus, service must be based on *physical* realities. For that reason, it is important to understand why none of President Obama's social engineering projects provoked more strenuous objections from the force than the transgender policy did. All four service chiefs opposed it.[1] When President Trump announced on July 26, 2017, his plan to reverse it and reinstate the military's prior, longstanding policy on gender dysphoria, the media quickly adopted the narrative that Trump was acting against the wishes of the military and simply out of bigotry. Soon they began reporting that the military was actually defying the commander in chief and refusing to implement his policy. *USA Today*, for example, ran a "Breaking" headline that declared in part, "Mattis freezes transgender policy."[2] The newspaper was far from alone. Even the conservative *Daily Wire* ran the headline "Navy Secretary Defies Trump: Transgender Troops Should Be Able to Serve."[3]

This narrative, useful for progressives, was pure fiction. In June 2017, a month before Obama's transgender policy was to take full effect, the commanding generals of the Army, Air Force, and Marines asked the Pentagon to delay expansions of the policy for one or two years.[4] A week earlier, the chairman of the Joint Chiefs, General Joseph Dunford, told a Senate committee that the new policy caused problems that "some of the service chiefs believe need to be resolved before we move forward."[5] In response, Secretary of Defense Mattis ordered an in-house review of the feasibility of the Obama policy. In a memorandum to President Trump, Mattis wrote, "[a]fter consulting with the service chiefs and secretaries, I have determined that it is necessary to defer the start of [the enlistment of transgender soldiers] for six months. We will use this additional time to reevaluate more carefully the impact [of the policy] on readiness and lethality."[6] (By "lethality," Mattis meant the ability of combat units to engage and destroy enemies in battle. Readiness, generally speaking, refers to the military's ability to win America's wars while losing as few American lives as possible.) All of this took place prior to Trump's announcement.

When Mattis became the secretary of defense, the service chiefs told him that they had not been consulted about the Obama Administration's transgender policy. In an exchange with Senator Kirsten Gillibrand at an Armed Services Committee hearing in April 2018, after Trump announced his intent to reverse the Obama-era policy, Mattis recounted this conversation with his top generals:

> They were asking me questions because we were coming up on the advent of the induction of [the] transgender [policy], and they wanted to know how they were going to deal with certain issues, basic training, deployability. I said, "Didn't you

get all of this when the policy was rolled out?"...They said "no." And I said, "Well did you have input?" And they said no, they did not.

He characterized that revelation as "very, very newsworthy."[7]

Mattis also pointedly noted that his predecessor, Ashton Carter, had prohibited military leaders from speaking publicly about any problems caused by the new transgender policy since doing so would violate the privacy of transgender service members.[8] At a separate meeting with reporters, Mattis questioned the validity of a RAND Corporation study, commissioned by the Obama administration, that concluded that the proposed policy change would have only a "minimal impact" on military operations. "I'm not willing to sign up for the [RAND] numbers," he told the assembled journalists.[9]

The media narrative about the Trump policy from day one has been that President Trump upended a settled policy that was uniformly accepted within the ranks by sending a few impulsive tweets. In fact, Trump's Twitter announcement—as unwise as the method may have been, and as abrupt and unexpected as it may have been to everyone, including the senior brass—came *in the midst of* a self-initiated Pentagon review about the wisdom and feasibility of the Obama-era policy change. The Pentagon was already holding weekly meetings at the highest levels to review the Obama policy when Trump announced his intent to change it, and those meetings continued well after Trump tweeted his intentions, according to a military source within the Pentagon with firsthand knowledge about the content and timing of the meetings. It was only after Mattis's internal review finished and the Pentagon sent its conclusions to the White House that formal policy changes were announced.

"They Definitely Started with an End in Mind"

It is important to understand how the Obama administration's initial policy change was made and what effects that policy would have on military readiness if it were fully implemented. On June 30, 2016, Secretary of Defense Ashton Carter announced the Obama administration's decision to allow transgender service members to serve under the standards of their "gender identity" instead of the standards designed for their biological sex.[10] The "first and fundamental reason" for the policy change, Carter said, was to ensure that the military could "avail [itself] of all talent possible in order to remain what we are now—the finest fighting force the world has ever known."

The new policy was the culmination of several years of planning and maneuvering. In 2013, top officials in the administration such as Valerie Jarrett and Secretary of Defense Chuck Hagel began using the term "LGBT" instead of "gay and lesbian"—most notably in their speeches at the 2013 Pentagon LGBT Pride Celebration. This change was correctly interpreted by many progressives and LGBT activists as a hint that a change in transgender policy was coming.[11]

Eric Fanning, while under secretary of the Air Force, publicly supported the policy change in 2013.[12] That same year, the Pentagon began changing the service records of transgender veterans to reflect their current gender identity instead of the sex that had been the context for all of their prior service.[13] Air Force Secretary Deborah Lee James followed Fanning's lead in 2014 and began publicly pushing for the policy change,[14] predicting that the Pentagon's longstanding policy was likely to "come under review in the next year or so."[15] Pressure came from Capitol Hill as well. In November 2014, the House Democratic leader, Nancy Pelosi, called for the Pentagon to change its policy.[16]

In 2015, Fanning, then secretary of the Army, removed the authority to dismiss transgender service members from commanders, centralizing it at the federal level with a senior civilian appointee.[17] The previous policy had recognized that unit commanders' familiarity with their soldiers made them best suited to decide on whether an individual's medical needs and other situational factors required separation from the military. Secretary of the Air Force Deborah James went a step further a few months later, placing discharge authority for transgender service members solely in the hands of the Air Force Review Boards Agency (the highest appellate review board in the Air Force) and authorizing discharges only in the rarest of cases, a standard that *Vox* celebrated as "unprecedented in the military."[18]

In February 2015, only days after his confirmation as secretary of defense, Ashton Carter abruptly announced that he was "very open-minded" about changing the military's transgender policy.[19] The president's press secretary responded, "We here at the White House welcome the comments of the Secretary of Defense."[20] The media reported that calls "for [a change] ramped up" after Carter's statement.[21] When asked what Carter's comments meant, a Pentagon spokesman said that the military began a "routine, periodic review" of medical standards for military service in February that would likely continue for roughly a year.[22]

President Obama remained formally neutral while the military supposedly studied whether the change was in the national interest. But in June 2015, long before any formal study had begun, he made his views clear by inviting two openly transgender active-duty service members and four transgender veterans to the White House. Considering that gender dysphoria was technically still grounds for discharge from the military, the commander in chief's gesture sent an unmistakable message—a "positive signal," *Politico* called it.[23]

In July 2015, Carter directed acting Under Secretary of Defense for Personnel and Readiness Brad Carson to "convene a working group to identify the practical issues related to transgender Americans serving openly in the Armed Forces, and to develop an implementation plan that addressed those issues."[24] The civilian secretary of each branch was responsible for supervising its participation in the working group. Deborah Lee James, for example, said that she "met regularly with members of the Working Group to discuss their progress and the Air Force's positions on the issues discussed."[25] In other words, the working group convened by the Pentagon to determine the feasibility of allowing transgender soldiers to serve according to their "gender identity" instead of their sex was supervised by political appointees who had advocated that change for years.

Later, in sworn declarations in support of lawsuits to prevent the reversal of Obama's transgender policy, those same political appointees affirmed that the new policy had received unanimous support from the members of the working group.[26] Yet the service chiefs were part of the working group, and according to Secretary Mattis's testimony before the Senate—also under oath—they told Mattis that they had not been consulted. These accounts are difficult to reconcile.

According to filings in the litigation, the working group's "process involved three steps: (1) *Understanding the medical needs* of transgender service members; (2) *identifying how those needs could be met* within the Military Health System; and (3) *developing policies and protocols to ensure transgender service members could serve openly* and have their medical needs met."[27]

In other words, the working group's conclusions were predetermined. And everyone involved knew it. A former chief of medical staff at a large military base who regularly interacted with and sought guidance from the DoD as the Obama policy developed told me that, in his view, "They very definitely started with an end in mind." And Carter himself later admitted in a press conference that he "directed the working group to start with the presumption that transgender persons can serve openly without adverse effect—impact, excuse me, on military effectiveness and readiness."[28] A general who was serving in the Pentagon at the time told me, "When [the Obama officials] were coming to the final decision" about the transgender policy, "it had to be the [service chiefs or assistant service chiefs] that went to the meetings—and no substitutes—because it was just that high-level, and it was just back-driven at that level of operation."

Roughly a year after it was established, the working group recommended a complete reversal of longstanding policy. It concluded (incorrectly, for reasons explained later in this chapter) that daily hormone replacement therapy and other medications had no effect on a service member's ability to deploy.[29] Carter, to no one's surprise, accepted its recommendation and announced a new policy authorizing transgender service members to serve openly according to the standards and requirements of their "gender identity" rather than their sex. Carter thus favored the recommendation of political appointees with no military experience over the vocal, repeated, and informed objections of generals who had more than a hundred years of combined military experience, including significant combat experience.

Ordinarily, one or more of the Joint Chiefs would appear with the secretary of defense at a press conference announcing a major policy change. It was telling, then, that no member of the Joint Chiefs appeared with Carter when he announced the transgender policy,[30] and the absence did not go unnoticed. As a general who served in the Pentagon during the Obama administration put it, this was "very subtle Pentagon messaging." Another senior general agrees:

> Ash Carter just came out [and] made an announcement, and I don't think any of the service chiefs really had input to it. They may have been able to be heard, but I don't think any of them would say that they ever actually influenced the position, and I think that's because at the time the position had already been made even before it got to the Pentagon. Then the Pentagon went on this kind of a show of a one-year listening tour, talking about how are we actually going to implement this policy. But again, I think it was mostly just kind of a show of listening. I don't think there was actually a lot of input to it.

After Carter's announcement, a journalist asked him, "Why [isn't] Chairman Dunford here to discuss this policy since it affects the uniformed military?" Because "[T]his is my decision," Carter replied. But the top generals supported his decision, Carter insisted—an assertion the service chiefs would later dispute, as we have seen, in conversations with Carter's successor and that Carter himself undermined in his very next sentence: "I actually made some adjustments specifically to take into account some of the desire by some of the chiefs to have a little more time on the front end, particularly for the commanders in training guidance, and so I agreed to that because I thought that was reasonable."[31]

Defending the policy change, Carter observed that "over a third of Fortune 500 companies, including companies like Boeing, CVS, and Ford, offer employee health insurance plans with transgender-inclusive coverage," a figure that was "up from zero such companies in 2000." This argument is absurd on its face. Whether a store manager at CVS has access to "transgender-inclusive coverage" tells us nothing about whether placing female-to-male or male-to-female soldiers in various stages of gender transition on the battlefields of Afghanistan enhances the military's ability to protect the nation. That the secretary of defense would make such a statement is a damning indictment of the Obama administration's credibility on military policy; it viewed the military as just another branch of the federal bureaucracy, with soldiers, sailors, airmen, and Marines no different from other government workers.

As one general said to me, "It's impossible to make [the] argument" that the Obama administration's policy change would make the military more lethal. In fact, it would make it less lethal, as we'll see.

Physical Standards Matter

The refrain from progressives and other supporters of the Obama-era policy is that "everyone who is qualified to serve should be allowed to serve." When President Trump announced on Twitter that he was reversing the Obama policy, former Vice President Biden responded by tweeting, "Every patriotic American who is qualified to serve in our military should be able to serve. Full stop."[32] This talking point, picked up and repeated by a great many well-meaning but uninformed people, obscures the issue. Nobody disputes that all qualified volunteers should be allowed to serve their country. The question is the meaning of "qualified."

Another common defense of the Obama policy is that "transgender troops were already serving" under the longstanding policy, proving that the policy changed nothing. This dishonest argument also obscures the issue. Yes, there were certainly some service members who identified as transgender before the change in policy, but they were serving *according to the physical fitness, grooming, and housing regulations that corresponded to their biological sex*. The Obama policy, by contrast, authorizes people to serve according to the standards of the sex that matches their "identity." No one was "already serving" under the standards authorized by the Obama policy.

Activists like to compare the transgender policy before Obama's change to the "Don't Ask, Don't Tell" policy that previously prohibited openly gay persons from serving, but the two policies deal with different issues and are predicated upon different reasoning. "Don't Ask, Don't Tell" was based on the premise that knowledge of lesbian and gay soldiers' sexual orientation would hurt unit cohesion and morale, thus supposedly degrading military readiness. It was overturned by an act of Congress and no one is trying to bring it back. The gender-identity policy, in contrast, is based on considerations directly related to *the individual soldier's* physical fitness, performance, and deployability and has nothing to do with *other* soldiers' opinions or attitudes about transgender persons. The transgender policy prior to Obama's change simply enforced the military's uniform combat readiness standards that apply to all servicemen and women. Furthermore, the policy of the Trump administration allows troops who identify as transgender to be open about their gender identity—it simply requires them to meet the physical fitness and appearance standards corresponding to their sex. A general who served during both the repeal of "Don't Ask, Don't Tell" and the Obama administration's transgender policy change told me that he thought the transgender policy was an obviously "different issue" from "Don't Ask, Don't Tell" and was surprised that it was not recognized as such. "I was scratching my head, thinking this is a no-brainer," he said.

The Obama policy allowed transgender service members to switch their "gender marker" in the Army's personnel database without undergoing sex-reassignment surgery or any other physical changes. All that was required was for a military or civilian doctor to certify that the person has achieved "stability in the preferred gender," and the service member can change the gender designation on a passport or birth certificate. From that point on, transgender soldiers were "expected to adhere to all military standards associated with their new gender" and "use the [corresponding] billeting, bathroom and shower facilities." Before President Trump rescinded the transgender enlistment policy, soldiers would have been able to enlist in the military under the gender with which they identify—regardless of whether they had undergone sex-reassignment surgery—as long as they had shown "stability in the preferred gender" for eighteen months or more prior to their enlistment.

The Obama transgender policy raises three problems for readiness. The first is the problem of evaluating transgender service members' physical fitness for duty not according to the standards for their sex but according to the standards for their "gender identity." A standard, by definition, applies to things that are comparable in a certain respect. *Physical* fitness standards are designed for groups of persons who share *physical* characteristics. The transgender policy's violation of common sense is explicit in the accompanying guidance to commanders: "For policies and standards that apply differently to Soldiers according to gender, the Army recognizes a Soldier's gender by the Soldier's gender marker in the Defense Enrollment Eligibility Reporting Systems (DEERS)."

So how does recognizing soldiers' gender identities instead of their biological sex for purposes of physical fitness standards play out in practice? An eighteen-year-old male soldier who has 21 percent body fat is considered a liability in combat and is non-deployable. Because healthy body fat levels differ for males and females, however, an eighteen-year-old female soldier with 21 percent body fat is considered fit for duty. Under the Obama policy, an eighteen-year-old soldier with 21 percent body fat and a male body but who identifies as female would be eligible for deployment even though the same soldier would have been non-deployable any other day if he identified as a male.

Even then, some of the service secretaries established exemptions for transgender service members who failed their physical fitness tests during their gender-transition process.[33] A memorandum from Secretary of the Air Force Deborah James exempted transgender airmen undergoing cross-sex hormone treatment from the Air Force's physical fitness assessments while in the transition phase (which can last more than a year)— that is, before they had fully completed their transitions and formally "switched" genders in the military personnel system. To obtain an exemption, airmen would have to provide evidence that they made good-faith efforts to pass the physical fitness test but failed to meet the standards of their current genders (that is, genders that correspond to sex and physical characteristics).[34] Airmen could also apply for an exemption that allowed them to use the housing, bathroom, and shower facilities that align with their gender identities even before completing the transition process and changing their gender markers in the military's personnel system.

In fact, the necessity of tying physical readiness standards to biological realities was precisely the reason the Mattis Report advised the White House to nip the Obama policy changes in the bud. The report argued that the approach urged by the Mattis DoD "will ensure that biologically-based standards will be applied uniformly to all Service members of the same biological sex. Standards that are clear, coherent, objective, consistent, predictable, and uniformly applied enhance good order, discipline, steady leadership, and unit cohesion, which in turn, ensure military effectiveness and lethality."[35]

What Physical Standards Should Apply to a Service Member Who Identifies as Neither Male nor Female? What about a Service Member Who Identifies as Both?

The premise of gender identity theory is that gender is distinct from and not necessarily related to sex. That is, a person's gender identity need not align with the person's sex, and it need not align with *either* sex.

Indeed, a virtually infinite number of gender identities can be posited. A growing number of transgender persons identify as "non-binary." Gender ideology has already begun to seep into governmental policies and records. The University of Vermont, for example, officially recognizes a third gender: "neutral."[36] In 2016, New York City's Commission on Human Rights released a list of thirty-one different gender identities that are protected by the city's antidiscrimination laws.[37] The gender identities officially recognized by the city include "Bi-Gendered," "Femme Queen," "Genderqueer," and "Gender Bender." California, Oregon, Washington, and New Jersey offer the choice of a "non-binary" option on birth certificates.[38] New York City offers a third option, "X." Three states now allow persons to identify as "non-binary" on their driver's licenses, and several public school systems permit students to identify as "non-binary."[39]

The military uses different body composition standards for males and females—which body composition standards should apply to someone who identifies as "X"? That is, what are the proper height, weight, and body fat standards for non-binary soldiers who identify as neither male nor female? If it is impermissible to hold biologically male service members to male physical fitness standards if they identify as female, what about biologically male soldiers who identify as non-binary or genderqueer? And what might the standards be for those gender identities?

If a recruit who is biologically male but whose legal gender is "X" enlists in the US military, should that recruit be held to the body-fat standards designed for males or those designed for females? If the answer is neither, must we come up with a third body-fat standard for "X"? If not, how is requiring the recruit to meet either the male standards or the female standards when the recruit is (legally speaking) neither male nor female any different from requiring a biological male who does not identify as male to meet male standards? And if we *do* come up with a third standard for "X," does that standard apply to every recruit who identifies as "gender neutral" or only to that individual recruit? Once we divorce military measurements of physical readiness from the physical characteristics of the persons we are evaluating, we no longer have any objective basis on which to judge troops' physical abilities in an equal or consistent manner.

Regardless of one's opinion about bathroom bills or any of the other culture-war flashpoints about gender identity, reasonable observers should acknowledge that in a military setting, this transgender policy is dangerously misguided. Transgender activists like to say, "Biology is not destiny." But even if that were true, physical realities still matter on the battlefield. An AK-47 round travels toward a soldier at 2,330 feet per second no matter how its intended target self-identifies. A six-foot, 180-pound anatomically male soldier can either pull his bodyweight over a wall, carry another soldier, and walk for miles with eighty pounds of equipment or he cannot. But under the Obama policy, a service member's combat-readiness depends on whether he identifies himself as the type of person who would be combat-ready in his situation. That's very millennial, but it's not a very good way to fight wars.

The Trump policy—which trans activists fought tooth and nail and which has been jammed up by unprecedented lower-court rulings—strikes a balance between concern for equal opportunity and the need to maintain combat readiness and deployability. Less restrictive than the transgender policy in effect before 2014, it simply requires that service members meet the physical fitness standards and live according to the regulations that apply to their biological sex, whatever they declare their "gender identity" to be. Gender dysphoria alone is not grounds for dismissal. Service members are free to live as they wish outside of duty hours. But an institution concerned first and foremost with physical outcomes must use physical, biological realities as its baseline criteria for evaluating eligibility for service.

There Must Be Legitimate, If Uncomfortable, Discussions about Mental Health

The second problem for readiness that the Obama policy raises involves mental health. In a tweetstorm after the announcement of President Trump's new transgender policy, J. R. Salzman, an Iraq veteran, argued forcefully that the uniquely stressful environment of combat can break even the most mentally and emotionally stable soldiers.[40] A world-champion lumberjack and log-roller and the ESPY Best Outdoor Sports Athlete of the Year in 2005, Salzman deployed to Iraq with his National Guard unit in 2006 and lost his right arm in an improvised explosive device (IED) attack.[41] His Twitter thread vividly conveys war's effects on soldiers:

> I served in Iraq in 2006. For the first five months, I was on a 12 man firebase out in the middle of nowhere in the desert. Everyday was Groundhog Day. Wake up and do the same patrols, the same shifts, every single day. It was so damn hot. 150° in the gun trucks. Tracer fire would go overhead occasionally at night. IED's on the road were a daily threat. We got resupplied food every 8 days. QRF [quick reaction force—reinforcements] was an hour away. After they made the minimum three gun truck rule after the guys got kidnapped, life got harder. The stress of being out there and doing the same job every single day eats away at you. The younger guys had problems with that over time. Any tiny little personal issue they had suddenly became a mountain. And that shit came out on that fire base. And they snapped mentally.
>
> After stepping on each other's nuts living in the same can for five months, guys were at each other's throats. The stress made it worse. Guys would literally snap over a dear John letter. Their personal issues came out and they were instantly combat ineffective. Now take someone confused about whether they are a man/woman. Take those psychological and emotional issues and put them in that environment. Take someone who is right off the bat not uniform or part of the same team. Give them special treatment because of their identity. Take that person, put them in that stressful war environment and watch what happens. It's a fucking ticking time bomb.

You can't teach someone to be a fearless warrior in a fucking PowerPoint. You either have it or you don't. You can hack it or you can't. We had guys who couldn't. When faced with combat situations they crumbled. They had mental and emotional issues. They were a liability. To be successful at war, you have to become a warrior mentally, physically, and emotionally. You can't fake it and go through the motions. In war if it comes down to kill or be killed, and you hesitate, you're dead. It's a simple as that. It's not a fucking video game. War is no place for people who are mentally, emotionally, or physically confused or in turmoil. You have your shit together, or you don't. And if you don't, you'll just get people needlessly killed. Political correctness has absolutely no place in the military.

Salzman's thread is compelling. Nearly half of transgender persons in the process of transitioning or after transitioning suffer from depression or anxiety.[42] More than one in five have considered suicide within the previous thirty days, and 41 percent do attempt suicide at some point.[43] These statistics are awful, and they merit greater attention and examination to reduce the suffering of those involved. But fragile mental health is simply not compatible with a deployment to a combat zone. Deployment, a close friend of mine observed while we were in Afghanistan, is "like an echo chamber of your own emotions." Deployment is not good for anyone's blood pressure, but it can be catastrophic for those who bring outside stressors with them. The military routinely screens out recruits who have a history of depression and anxiety, despite their admirable desire to serve, and it does so under the principle that "everyone *who is qualified* to serve should be allowed to serve."

"You Can't Have an Endocrinologist Who Specializes in Reproductive Endocrinology Downrange"

The third problem with the Obama policy is a matter of simple logistics. Deploying soldiers who require a steady, if not daily, regimen of hormone treatments to stay healthy raises undeniable logistical problems. A former chief of medicine at a major military installation put it this way: "What do you do? You can't have an endocrinologist who specializes in reproductive endocrinology downrange. It just doesn't make sense." Soldiers in basic training are not even allowed to keep personal bottles of Advil because the military is designed to produce warriors who can function independently in austere and primitive environments and must weed out those who cannot do so.[44]

The working group's conclusion that providing hormone therapy to deployed service members presents no challenge—even if you assume for the sake of argument that this assessment is accurate, which it isn't—assumes that we will always be conducting low-intensity stability operations in places where we have forward operating bases and a well-established supply chain. Not every war will be like Afghanistan in 2016. If a transgender soldier is serving with a unit assigned to a remote observation post in Syria, carrying only rucksacks and weapons, should resupplies of hormone injections be flown in for the transgender soldier? Should the medic remove other medical supplies from his med-bag to make room for two weeks' worth of injections or patches? If the answer is yes, is it fair to the pilots who may have to expose themselves to anti-aircraft fire to fly resupply missions if the supplies of those medications run low or to the medics who now must carry extra supplies or to the platoon that may have fewer pressure dressings with them? For those very reasons, the military does not deploy soldiers who require ongoing treatment for a vast array of medical conditions, however ardently they wish to serve. Furthermore, if the answer is "No, the transgender soldier cannot deploy," is it fair to the next service member who must take that soldier's place? And if there is no service member to replace the transgender soldier, is it fair to the rest of that individual's squad and platoon that now must deploy with at least one fewer soldier or Marine than they planned?

Even persons who forego hormone replacement therapy frequently experience long-term complications from sex-reassignment surgeries that are incompatible with the potential requirements of extended ground combat missions.[45] Indeed, the Obama policy authorized transgender service members who are in the process of transitioning to take extended leave while they complete the process,[46] a necessary addition to the transgender policy because the consuming demands of the transition process are simply incompatible with the daily requirements of service in a military unit in many cases. The *Washington Post* article "Tyler Becomes Taylor: A Transgender Coast Guard Officer in Transition," which followed an officer through the transition process, unintentionally revealed just how incompatible the gender transition process is with basic military life.[47] "[Lieutenant] Miller's transition includes painful facial and genital hair removal, constant medical appointments and staggering medical expenses," the *Post* told readers. The process was interrupted by "outpatient [mental health] care for a month" after Miller suffered a panic attack on duty.

The *New York Times* op-ed "My New Vagina Won't Make Me Happy" by a person preparing for the transition from male to female likewise highlights the inherent complications of sex-reassignment surgery: "Next Thursday, I will get a vagina. The procedure will last around six hours, and I will be in recovery for at least three months. Until the day I die, my body will regard the vagina as a wound; as a result, it will require regular, painful attention to maintain."[48]

These intensive medical procedures are simply incompatible with wartime service. And if soldiers who require ongoing treatment are not deployable, why sign them up? How does that make our country safer? And if we make an exception for one small segment of society—those who identify as transgender—why not for other people who cannot deploy, like patriotic asthmatics? The military's mission is singular and exclusive: to be as lethal and efficient as possible so it can protect this nation by defeating its enemies on the battlefield. We should pursue every policy that makes us more effective—and reject any policy that fails to do so.

"Understand That You May Encounter Individuals in Barracks, Bathrooms, or Shower Facilities with Physical Characteristics of the Opposite Sex Despite Having the Same Gender"

Apart from questions about transgender service members' physical and psychological ability to serve in wartime and the feasibility of such deployments, the policy authorized by the Obama administration—and reversed by the Trump administration—also raises serious privacy questions. The Army's "Tier Three Transgender Training" brief, given to all soldiers in the force, tells soldiers to "understand that you may encounter individuals in barracks, bathrooms, or shower facilities with physical characteristics of the opposite sex despite having the same gender marker in DEERS." The next bullet point adds that "all Soldiers should be respectful of the privacy and modesty concerns of others. However, transgender Soldiers are not required or expected to modify or adjust their behavior based on the fact that they do not 'match' other Soldiers." This is a first. The military is normally in the business of telling soldiers to "modify or adjust their behavior" *all the time.*

Consider what these policies mean in real life: Most army showers look like a prison cell with several showerheads on the wall. Anyone who has dealt with the practical challenges of funneling thirty people through them in ten minutes understands that "privacy" is impossible. And female soldiers who feel uncomfortable exposing themselves to persons who still have "physical characteristics of the opposite sex" will just have to put up with it. The adjustments to billeting are equally intrusive. Modern barracks resemble college dorms, with two soldiers of the same sex—now "gender marker"—sharing a room just large enough to accommodate the basic necessities of military life. The training brief forbids any commander from ordering a transgender soldier to occupy a billet that is inconsistent with the soldier's "gender marker" and rejects separate quarters for transgender soldiers. If there are separate facilities of any kind, they must be for soldiers who are unwilling to share quarters with transgender service members of the opposite sex. In short, the rest of the unit must adjust, not the individual transgender soldier.

The changes also affected drug testing procedures. Department of Defense Instruction 1010.16 requires urine specimens to be "collected under the direct observation of a designated individual of the same sex as the Service member providing the specimen." To be blunt, "observers" must watch the urine sample leave the tested soldier's body and enter the collection cup. Under the new rules, however, "absent an exception to policy, the observer will be the same gender as the Soldier being observed (*as reflected by the gender marker* in DEERS)." The change is justified by interpreting the term "sex" in existing drug testing regulations to have the same meaning as "gender." In other words, an eighteen-year-old female soldier may be forced to drop her pants and urinate in a cup in front of a male non-commissioned officer who identifies as female, and a female may be forced to observe a soldier who has a penis but identifies as female pee into a cup, "absent an exception to policy."[49]

How can the military justify these requirements to survivors of sexual assault, who very understandably may be averse to undressing in close quarters with someone who has the genitalia of the opposite sex? These policies represent a judgment that the feelings of soldiers who identify as transgender are more important than those of soldiers who may have survived sexual assault.

Furthermore, the very idea of "training" more than 99 percent of the force to accommodate the demands of less than 1 percent runs counter to basic military principles. Since when do we "train the force" (to use Ashton Carter's phrase from his press conference) to accommodate individuals? And if the policy simply codifies existing practices, as its proponents say, and if the change will have no effect, why is it necessary to train the entire force to prepare for it?

Some of the same persons who promoted these transgender regulations also promoted—rightfully—greater scrutiny of sexual assault allegations within the services. When the media reported that a male soldier secretly filmed other soldiers in a women's locker room, for example, Senator Kirsten Gillibrand characterized the story as proof that the military has a "sexual assault problem."[50] But at the same time, Gillibrand, a Democrat from New York, was forcefully advocating a policy that would place males who "identify" as female in women's locker rooms, with no recourse for women who objected. The cognitive dissonance required to support these policies simultaneously is astounding. Either Senator Gillibrand was unaware of the practical consequences of the policy or, bowing to pressure from the far left, she chose to ignore those consequences.

These radical changes will inevitably have secondary effects that extend beyond the direct problems discussed earlier in this chapter. Servicemen and women join the armed forces to fulfill a dangerous and at times thankless mission. When the armed forces themselves undermine that mission, they erode service members' respect for the mission and their confidence that their commanding officers take that mission seriously too. In late 2016, for example, I spoke to a close friend who was an Army captain deployed to Afghanistan at the time and was slated to take command of a military intelligence company, a coveted assignment for intelligence officers, upon redeployment. He told me he was foregoing his command and leaving the Army after that deployment because he could not "morally accept [the transgender policy's] adverse impact on readiness." He did not believe that he would be able to "wholeheartedly advocate for the welfare" of his future soldiers—including soldiers who may be transgender—under the policy. He had direct combat experience, a top-secret clearance, and foreign language abilities. In other words, he was exactly the type of skilled leader that our military must retain to keep its edge over its adversaries in future conflicts, but he left the force because of social engineering policies of progressive political appointees. He's now getting an MBA.

Australia and Other Countries Show Where This Leads

Because there are so few transgender service members, some hope the issues raised will be "minimal" and justify avoiding this uncomfortable debate. But there is no such thing as a "minimal" effect on readiness at the level of the individual soldier; and the experience of other Western militaries that have already embraced gender ideology offer further warnings.

As those who have followed the gender-identity disputes over the past handful of years can attest, policy changes are never confined to the tiny minority of persons who identify as transgender and those who interact with them. No, gender identity policies generally demand that all of society actively affirm the "lived reality" of trans persons. Twitter, for example, has banned a Canadian feminist for tweeting—to no one individually—that "men are not women."[51] Western countries' militaries are being drafted into the effort to compel acceptance of the "gender identity" ideology. New directives in Australia, for example, warn that soldiers can be punished for using "non-inclusive language" such as failing to use another soldier's preferred pronouns.[52] In other words, it is not enough to allow transgender persons to serve according to the standards of their gender identities instead of actual biological sex; everyone else must affirm their trans identities or potentially suffer the consequences. The experiences of other Western militaries are particularly relevant to this debate because the DoD explicitly asked the RAND Corporation to consider the experiences of foreign militaries when it conducted its "study," and prominent advocates for the policy change within Defense like Deborah James have pointed to foreign military practices to support their position.)

Australia is far from an isolated example. In the United Kingdom, troops were ordered to stop using language that was considered non-gender-inclusive. "Phrases such as 'mankind' and 'sportsmanship' have been banned amid fears they discourage" transgender persons and others from enlisting. "The new guidelines have been found pinned to the walls of toilets at the Defence Academy at Shrivenham which trains the Army, Navy and [Royal Air Force]," the *Daily Mail* reported.[53] The phrase "gentleman's agreement" was also banned, to be replaced by the more gender-inclusive "unwritten agreement." Unsurprisingly, the new directive did not go over well with British soldiers preoccupied with more important considerations such as fighting wars. "'It's the daftest thing ever,' said one soldier. 'We're building leaders not politically-correct droids.' 'We should be spending more time on tactics than worrying about the niceties of modern language,' said another."

If you doubt that the US military is susceptible to such absurdities, consider that the US Navy's "Commanding Officer's Toolkit [for] Transgender and Gender Transitioning" sailors warns naval commanders that "it is inappropriate to intentionally mix pronoun usage."[54]

There Is a Reason Why No Generals Appeared with Ashton Carter When He Announced the New Policy

Every Obama-era general I spoke to for this book expressed the same misgivings about the Obama administration's policy. One called it "craziness" before pointing out that "we'll tell somebody who's got a chronic condition like diabetes, or even somebody who's got a deviated septum that they can't join." Another said, "common sense wasn't factored into this. It was purely an emotional, agenda-driven political decision." Yet another remarked, "The Department [of Defense] and others have done a pretty good job of laying out why it doesn't make a lot of sense.... [I]t's just pandering to a particular group of Americans for political purposes."

A senior leader in the Air Force Medical Corps relayed his experience dealing with the policy change: "I talked to [senior Air Force officials in the Pentagon], just saying, you know, 'what are we thinking about doing here?' They said, 'this is the policy that's coming down from the head of the Air Force, and we need to—you know, viewpoints are changing on this subject.'" Then he put it another way: "The culture was changing, and the military was expected to change with it without a good look at how this would affect the mission.... And that's why I think it sort of caught, I think, a lot of people in the service unawares because before that it was not something that we ever dealt with." He added that political correctness seemed "to be more important than medical readiness, I think, in a lot of ways. Or combat readiness."

When I asked this officer, a physician, to summarize how the policy came about and why he disagreed so strongly with it, he said:

> I got that impression that there were concerns about the kind of social engineering that was going on on the outside and starting to go into the military. And the issue was that we have a very specific mission, and what could be acceptable in a civilian job, in a civilian setting, is not acceptable in the military. I mean, if you're worried about making sure you take your estrogen [while] you're, like, riding around in an MRAP [a tactical military vehicle commonly used in Afghanistan and elsewhere], you know—that's not what you should be worried about at the time. Eyebrows were being raised. Like, wow, what are they thinking?

But You Cannot Reason Committed Ideologues out of Irrational Conclusions

Nearly every general the Obama administration consulted about the proposed transgender policy said it was a terrible idea. But the ideologues pushed it ahead anyway. The Department of Defense issued a training handbook instructing service members and commanders about what to expect from the new policy and what would be expected of them. Among other things, troops were told to be sensitive to pronoun use.[55] Similar instructions were given to midshipmen at the Naval Academy, who received "Transgender 101" training from two Google employees,[56] one of whom identifies as gender-neutral and uses the pronoun "ze."[57] The Navy issued a "toolkit" to its officers, which prohibited commanders from refusing transition care to sailors and allowed sailors to begin or complete their transitions while they were at sea.[58] The Pentagon also created an open-bathroom policy at all Department of Defense schools for children of service members and contractors stationed at overseas bases, allowing students to use the bathrooms that corresponded with gender identity as opposed to sex.[59]

The Pentagon also modified military healthcare regulations to authorize gender-transition treatments for children of service members,[60] taxpayer-funded hormone treatments to suppress puberty in military dependents diagnosed with gender dysphoria.[61]

The Obama administration's decisions were justified in large part by a RAND Corporation study commissioned by Secretary of Defense Carter, which purported to evaluate whether changing the longstanding policy on gender dysphoria was compatible with the military's broader mission of fighting and winning wars. In reality, the study was a whitewash that, like so many other "policy evaluations" in the Obama era, began with the administration's preferred conclusion and worked backwards from there. The study frequently and uncritically repeats assertions and "research" from the Palm Center, an advocacy group long-dedicated to reversing the military's transgender policy.[62] The authors of the RAND study have been falsely portrayed as neutral, objective "experts." In fact, most of the seven authors had no military experience. At least one of the supposedly nonbiased "experts" advising the Obama administration was a member of President Obama's National Security Council who left to join RAND and "advise" the administration to adopt the policy it already desired. Another has since publicly called for the Department of Veterans Affairs to provide "medically-necessary" gender-transition surgery to veterans and has declared medical arguments against sex-reassignment surgery "thoroughly refuted."[63] When President Trump and Secretary of Defense Mattis announced limitations on the Obama-era policy, the authors of the policy were interviewed and uncritically quoted in the media as if they were experts on the subject, but the truth is that the Obama administration's allies at RAND cooperated with the administration, giving its preferred conclusions a veneer of objectivity.

The RAND study's highly debatable conclusion was that changing the military's policy would have a "minimal impact on readiness,"[64] which Carter repeated in his press conference. In any case, a "minimal impact on readiness" implies *some* impact on readiness, contradicting Carter's assertion that the "first and fundamental" reason for the policy change was to maintain or improve our current readiness levels and ensure that the US military remains the finest fighting force the world has ever known. "We have to have access to 100 percent of America's population for our all-volunteer force to be able to recruit from among them the most highly qualified and to retain them," he said. In other words, the Obama administration thus argued that the policy was necessary for *improving or maintaining* military readiness while simultaneously arguing that the policy would harm readiness only a little.

Military readiness is not an abstract concept. It is a way of describing the degree of likelihood that *young servicemen and women on the ground or at sea, in uniform, will be hurt or killed if they engage with their enemies.* Marginal fluctuations in readiness are not inconsequential. Arguing that a change in policy "will only have a minimal impact on readiness" amounts to saying that the change will make America's men and women in uniform only slightly more likely to die when they meet the nation's enemies in battle.

Final Thoughts

To be clear, I am addressing the question about transgender service members solely from the standpoint of the policy's effect on the military's ability to accomplish its sole mission: defending the country by fighting and winning America's wars. And those who are doing the fighting are the greatest skeptics about the policy. A poll conducted in December 2016 by the *Military Times* found that only 12 percent of active-duty troops thought that the Obama administration's change in policy would improve readiness.[65] No one knows better than they do.

THE REAL RANGER SCHOOL STORY

*"There was a perception that we were being scrutinized
and observed pretty hard to pass them."*
—A Ranger Instructor who was present at the first integrated Ranger
School class

On August 21, 2015, the Army announced that for the first time in history, two females had passed the Army Ranger School course and would graduate with the Ranger tab. They were among the first nineteen women to attempt the course, and the media had followed their ordeal with keen interest. The announcement was not without controversy, however. Rumors of special treatment and lowered standards at the first sex-neutral course had swirled for weeks among many army communities. In fact, so many former Ranger School graduates and other veterans took to online message boards to voice their suspicions and share scuttlebutt about the Army lowering its standards to accommodate the historic graduates that the top brass took the stage at the graduation ceremony to dispel "the nonsense on the internet."[1] The standards, they insisted, had not changed in the slightest.

A month later, freelance journalist Susan Katz Keating published an explosive story in *People* magazine that contradicted the Army's talking points about a level playing field. Keating relied on a number of sources, including several Ranger instructors, who asserted that the training and evaluations had been tilted in the female candidates' favor in a number of important ways. Keating alleged that, prior to the course, the female candidates were placed in a separate platoon, where they received supplementary individualized training from Ranger School graduates. Unlike male candidates, they were allowed to remain in the "pre-Ranger" screening course despite failing critical tests. And the instructors felt intense pressure to make sure the women passed, pressure that led to sharp departures from normal Ranger School standards. Keating's story undermined the Army's narrative.

The Army's chief of public affairs at the time, Brigadier General Malcolm B. Frost, issued a statement denouncing the story in harsh and personal terms, labeling it "pure fiction," emphatically denying nearly every assertion, and accusing Keating of refusing to talk to Army leadership before she published her story. The statement concluded with a shot at Keating's professionalism: "Celebrity gossip may not require fact-checking, fairness or objectivity, but serious journalism does. On that count, Ms. Keating has failed PEOPLE magazine, its readers, and, quite frankly, every man—or woman—who has ever earned the coveted Ranger tab."[2]

General Frost's statement was published on the Army's Facebook page and on his personal Twitter account, provoking a storm of social media attacks on Keating.[3] Keating responded forcefully on Facebook with two statements:

> Gen. Frost, this statement is a lie, and you know it. Stop instigating an online mob attack. It's not in keeping with Army values.... Instead of obfuscating and making a personal attack, please respond to my requests. My sources in [Ranger Training Brigade] are in fear for their careers, because they

have been told to remain silent about a nonclassified program. I repeat: Allow me to speak to the [Ranger instructors], cadre [senior officers who oversee the instructors], students, and medics alone and without fear of retribution to them. I am available all week. When can they meet?

After three days passed with no response from the Army, Keating issued the second statement:

Gen. Frost, one of the commenters on this thread says I should be put in front of a firing squad. I have been held at gunpoint while reporting a story in a conflict zone, and I know what that feels like. So I don't quite get the joke. Nor do I understand why the U.S. Army would leave that comment up on their FB page. Is this what you meant to stir up? Please explain. Please tell the 8K+ people who liked this post and the 900+ people who shared it why, instead of supplying the interviews and information requested of you, you chose to make a personal attack and level charges that you know to be untrue.

As I write, the statement remains on the Army's Facebook page, and the Army has never addressed Keating's response.

Keating called the experience "surreal" during one of our several conversations about the ordeal. Frost's attack on her credibility was especially jarring, she said, because she had "longstanding good relations with the Army, writing about combat and highlighting heroism." A founding trustee of the National Museum of Americans at War, Keating has run a charity that delivers laptops to wounded soldiers at Walter Reed National Military Medical Center, and her reporting has unmasked persons who falsely claim to be war heroes.

Keating says that she initially had no intention to write an exposé. In fact, her very first article about the female graduates was a uniformly positive piece about the Ranger School press conference announcing their success.[4] Her second article about the event was equally as positive.[5] But when reports emerged that standards had not been followed, she contacted her sources at Ranger School and dutifully followed the troubling evidence that emerged. "If the women had gone through the course fairly and under their own steam, I would have written that," she told me. But "the evidence and my sources said otherwise. So that's what I wrote."

The Army's leadership invoked the moral authority of a brigadier general to discredit a journalist who had a track record of covering the heroism of American soldiers, male and female. It depicted her as a fabulist at worst, and a shoddy journalist with a motivation to undermine the success of America's female warriors at best. (Note: it is not clear whether General Frost was aware that some of the contents of his press release were inaccurate, or if he was simply relying on the assurances of Ranger School leadership.) But overwhelming evidence gathered over a twelve-month period proves that senior Defense Department officials—uniformed and civilian—misled the American people about what happened at Ranger School in the summer of 2015 and about Susan Keating's story.

The firsthand accounts of Ranger instructors (RIs), screenshots of contemporaneous messages exchanged among roughly half a dozen RIs during the female candidates' graded patrols and other exercises, a copy of the grading sheet for one of the graduating female candidates' patrols, an internal Army report about the preparation and execution of the test class, and interviews with other sources with firsthand knowledge of events at the course tell a vastly different story from the one that has been presented to the public. I am aware of the vast number of rumors surrounding this event—I heard plenty of them, ranging from the semi-plausible to the absurd, while working on this book—and want to emphasize up front: the only sources I cite to describe what happened during the course were individuals who were physically present at the course itself, and I did not cite information I could not corroborate. To the best of my knowledge, none of my sources who were at the course overlap with Keating's. We did not share details about our respective sources because we both promised them full confidentiality.

The Real Story

The purpose of this story is not to demean, denigrate, or depreciate the female candidates who trained for Ranger School or attended the course. There is no reason to doubt their fitness, motivation, or grit. Quite the opposite. Ranger School is brutal; the average graduate loses thirty to forty pounds. Ranger candidates subsist in the mountains of northern Georgia and the swamps of the Everglades on little food, even less sleep, and no contact with the outside world. Anyone who endures that environment for several months deserves profound respect, but the impressive accomplishment of the female graduates is not a reason to hide the truth about what their superiors did. Nor am I arguing that none of the subsequent female graduates from the course did so under their own steam, or that it's somehow impossible for any female candidate to graduate. I do not believe those things, and neither did multiple sources with whom I spoke. In fact, if anything, the misfeasance by the higher-ups at the test class did the greatest disservice to any female candidates who came after the first graduates because any success has now been met with suspicion in many quarters.

No, the real story here is about undue command influence and an apparent cover-up of the same. It is a story about political appointees and a few career-minded officers who placed their thumbs on the scale at one of the military's premier courses. They manipulated the process in pursuit of their own goals. Their actions evince disrespect for every Ranger candidate.

It is a story that should be told.

What Life at Ranger School Looks Like

For decades, Ranger School has been the Army's premier combat course. A 2010 Discovery Channel documentary called it "the hardest combat course on the planet."[6] The name comes from the colonial company Rogers' Rangers, commanded by Major Robert Rogers in the French and Indian War. His "Twenty-eight Rules of Ranging" still appear at the beginning of the Ranger Handbook. Rule One is "Don't Forget Nothing." (I will always remember Rule One. During Ranger School, I forgot a piece of equipment and paid for my negligence by spending an ungodly amount of time in the "front leaning rest" position repeating the rule.) The motto "Rangers lead the way" originated at Omaha Beach on D-Day when Colonel Norman Cota of the Twenty-Ninth Infantry Division, encountering Major Max Schneider in the waves, asked which unit he was leading. Schneider told him "Fifth Ranger Battalion," and Cota replied, "Well, Goddammit then, Rangers, lead the way!" (Cota is also credited with another famous line at Omaha Beach. On the beach and under fierce shelling from Nazi defenses, he reportedly looked at his men and said "Gentlemen, we are being killed on the beaches. Let us go inland and be killed.")

Ranger School is institutionally distinct from the 75th Ranger Regiment, but the Ranger Tab has always been an entry requirement for all officers and noncommissioned officers in the 75th. Before a specialist can become a sergeant and take on a leadership role in the 75th, for example, that soldier must first have a tab. And even to be considered for acceptance into the 75th, officers must have already earned their Ranger tab. In many of the Army's most prestigious light infantry units, such as the 82nd Airborne and the 101st Airborne, a Ranger tab has traditionally been a non-negotiable prerequisite for lieutenants seeking platoon leader assignments.

The school itself consists of three main phases: Darby Phase, Mountain Phase, and Florida Phase, in that order. Before candidates reach any of those phases, however, they must first pass "RAP Week"—the Ranger Assessment Phase, which entails physical fitness and land navigation tests, repeated physical exercise, and meager food and sleep. Its intensity is legendary. This is when the vast majority of candidates who fail the course are dropped. The Darby Phase (named for Camp Darby, the Fort Benning, Georgia, outpost where it occurs) evaluates candidates' basic infantry skills—such as their ability to disassemble and reassemble various weapons systems within an allotted period of time—and assesses their ability to lead squad-level missions involving up to nine soldiers. The Mountain and Florida phases primarily test candidates' endurance, teamwork, leadership, and tactical abilities. They consist entirely of platoon-level tactics, and candidates are evaluated on their performance in tactical leadership roles within the platoon.

Two slates of candidates are graded during each mission. The first is evaluated during the "planning phase" of the mission on how well they plan the mission itself (including choosing and requesting the appropriate resources), their ability to brief the mission to their subordinates and conduct the appropriate rehearsals, and their ability to navigate from the platoon's patrol base to the objective rally point ("ORP") chosen by the platoon leader close to the location of the mission's target. The ORP is where the platoon hunkers down while the platoon leader and several other members perform a brief reconnaissance of the mission objective. It is also where the second slate of candidates replaces the first. Candidates in the second slate—called the "actions-on" candidates, short for "actions on the [mission] objective")—are evaluated on their ability to execute the mission planned and prepared by the first slate.

The final two phases are characterized by long ground movements that span several miles. In Mountain Phase, those movements often occur on inclines so steep that you can reach forward and touch the earth in front of you while walking uphill, carrying anywhere between sixty and more than one hundred pounds of equipment depending on your position within your platoon. Florida Phase entails trekking through tangled, chest-deep swamp water while trying not to trip on submerged logs or roots, and paddling zodiac boats for hours while mosquitos make a buffet out of your face. Both phases are thoroughly unforgiving and entirely miserable. (An Army friend of mine once described his decision to go to the course as "volunteering to get kicked in the nuts every hour for months.")

For the sixty-two days of the course, candidates train for up to twenty hours a day and subsist on little more than a thousand daily calories. Anyone who has gone to Ranger School has numerous stories about classmates who fell asleep standing in formation or walking on patrol. During multi-day field exercises, platoons sleep in tight patrol bases with a single "slit trench" running down the middle, into which candidates relieve themselves just feet away from their platoon-mates and in full view (at least until recently—post-2015, ponchos are hung around the slit trench to provide a small measure of privacy for the male and female candidates). Any candidate who has made it to the Mountain or Florida Phase has at least a few memories of resting on one knee and trying to focus on the platoon leader outlining his plan in the dirt instead of on the platoon-mate bear-hugging a tree and taking a dump into a shallow hole a few yards away.

At least, that is how a *normal* Ranger School training cycle is conducted. But from the outset, there was nothing normal about this cycle. By the Army's own admission, the results of the integrated Ranger School classes would be used "to inform future decision making" about whether to create sex-neutral infantry units.[7] Thus, this class would be different. "Observer-advisors" (OAs)—female officers and NCOs from other parts of the Army who because of the previous restrictions had not attended Ranger School—were appointed to monitor the RIs' evaluations of the female candidates to ensure that they were grading according to Ranger standards. The glaring flaw in the plan was either overlooked or ignored: How can officers who never attended Ranger School and who have no combat-arms background know whether training meets the "Ranger standard"?

The policy was "a catastrophe to say the least," said one RI. "The worst choice that could have been made was to allow untrained individuals to get read on to the course.... [T]hey were able to oversee the course, how we grade [and] everything. They were a hindrance and distraction to Ranger instructors who were just trying to do the right thing," he continued. "All of the RIs just wanted the...drama to stop." An internal Army report—titled the Ranger Assessment Study—confirms this assessment, finding that RIs "did not appreciate the constant presence of female observer/advisors (O/As) who were not cadre or students." The use of

OAs, it concludes, "produced resentment among both students and cadre for a variety of reasons."[8] One RI recounted for me a disagreement he had with an OA in the middle of a field exercise. The OA, an officer, publicly "locked him up" at the position of attention—an example, perhaps, of why the RIs failed to "appreciate" the contributions of the OAs.

The Ranger Assessment Study also noted that RIs "reported that repetitive senior leader visits did not set positive conditions."[9] The report was completed on August 10, 2015, several days before the test-class completed the final training exercise of the Florida Phase and eleven days before the historic graduation. Curiously, after rehearsing a litany of problems with the test course—and before the first integrated test class had been completed—the report labeled the pilot program a success and recommended that it continue.

Other characteristics of the course changed as well. Previously, RIs were assigned to "walk" candidates (that is, evaluate their patrols) according to their respective specialties and the tasks that would be evaluated. Specific RIs were not assigned to specific candidates. Now, Ranger School leadership reportedly reviewed RI's reports from earlier courses before assigning them to new candidates. (Course leadership periodically checks the RIs' grading histories to ensure that individual instructors are not being too strict or too lenient, so the review itself was not entirely "out of the norm," a source told me. What set this review apart was that the information was allegedly used to assign graders to specific candidates.) An RI told me that instructors normally do not know who they are grading until the morning of the patrol or the day prior, but at least one R.I. was told he would grade one of the candidates before the phase even began. There was also painstaking, and unusual, review of current (and sometimes longstanding) course practices for conformity with the letter of the law. According to one of the RIs, "A lot of this was perceived to see where we could make things easier for women to see if we were being too hard."

RIs across all three phases of Ranger School reported feeling pressure to pass the female candidates. One RI in the Darby Phase told colleagues that his leadership repeatedly inquired by phone and text message about a female candidate's progress while the RI was grading her patrol. "There was a perception that we were being scrutinized and observed pretty hard to pass them," another said. The instructors' comments align with statements other instructors gave to Keating in 2015. One of her RI sources told her that they "were under huge pressure to comply." "It was very much politicized," he added.[10]

After the first female candidates successfully graduated, an Army spokesman told the press, "There was no pressure from anyone to lower any standards—the standards remained the same and the Soldiers that graduated with their Ranger tabs on August 21, 2015, in Ranger Class 8-15 accomplished the very same demanding standards of Ranger School as previous classes."[11] But as we will see later in this chapter, that statement is explicitly contradicted by correspondence exchanged between RIs during the course of the class.

Methods also changed at the Ranger Training and Assessment Course (RTAC), commonly referred to as "pre-Ranger," which screens recruits with non-infantry backgrounds for entry into the course itself. The Ranger Assessment Study admits as much: "MCoE [the Army's Maneuver Center of Excellence, the headquarters unit with ultimate oversight of Ranger School] leadership provided women the option to remain at RTAC after failing an event, while male student failures returned home."[12] This is one of several instances in which internal Army documents explicitly contradict the Army's statements and its characterization of Susan Keating's reporting. (The press release issued by General Frost stated, unequivocally, that Keating "claimed that women were allowed to repeat a Ranger training class until they passed, while men were held to strict pass/fail standard. That is false."[13])

The report also found that "male RTAC graduates progressed immediately to Ranger School with no interim break, while female graduates of five RTAC Classes…had a break between the courses."[14] This discrepancy in the treatment of male and female candidates is far more important than would appear at first glance. RTAC mimics the conditions of the first two weeks of Ranger School (except for the food deprivation) and so breaks students down physically. Candidates who successfully complete RTAC normally have only forty-eight hours to reset mentally and physically before they begin Ranger School. Merely having an extra week between RTAC and Ranger School to regain lost sleep, allow taxed muscles to recuperate, and otherwise recover physically would make a huge difference. Instead of having forty-eight hours, or even a week between RTAC and Day One of Ranger School, however, the first female class of candidates had two to three months of additional recovery and preparation time before signing in for the first day of the course.[15] If that recovery period were granted to every graduate of RTAC, it would be safe to assume that the graduation rate of candidates who attended RTAC before Ranger School would increase substantially. The report continues:

> These differences contributed to negative views of integration from male RTAC students and cadre. Many men perceived an unequal training environment because women were allowed to remain at the course after failing an event, to repeat consecutive courses, and for those who passed the first three RTAC classes, an extended recovery time prior to starting Ranger School. These training opportunity differences placed an unfavorable focus on the female students at RTAC and led to some hostility towards the women from the cadre who felt [Army] leadership was giving special treatment to female students.

When the first integrated class started on April 19, none of the nineteen female candidates made it through the Darby phase of the course. Eight were "recycled" back to the beginning of the phase to take a second crack at the course with the next class to show up, which is an entirely normal procedure. None of the eight passed on the second try. Of those eight, three candidates were given a third try but were required to start back at the very beginning and re-do RAP week, in what is known as a "Day One" recycled (as opposed to joining the next class after it completed RAP week, which is how the average recycle usually works).[16] Getting a third attempt at the course is certainly unusual, but it's not unheard of. The opportunity is offered on relatively rare occasions to candidates who have performed well in most aspects of the course but struggled with a single test or task. In this particular class, three of the eight female candidates remaining were given a third try, as were two male candidates who had passed RAP week but failed Darby twice. (At this point, it's worth mentioning two things. First, the two male candidates did not take the offer for a third chance as Day One recycles; all three female candidates did. Second, RAP week consists largely of pass-fail physical tests that have objective and essentially unfudgeable metrics of success—you either run five miles within the time limit, for example, or you don't; you either complete the twelve-mile weighted ruck march on time, or you don't. Many people don't pass all those tests even when entering the course for the first time in peak physical condition. The female candidates did, and they did it despite having already been subjected to the exhaustion and malnutrition of Darby Phase twice. Day One recycles are viewed by a lot of candidates as something close to a death sentence for your chances of passing the course for exactly that reason. That the female candidates passed RAP week events under those conditions speaks to their level of physical stamina and conditioning.)

All of the changes I mentioned above led to perhaps the most egregious departure from Ranger School's normally strict standards: the grading of candidates' training missions during the course itself. The messages exchanged between RIs in the immediate aftermath of a female graduate's patrol in the Mountain Phase of Ranger School, reproduced below, are a perfect illustration. The candidate was graded for her performance as the platoon sergeant for a nighttime raid. In non-training environments, the platoon sergeant is the senior enlisted soldier in the platoon, second in rank to the commissioned officer who serves as the platoon leader and, as any honest officer will tell you, second to none in authority. During dismounted operations, one of the platoon sergeant's primary jobs is to account for all of the soldiers in the platoon, making sure no one is missing or left behind. In Ranger School, that role becomes even more critical at night, when the platoon is moving through dense terrain in the dark. The platoon sergeant will often move to the front of the platoon as it moves in single file and physically tap every soldier who passes. When the final elements of the patrol have passed, the platoon sergeant reports his head count.

The following two exchanges took place after the nighttime patrol, when the instructors had just learned that the female candidate had received a passing grade. The reason for the incredulity expressed in the messages was that the female candidate had been graded in the platoon sergeant role, a grade based almost entirely on her ability to keep track of all of the members of her platoon as they moved through the woods. But she lost a member of the platoon. In fact, the missing soldier was so thoroughly separated from the rest of his platoon that the RIs had to shut down the entire mission, telling the platoon to go to sleep where they were while the RIs searched for the missing candidate. The platoon never had the chance even to attempt its assigned mission. But the candidate who had served as platoon sergeant, despite a failure in her performance that ended the mission, received a passing grade.

The first text exchange describes what happened during the mission (a contemporaneous conversation that is confirmed by the leaked observation report of the same patrol):

Text Exchange One:
Ranger Instructor 1: Female got a "go" last night. I was out there.
      She shouldn't have. But it happened and [redacted]
Ranger Instructor 2: Why did she get a go then?
Ranger Instructor 1: I was out there until actions on [that is, the raid or ambush the platoon was supposed to conduct]. Never happened because they missed their hit time. 1SG recocked them [that is, reset the mission conditions and gave them the

chance to start over]. That never happened because she gave a bad head count three times. We finally realized their [sic] was a missing student.

Ranger Instructor 1: Had to lock the [platoon] down and find this kid.

Ranger Instructor 3: That's a definite go haha

Ranger Instructor 1: I thought after that the last nail was driven into the coffin. So I left.

Ranger Instructor 1: [The grading instructor] gave her a go at the end of the night. . . .

The second exchange is between two RIs discussing the pressure on the instructor to give the female candidate a passing grade on the patrol even though the candidate failed to accomplish the objective requirements of her position:

Text Exchange Two:

Ranger Instructor A: Another patrol in blue [that is, the candidate received a passing grade] get the fuck out of here

Ranger Instructor A: That's a fail

Ranger Instructor A: That dudes [the grading instructor's] spelling is like a 5th grader no wonder he got pressured into it

Ranger Instructor B: [Redacted.]

Ranger Instructor B: It's all bullshit. On 8-35 [the mission they were on], they walk [sic] the road back into camp under RI control [that is, RIs took over from the candidate leadership and led the platoon to its destination on an open road rather than through the woods]

Ranger Instructor B: And lost a Ranger

The RI's written evaluation of the graded patrol reveals the source of the instructors' frustration:

[The candidate] passed her patrol primarily due to actions in the ORP *and a high level of motivation throughout the patrol.*

PASSED HER PATROL PRIMARILY DUE TO ACTIONS IN THE ORP AND A HIGH LEVEL OF MOTIVATION THROUGHOUT THE PATROL. AFTER TAKING OVER IN THE ORP, RGR EFFECTIVELY COMPLETED ORP TASKS ON A SEVERELY RESTRICTED TIMELINE. DUE TO FAILURE ON THE PART OF THE LEADER'S RECON ELEMENT, THE PLATOON FAILED TO MAKE THEIR HIT TIME. A LOST RANGER DURING RETRAINING PUT AN END TO RETRAINING. PRIOR TO MOVEMENT, RANGER BRIEFED THE SQUAD LEADERS ON THE ROUTE. THROUGHOUT MOVEMENT, SHE CONSTANTLY MOVED UP AND DOWN THE FORMATION, ATTEMPTING TO KEEP THE PLATOON TOGETHER, A DIFFICULT TASK CONSIDERING THE TERRAIN AND OVERALL CONDITION OF THE PATROL, SHE MAINTAINED S.A. BY PACE COUNT AND DISSEMINATED IT AT CHOKE POINTS WHILE MAINTAINING 100% ACCOUNTABILITY. UPON REACHING THE PATROL BASE, THE PLATOON WAS NON-FUNCTIONAL AND WAS PUT TO SLEEP, NEVER GOING THROUGH THE PB ESTABLISHMENT PROCESS.

Leaked patrol evaluation

After taking over in the ORP, Ranger effectively completed ORP tasks on a severely restricted timeline. Due to failure on the part of the Leader's Recon element, the platoon failed to make their hit time. *A lost Ranger during retraining put an end to retraining.* Prior to movement, Ranger brief[ed] the squad leaders on the route. Throughout movement, she constantly moved up and down the formation, *attempting* to keep the platoon together, a difficult task considering the terrain and overall condition of the patrol. She maintained S.A. [situational awareness] by pack count and disseminated it at choke points while maintaining 100% accountability. [**Author's Note: The report itself already admitted that the candidate "lost" another candidate, so obviously there was not "100% accountability".**] Upon reaching the patrol base, the platoon was non-functional and was put to sleep, never going through the [Patrol Base] Establishment Process. (Emphasis added.)

According to multiple sources with firsthand knowledge, the candidate who became separated from the patrol was dropped from the course, as is standard practice, but the candidate responsible for ensuring that he did not become separated advanced to the next phase. According to the Ranger School grading standards drilled into every Ranger instructor, when a member of the patrol becomes separated from the platoon and cannot be located, the platoon sergeant not only fails the patrol but also receives a "major minus" (essentially a "strike" in a "three-strike" policy), RI sources told me. As a source confirmed, "maintaining accountability [of the soldiers within the platoon] is basically the entire job," and she failed to do that. (Moreover, passing a graded exercise in Ranger School depends on fulfilling a threshold number of specific technical and tactical tasks upon which candidates are evaluated, and motivation is not one of them.)

Every candidate who was evaluated during the mission reportedly received a failing grade except for the female candidate, even though the mission was suspended because of a missing Ranger—a situation for which the female candidate was primarily responsible. Ninety percent of the observation report (OR) is a description of the different ways the candidate failed her patrol, but it concludes—inexplicably—that she nevertheless passed. The patrol was one of the last graded exercises of Mountain phase and therefore the candidate's final opportunity to advance. Candidates typically get only two chances to pass a graded patrol, and the rules prevent a candidate from getting those chances back to back.

There were similar incidents during the Florida Phase—the third and final phase of Ranger School—as well. An RI with firsthand knowledge of the candidate's evaluation explains, "During clearance of the [objective], she lost control of her squad, leading to fratricide" (i.e., leading to what would have been a friendly-fire incident if live rounds were being used in a non-training environment.) Understandably, this normally earns a failing grade (an "immediate no-go"). But it didn't here. He also said the squad left the casualty behind when it withdrew from the mission objective, normally another automatic no-go. The mission, he said, was a disaster. Nevertheless, the instructor overseeing the female candidate's patrol gave her a passing grade. Every candidate on the mission reportedly received a no-go, except one—the female. (The fratricide issue seemed to fit a pattern with the candidate's first patrol in the Mountain Phase, which was an ambush that also resulted in fratricide. The candidate's evaluation for that mission listed "fire control measures" as a weakness.) After the Florida mission, a verbal altercation reportedly broke out between RIs when some of the other instructors learned that the candidate in question had been given a passing grade despite committing errors that would objectively have caused an average candidate to fail.

Even after passing patrols, however, graduation is not guaranteed. If a Ranger candidate receives three "major minus" spot reports from instructors during a single phase—penalties for infractions like showing up late to morning formation or forgetting an item on a packing list—he or she normally must repeat the phase. A major minus can be offset, however, by a "major plus," which is occasionally given to candidates who perform a task exceptionally well or go above and beyond during a patrol. In this case, even after receiving a "go" on her second patrol, one of the female candidates already had three major minuses during the Florida phase, putting her graduation in jeopardy. The candidate reportedly received a "major plus" spot report on the final day of the exercise for helping to evacuate a casualty, however, "a fairly standard task in Ranger School" that doesn't normally merit a major plus, according to an RI. She eventually graduated.

It is important to emphasize once again that those whom I interviewed expressed admiration for the graduating females' grit and perseverance and were not critical of the female candidates' character or commitment. The officers and enlisted soldiers I spoke to uniformly respected the female candidates' efforts and willingness to put themselves through the rigors of Ranger training. They repeatedly emphasized that their critiques were intended simply to highlight how systematic political pressure forced changes to the legendary Ranger course, damaging its integrity, just as political pressure forced detrimental changes at every level of the military during the eight years of the Obama administration.

The Bigger Issue

The Department of the Army's reaction to the allegations is more important than the allegations themselves. The impetus for Keating's story in *People* was a letter sent by a member of the House Armed Services Committee, Congressman Steve Russell of Oklahoma, to Army Secretary John McHugh. Russell was a highly-decorated infantry lieutenant colonel and Ranger School graduate who had a distinguished career of more than twenty years in the Army (including commanding a battalion that played a central role in capturing Saddam Hussein) before retiring and becoming a member of Congress. Russell's letter asked the Army to provide all internal Ranger School documents related to the female candidates' training and assessment, including "test scores, evaluations, injuries, pre-training and more."[17] Russell had spoken to several RIs who told him one story—that standards had been lowered and senior Ranger Training Brigade officials had unduly influenced the outcome of the course—while the Army was telling him another—that everything was the same as always. "The training of our combat warriors is paramount to our national defense," Russell wrote to Secretary of the Army John McHugh. "In order to ensure that the Army retains its ability to defend the nation, we must ensure that our readiness is not sacrificed."[18] (It's worth noting that Russell also went out his way to emphasize in his public statements that he did not, and would not, question the abilities or records of any of the individual candidates themselves.[19] His concern was solely about the possibility that officials with their own agendas had improperly influenced the course and about the effects their actions would have on the Army.)

McHugh's office responded to Russell's letter one day before the due date and asked for additional time to complete his request. Nine days after that, Army officials informed Russell that nearly all of the training records (including, presumably, the observation report reproduced above) had been destroyed. The only documents preserved were the candidates' "green cards"—four-by-six-inch cards containing a thumbnail sketch of their time at the course and listing their graduation status. Although it is standard practice eventually to dispose of peer evaluations and patrol observation reports and to preserve only the green cards, it is unclear whether those documents had already been destroyed when Congressman Russell asked for them (only weeks after the course ended) or if they were shredded after his request. Rep. Russell sent a second letter to McHugh after the Army's response, informing the secretary that he was "somewhat puzzled by the Army officials informing me that many of the documents I am requesting might not be delivered as they may have been shredded."[20]

The Army's request for additional time to respond to Russell's request is curious, since the documents in question were readily identifiable and would have been meticulously filed until erased. In other words, they were the type of records that officials should have had no difficulty locating within a day, much less three weeks. Multiple RIs made that point independently and without prompting during my conversations with them. Moreover, the initiative of several RIs to preserve copies of these records and to keep them for several years afterward suggests that they were worried about the integrity of the process and feared that it was being manipulated on behalf of a political agenda. They wanted to have the evidence, if asked.

One would think that concerns expressed by a member of Congress serving on both the House Armed Services Committee and the House Oversight Committee—a highly decorated career military officer no less—about potentially serious integrity violations and reduced training standards at one of the military's premier courses would prompt significant inquiries and be treated with the level of gravity they deserve. But that is not how the Army leadership responded. Army officials sent Russell an "information paper" providing a sampling of some records and an analysis of those records, but never turned over any of the specific documents he requested.[21] (And in a meeting with Army senior uniformed leaders, the officers demanded to know Russell's sources and even suggested that his only source was a retiree. Russell's sources, in fact, were both officers and enlisted soldiers from every phase of the course.)

Russell stated that John McHugh and his staff "slow walked" the process to simply run the clock out on any potential investigation. McHugh put off meeting with Russell for months—with his staff saying he was tied up in other matters and stonewalling all of Russell's requests—before finally sitting down to discuss the issue a single time. A congressional source with direct knowledge of the situation told me that Rep. Russell repeatedly demanded a meeting to discuss the evidence that whistleblowers provided—even questioning on what basis a refusal to meet with a member of Congress was in order—but received little to no meaningful response from the secretary of the Army and his staff. When McHugh finally did meet with Russell, he was preparing to leave the administration and was literally placing his personal effects in boxes both before and after the meeting.

After McHugh was replaced by an even more politically-driven appointee, Eric Fanning, it became clear that the issue was going nowhere with the Army's senior civilian leadership. At best, it appears that

McHugh and company were simply uninterested in finding out whether the allegations the RIs brought to Russell were true; they got the result they desired, and that was what mattered, the integrity of the course— and fairness to any future female candidates whose potential success would now be met with skepticism—be damned.

Keating told me that as the controversy heated up, her RI sources, concerned that their careers were in jeopardy, became increasingly fearful—even paranoid—about communicating with her, and a few even started to believe that their phones were tapped. Most stopped answering her calls. They had good reason to be worried. At least two qualified and decorated RIs were reportedly subjected to what amounted to potentially career-crippling disciplinary action for "publicly" describing details about the female candidates' performance in a private Facebook group limited to fellow instructors. The Ranger School leadership responded to the discussions on the Facebook group by putting all records relating to the female candidates "under lock and key," available only to senior leaders, according to an RI with direct knowledge.

Keating's description of the instructors' fear of retaliation matches what I observed in my own (separate) sources. Until I earned their trust, nearly all of them communicated with me only through intermediaries. Even then, we developed fairly elaborate systems for sharing information. Whether all of our precautions were necessary I have no way of knowing, but the fear and intimidation I witnessed were eye-opening. The atmosphere was so stifling, in fact, that even some of my most forthcoming sources were astonished that one of their peers leaked a female candidate's OR. "Whoever that dude is, he's fearless," one RI said.

After Keating's story broke, senior Defense Department officials and Army leaders asked her to disclose her sources. Keating refused. The Army then invited Keating to a meeting with senior leaders throughout the Ranger School chain of command, including Colonel David Fivecoat, the commander of the Ranger Training Brigade. The assembled leaders told Keating that her sources needed to identify themselves if their concerns were genuine, promising that they would suffer no recrimination. The RIs' careers were on the line, of course, and no one was willing to bet on the chain of command keeping its word.

Indeed, because of the need to protect the dedicated career professionals involved, some of the specific allegations of misconduct were never even discussed publicly. There is evidence that certain records were altered to remove information that would be inconsistent with one of the candidates' successful completion of the course overall, for example, but details of those records are too sensitive to describe in further detail without jeopardizing sources' anonymity. I reached out to both Susan Keating and Congressman Russell, and both confirmed that they were aware of that evidence when the controversy first erupted but chose not to publicize it, due to their respective obligations of confidentiality to their sources.

Fivecoat drew intense criticism from former instructors and graduates of Ranger School after the first female candidates graduated. His critics speculated that he had watered down parts of the course to gain the favor of the Pentagon and White House officials who would determine whether he "got a star" (i.e., a promotion to brigadier general). Several of my sources voiced similar beliefs. Right up until he relinquished command in 2016, Fivecoat maintained that there had only been one standard for Ranger School and it had been met.[22] He retired the following year.

The Process Undermines the Premise

From the day the Army News Service announced that "the Army's Ranger School will be open to any female soldiers who meet the criteria,"[23] senior political appointees in the Obama Defense Department insisted repeatedly and emphatically that standards would not change, and no one would receive special treatment. Giving every soldier in the Army, male or female, the chance to pass the unforgiving course, they said, would merely expand the pool of potential candidates. It was, of course, all nonsense.

Before the first thumb was placed on the scale at the Ranger School itself, the Army was taking extraordinary measures to ensure that women would pass. The premise of the policy change was that the Army needed to expand its talent pool. To give every soldier an equal chance to pass, solely on his or her merits, which Secretary of the Army John McHugh and many others said was the plan, all that was necessary was to open the applicant pool. But that's not what happened. Sparing no expense, the Army gave a select group of female candidates extra preparation far beyond that given to their male counterparts. The intensity of the administration's effort to produce a female Ranger belies its assertion that the only motivation for the new policy was to simply tap a promising source of additional candidates.

The vehemence with which the Pentagon denied all reports of extensive and unprecedented special preparation for the female candidates only reinforces the impression that such special preparation undermined the justification for the new policy. Keating's initial story reported that, "in response to questions that included a request for confirmation that the women were placed in the special platoon, [an Army spokesman] said 'the allegations are not true.'"[24] In fact, it was that blanket denial which was untrue. A few days later came General Frost's press release about Keating's journalism and his denial of special preparation. He acknowledged that the female candidates were placed in their own platoon, contrary to the Army's earlier blanket denial of her story but said that arrangement was "part of routine continuing education and training in preparation for Ranger School." Frost insisted that rather than helping the female candidates, being in a separate platoon "quite frankly…placed them at tremendous disadvantage."[25] But those statements were not entirely accurate, either.

They were trained by Sergeant First Class Robert Hoffnagle, a former member of the 75th Ranger Regiment who had previously competed in the Army's Best Ranger competition.[26] Social media posts and messages confirm that Hoffnagle prepared members of the platoon for Ranger School during the intervening period between their attendance at RTAC and when they began the course on April 19. (Hoffnagle's role, by the way, is yet another detail from Keating's story that I was able to independently confirm.) Furthermore, the comparison of the special platoon—taken from active-duty units across the Army—to the brand-new second lieutenants who had just graduated the infantry officer's course and were waiting for a slot to attend Ranger School is simply not a one-to-one comparison. The appropriate comparison is between the preparation received by the special platoon of female candidates drawn from active duty units and the preparation given to similarly situated male candidates from non-combat arms backgrounds who were also selected from active-duty units to attend the course.

Unsurprisingly, the disparity between the Army's treatment of male and female Ranger candidates spurred resentment within the ranks. The experience of one officer I interviewed in 2018, who attended the Infantry Basic Officer Leadership Course ("IBOLC") for new infantry lieutenants and prepared for Ranger School at the same time as a former classmate who was a female infantry officer, perfectly illustrates the double-standards at play. The officer went to Ranger School and passed on his first try. Many of his male peers did not. Most but not all of them were given a second crack at the course, he told me. But there were no third chances for male candidates who failed a second time. What about the female candidate, his classmate, I asked. He hesitated for a moment, asked me to confirm for the fourth time that his identity would remain a secret, and then said, "She got, by my count, four tries at Ranger School. Which I have never heard of any of the guys who were at IBOLC—maybe they get two tries, but that's it. But the girls' standard routine is they get three or four.... For her case it was the chin-ups. She always failed the chin-ups."

I asked him if that disparity ever became a point of friction or resentment among the rest of the officers preparing to go to Ranger School. The tone of his answer made it plain he thought that was a stupid question. *Of course* it was a source of resentment, he replied—the topic was raised daily in private conversations. But, he added, "you can't really complain because they're like, 'Get with the fucking program, soldier.'"

CHAPTER
5

THE MARINES OVERRULED

"Our future enemies will be the ultimate arbiter of such decisions—when the lives of our Marines are in the balance. Those who choose to turn a blind eye to those immutable realities do so at the expense of our Corps' warfighting capability and, in turn, the security of the nation."
—*Memorandum from Brigadier General George C. Smith, USMC, to Commandant General Joe Dunford, recommending no changes to the Marine Corps policy regarding infantry units*

On January 24, 2013, Secretary of Defense Leon Panetta and the chairman of the Joint Chiefs of Staff, General Martin Dempsey, announced that the services would begin "investigating" the feasibility of integrating women into ground combat positions such as special operations units and the infantry. If any of the services concluded that a branch should remain closed to women, then it needed to explain why.

In subsequent discussions between some of the most senior leaders in the Marine Corps, the assembled officers decided that the best way to begin implementing the Obama administration's directive was to integrate two infantry companies at the Corps' training center in Twentynine Palms, California, and compare their combat capabilities with those of existing Marine infantry units.

The companies would be evaluated over several months while they conducted standard training tasks. The Marine Corps would measure everything meticulously—injury rates, the speed at which the companies evacuated causalities on the ground, marksmanship scores, and dozens of other measurements. According to one of the participants in those discussions, most of the Marine leaders believed that if they gave the administration hard evidence that sex-neutral infantry units would be less effective in combat than the Marines' all-male units, then the administration would surely defer to the commanders' judgment. One of the generals, however, saw the handwriting on the wall. "It's good that we are doing this, and it's the right thing to do, but it won't matter what we say. They know the end state they want," he warned his peers.

Shortly afterward, a Marine Corps major—I will call him "Major X"—received a call from an old boss, the colonel overseeing the Marines' study, who asked him to lead one of the four test rifle companies at Twentynine Palms. Major X is a battle-hardened infantryman with more than a decade in the Corps and multiple deployments. He knows that combat is unforgiving and that seconds can mean the difference between life and death. Training Marines to the Corps' standard holds special importance to him, he told me, because he attributed the muscle memory acquired through proper training with saving his life in combat; muscle memory broke through the fog of war. "[During] my first firefight, everything went dark," he said. "And then, all of a sudden, I started hearing voices in my head telling me what to do. [Proper training] teaches you how to embrace adverse situations and then be comfortably uncomfortable."

"General Dunford [then the commandant of the Marine Corps] never told us to look for a certain outcome" in the testing at Twentynine Palms, X said. The data he and the other Marine officers compiled would determine whether the Marines would recommend that the Obama administration stick with the status quo or begin integrating its ground combat units. Hanging on Major X's wall is a personal letter from General Dunford thanking him for his role in the study. He called it one of his "prized-possessions from the Marine Corps." After reciting Dunford's accomplishments and attributes—which include graduating from both the Marine Corps' Amphibious Warfare School and US Army Ranger School, multiple tours in both Iraq and Afghanistan, and substantial ground combat experience—the Major concluded, "You know, you're going to listen to a guy like that." He paused. "But *they* didn't. Of course."

"They" are the Obama political appointees who would make the ultimate decision. General Dunford's professional opinion about warfighting, informed by years of grueling firsthand experience, would be overruled by Secretary of the Navy Ray Mabus and Secretary of Defense Ashton Carter, the latter a former Rhodes Scholar and theoretical physicist with no firsthand military experience. Carter would tell *Time* magazine that the Marine Corps' data and its corresponding recommendation to the Pentagon were "just not definitive, not determinative."[1]

Hard Data, Purposely Ignored

The Marine Corps Research Department analyzed the units' performance in a variety of essential tasks, including casualty evacuation, long-distance foot patrols, squad maneuvers, and preparing fortified fighting positions, to name only a few. The Marines—the tactical experts—designed the tasks on which the units would be tested, and a collective of civilian academics they hired—data experts who formed the experiment's self-described "nerd squad"—crunched the numbers.[2] The nerd squad made sure that no variable was left uncontrolled. To eliminate inconsistencies in the casualty evacuation drills and avoid the possibility that human "casualties" might subconsciously assist or hinder the squad trying to evacuate them, for example, the nerd squad used the same life-like crash dummies that automakers use in safety tests.[3] (They nicknamed one of the dummies "Corporal Carl."[4]) And to obtain more precise data from the live-fire exercises, they designed interactive targets that logged not only whether the targets had been successfully engaged, but which Marine had fired each successful shot during the mission and how often.[5] The nerd squad also outfitted every Marine in the experiment with heart-rate monitors that sent the results directly into a research database so they could measure how hard each Marine had to work to accomplish the tested tasks and whether some Marines were slowing down to accommodate others.[6] Former Marine Captain Jude Eden, herself a combat veteran of Afghanistan, summarized what they found:

> [A]ll-male units outperformed coed units in 69 percent of the 134 combat tasks.... If the figure had been even a mere five percent difference it would have been ample reason to maintain women's exemption, since five percent is easily and frequently the difference between life and death in offensive ground combat. But in fact the figure was 69 percent! Ignoring that makes no sense! It's catastrophic for the combat arms, but Secretary Carter will not be the one paying the price.[7]

Merely stating this figure as a headline or a statistic ("all-male Marine rifle companies outperform sex-neutral companies seven out of ten times") minimizes its significance. It must be evaluated in the context of the details provided by Major X. When mere seconds can determine the difference between life and death, sending into combat units that we know are less effective 70 percent of the time is almost criminal. What purpose does that policy serve? Is reducing the survival chances of both male and female Marines, who will serve in these new units together, a reasonable price to pay for achieving equal outcomes on paper?

To supplement the Corps' own experiments, the Marines also commissioned several independent feasibility studies from Michigan State University, George Mason University, the University of Pittsburgh, and other institutions. The results were unanimous, and they were not the results the administration wanted. On August 18, 2015, Brigadier General George W. Smith, the director of the Marine Corps Innovation

Office, delivered to General Dunford a memorandum summarizing the findings. The memorandum concludes:

> Based on the body of evidence developed in support of this research, as well as existing related research, the integration of females into the combat arms MOSs [military occupational specialties] and units will add a level of risk in performance/effectiveness and cost. While this risk can be mitigated by various methods to address failure rates, injuries, and ability to perform the mission, the bottom line is that the physiological differences between males and females will likely always be evident to some extent.[8]

In short, the studies confirmed what most people already know but that politically correct bureaucrats want us to ignore: there are real and substantial physiological differences between men and women. That doesn't imply that one sex is somehow superior to another in any form. It's merely a statement of a long-accepted biological fact; it means that men and women have different physical constitutions and therefore different skills. A clear-eyed national defense policy that aims to keep as many people alive as possible should take those differences into account instead of purposefully ignoring them. In close combat situations, those physical differences can mean the difference between life and death—for both the men and women involved.

To be sure, the study did not conclude—and no reasonable person would contend—that there are no female Marines who could outperform any male Marine, in any metric, with regard to the physical requirements of being in the infantry. Out of all of the sources I spoke to, a group with a collective military experience that easily exceeds several hundred years, not one of them made that assertion and a significant number went out of their way to state the contrary. Rather, their concern was about both the vastly higher rate of serious and potentially career-limiting injuries suffered by female Marines serving in those positions (as explained in the pages to come), as well as the data showing that, over the course of a broad statistical sample, the mixed units simply did not perform as well. In other words, their conclusion—informed by statistics that unequivocally demonstrated that sex-neutral units were significantly less effective—was "not based on individuals, but on the collective" effects of such changes, as an officer familiar with the experiment and the Marines' recommendations explained.

To members of a ground combat unit like a Marine rifle platoon, these statistics represent more than abstract research. The issue isn't politics but about things like the "golden hour": if a gravely-wounded Marine's buddies do not get him or her off the battlefield and onto the operating table within an hour, that Marine's chances of survival plummet. When seconds count, extra minutes can be deadly.

To use another example, if a Marine Amphibious Assault Vehicle (AAV) hits a mine or an IED and the vehicle commander sitting in the turret becomes incapacitated, the rear crewman must get up and open the roof hatch of the vehicle and pull himself up "nearly six feet" to reach the roof of the vehicle, from where he will evacuate the incapacitated crew member by reaching back inside of the vehicle and "grabbing the shoulder straps on his body armor" and pulling him up and out.[9] (This is one of the many tasks the Marines measured.[10]) For an average-sized Marine infantryman wearing body armor, that's a load of nearly two hundred pounds. And if that vehicle is on fire—which is not uncommon when a vehicle encounters an explosive device—the additional seconds or minutes required to evacuate the vehicle commander can make the difference between whether he lives or dies.[11] (To paraphrase one Marine I spoke to, it's the difference between meeting every year to memorialize a friend who passed away or getting a beer with him or her to recall that Really Bad Day you shared together.) The data crunched by the nerd squad showed that the mixed infantry squads took up to 159 percent longer to evacuate casualties.[12]

General Smith's memorandum quotes a passage from the report of a presidential commission that examined the same issue in 1992 and concluded that "when it comes to combat assignments, *the needs of the military must take precedence over all other considerations*, including the career prospects of individual service members" (emphasis added). Smith stressed, "This fundamental tenet that is as relevant today as it was nearly a quarter century ago must remain at the forefront of any decisions on integration, despite the significant cultural shifts within our nation.... To move forward in expanding opportunities for our female service members without considering the timeless, brutal, physical and absolutely unforgiving nature of close combat is a prescription for failure."[13] The "failure" Smith refers to means greater danger and decreased chances of survival for the privates, lance corporals, and other Marines assigned to infantry squads engaged in close combat.

Smith concluded his memo with a warning: "Our future enemies will be the ultimate arbiter of such decisions—when the lives of our Marines are in the balance. Those who choose to turn a blind eye to those immutable realities do so at the expense of our Corps' warfighting capability and, in turn, the security of the nation." The "immutable realities" General Smith and many of his peers emphasized during this discussion cannot be hidden for political gain or wished away on the battlefields onto which we send our young men and women. In the words of an Army three-star I interviewed, "I just think that this is…done in the interest of 'fairness.' Well, here's a revelation. 'Fairness' only exists in the minds of five-year-olds and politicians. Otherwise, life is not fair. Period."

Life is not fair. Battlefields certainly aren't. Feel-good bumper-sticker slogans espousing social justice ideals cannot serve as body armor. Although they may appeal to the public at an abstract level, they do nothing to save service members' lives when it counts. Are we willing to risk our male and female service members' lives for the sake of political correctness? For officers and NCOs leading ground combat units, that is no abstract question.

The Data Show That Female Infantry Marines Are Much More Likely to Suffer Serious Injuries, but the Pentagon Won't Warn Them about the Risks

Researchers from the University of Pittsburgh conducted a comparative analysis of all-male and mixed-sex infantry units' performance in critical battle drills and corroborated the findings of other teams. In a thorough analysis of the injury reports from each of the training exercises, the researchers also discovered that the injury rate for female Marines during weight-carrying exercises was more than twice that of their male counterparts.[14] Their statistical analysis confirms what Major X told me when I asked him about injury rates. "We were—obviously unintentionally—we were breaking people," he said.

Another intriguing observation of the University of Pittsburgh team suggests why the results of both the Marines' study and the independent studies they commissioned were almost inevitable. The "overall load" carried by each infantry Marine equals his standard eighty-one-pound combat load plus his body fat. The overall load carried by male Marines almost never exceeded their lean body mass, but the overall load carried by female Marines exceeded their lean body mass in 75 percent of the cases.[15] In other words, the average female carrying the infantry's standard combat load is carrying equipment that outweighs her functional body mass. What is the effect of this daily overload over an event like a fifteen-day, dismounted training exercise? More than 40 percent of the female Marines who participated in the study suffered musculoskeletal injuries.[16]

The fact is, putting women in infantry units may be devastating for their long-term health, especially in their lower extremities, which bear most of that weight and pressure. And a substantial body of academic, peer-reviewed research explains why. Colonel Sonja Thompson, the chief of surgery at Carl R. Darnell Army Medical Center at Fort Hood, Texas, the largest base in the Army, observed in 2012 that the "combination of anatomy and physiology appears to predispose women to a higher risk of pelvic stress fracture" when they are carrying heavy loads for long periods.[17] In 2015, a team of Israeli medical researchers conducting a review of peer-reviewed medical studies crunched the numbers provided by Colonel Thompson and discovered that female soldiers carrying the same combat loads as their male peers for an extended period were roughly one hundred times more likely to develop pelvic stress fractures.[18]

One of the reasons for the substantial difference in male and female injury rates, the researchers concluded, is that upon "increasing loading [that is, shouldering a greater amount of weight], women tend to decrease stride length and increase cadence, whereas men maintain gait length and cadence over a wide range of loads carried. Women also dramatically increase the amount of time spent with both feet on the ground (double support time) as load increases, a phenomenon much less apparent in men." In other words, because the weight of the ground combat load is often greater than their lean body mass, female service members in ground combat units do not shift the pressure of that load from one leg to another the way the human body usually does when unburdened or carrying an appropriate load. Consequently, those female Marines' backs, hips, knees, and ankles are continuously absorbing far more pressure than those of their male counterparts and far more pressure than they would if they were carrying combat loads of Marines who are not in the infantry.

While the Marines were conducting their study—and observing the same phenomena summarized by the Israeli researchers in 2015—many female veterans, citing their own experiences with precisely the types of injuries the Marines warned about, wrote opinion pieces in the press opposing any change to the policy on women in combat units.[19] One of them, former Marine Captain Katie Petronio, who had deployed as a combat engineer officer in support of a Marine reconnaissance battalion in Afghanistan, documented the physical toll that ground combat operations took on her body. She asked whether society was "willing to accept the attrition and medical issues that go along with integration." (Of course, society must be *informed* of those risks to accept them.) "As a young lieutenant," she wrote, "I fit the mold of a female who would have had a shot at completing IOC [the Infantry Officer Course], and I am sure there was a time in my life where I would have volunteered to be an infantryman. I was a star ice hockey player at Bowdoin College.... At 5 feet 3 inches I was squatting 200 pounds and benching 145 pounds when I graduated in 2007. I completed Officer Candidates School (OCS) ranked 4 of 52 candidates." But "[f]ive years later, I am physically not the woman I once was and my views have greatly changed on the possibility of women having successful long careers while serving in the infantry." She continued:

> By the fifth month into the deployment, I had muscle atrophy in my thighs that was causing me to constantly trip and my legs to buckle with the slightest grade change. My agility during firefights and mobility on and off vehicles and perimeter walls was seriously hindering my response time and overall capability. It was evident that stress and muscular deterioration was affecting everyone regardless of gender; however, the rate of my deterioration was noticeably faster than that of male Marines and further compounded by gender-specific medical conditions. At the end of the 7-month deployment, and the construction of 18 PBs later ["PBs" means patrol bases, which are primitive outposts that are physically demanding for a unit in the field to build—and guard and defend while building—with only the most basic equipment and on a constricted timeline], I had lost 17 pounds and was diagnosed with polycystic ovarian syndrome (which personally resulted in infertility, but is not a genetic trend in my family), which was brought on by the chemical and physical changes endured during deployment.[20]

Petronio was a highly capable Marine by anyone's standards, and she earned the respect of the Marines she served with, but she nearly destroyed her body in the process. Future soldiers and Marines like her deserve to know about that risk before they expose themselves to similar lasting damage.

The injury rates observed by the Marines' ground combat study are backed up by internal injury statistics tracked by the Army during basic training and advanced individual training for soldiers in newly opened MOSs. The records were obtained by the Thomas More Law Center through the Freedom of Information Act. For certain jobs that required repetitive heavy lifting, such as field artillery or air defense artillery, the injury rate for female service members was up to 114 percent higher than for males.[21] And those jobs aren't nearly as physically punishing as being in the infantry.

But when Ashton Carter, announcing that the exclusion of female service members from ground combat units would be reversed with no exceptions, was asked directly by Pentagon reporters about the higher risk of injuries to female soldiers and Marines in ground combat units, he acknowledged that the risks were real but said they were no reason to keep the current policy in place. Carter simply said that proper "implementation" of the policy would address those risks, an unfounded statement that the studies themselves disproved. Carter never specified what that proper implementation would look like or how it would mitigate the effects of basic physics on female service members' bodies:

> *Reporter*: And also, I understand, one of General Dunford's concerns was, since women—women in the experimental unit suffered more injuries than men, that—he was concerned that you would lose some hard-charging women Marines, and what did you think about that?
>
> *Secretary Carter*: Yes. There are a number of studies that indicated that. Again, that's something that doesn't—doesn't suggest to me that women shouldn't be admitted to those specialties, if they're qualified. But it's going to—something that's—needs—that's going to need to be taken into account

in implementation. So these are real phenomena that are—affect gender—that are, rather, affected by gender and need to be taken into account in implementation.[22]

High injury rates for female Marines have both short-term and long-term effects on combat readiness. In the short term, losing a female Marine to injury leaves her squad operating down a Marine. In the long term, the sky-high injury rates for female Marines who join the infantry will mean that some of the best female Marines—the ones who are seeking out these challenging positions—are more likely to sustain serious injuries and be forced to leave the Corps prematurely. The Marine Corps report explicitly concluded as much, warning that the "Marine Corps risks losing a number of highly talented female Marines prematurely due largely to the often extreme physical demands of these infantry, reconnaissance, and special operations occupations."[23]

But the issue would be no less critical even if it somehow had no effect on readiness—because it, too, affects the health and safety of those protecting the nation in uniform. Is it moral for a Defense Department that is aware of serious health risks to female service members to withhold information about those risks solely to maintain appearances and appeal to progressive orthodoxy? If the sole purpose of this policy is to provide equal professional opportunities for female service members, how can the Pentagon justify dismissing evidence that putting female service members in particular positions will decrease their chances of completing a full twenty-year career while increasing their chances of developing serious health problems, including infertility? How freely are they choosing to join ground combat units if information about the long-term effects on their health is withheld from them? Embracing a policy change that has the potential to damage both combat readiness and the health and military careers of the women it ostensibly benefits solely because it appeals to the progressive left is mindless, at best.

The Chairman of the Joint Chiefs Refused to Approve
the Policy Change

General Dunford, who had become the chairman of the Joint Chiefs of Staff in October 2015, submitted the thirty-two-page "United States Marine Corps Assessment of Women in Service Assignments: Recommendations for the Secretary of the Navy" to Ray Mabus, detailing the extensive research conducted by "both internal Marine Corps agencies and a number of external civilian research entities." The memorandum informed Mabus that although opening certain jobs to female Marines (such as tank crewman) would not diminish combat readiness, introducing women into ground combat units would reduce those units' effectiveness.[24] The Marine Corps therefore opposed the new policy and requested an exemption.

The Pentagon never made the content of Dunford's memorandum public. There is a reason for that: It obliterates the Obama administration's talking points on the issue. I obtained a lightly redacted copy through the Freedom of Information Act.

Dunford begins by advising Mabus that the Marines' analysis "focused principally on the unique physical and physiological demands of service in ground combat occupations and units." He later notes that he "fully understands and appreciates that many view this policy principally through the lens of equal opportunity for female members of the Naval Service," and he goes on to expose the Orwellian rhetoric of the Obama administration and its progressive allies in the debate:

> I do not view gender integration as an issue of women in combat, as many have attempted to frame this change in policy. Frankly, to describe it as such does our female Marines a tremendous disservice, especially those who most recently have served, fought and, in a number of cases, died in the non-linear operating environments of Iraq and Afghanistan. Simply, our female Marines have performed magnificently in those combat environments and are fully

part of the fabric of a combat-hardened Marine Corps on
the back-end of the longest period of continuous combat
operations in our history.

Framing the debate in terms of whether women can be "in combat"
minimizes the contributions of female soldiers, airmen, and Marines over
the past eighteen years of war. In the non-conventional wars of the post-9/11
era, there are no traditional "front lines." The question then is not whether
women service members will be in combat or exposed to it, but in what
capacities they will serve. And the most extensive and thorough study of
its kind concluded that while 96 percent of Marine Corps jobs can be open
to both sexes, a few jobs, because of the "extreme physical demands and
brutal nature of [their] fundamental mission," should not be. Those jobs,
in Dunford's words, impose "the unique physical demands associated with
direct ground combat—where the Marines of our ground combat element,
and particularly the infantry, make their violent bid for success."

The portions of the memorandum in which Dunford details the
evidence supporting his recommendation are, tellingly, redacted. The
ideologically driven appointees who rammed the policy change down
the Marines Corps' throat have no interest in making that kind of information freely available.

The Chairman of the Joint Chiefs Was Overruled by a Theoretical Physicist

As he did when the military's new transgender policy was announced,
General Dunford declined to endorse the Obama administration's social
engineering by joining the secretary of defense at the press conference
announcing the integration of women into ground combat units. Having
overruled the Marine Corps' objections to the policy, Carter could defend
it without the general's help. The press noticed. First, they pressed Carter
to explain why he had overruled the Marine Corps legend. Carter replied
vaguely and tried to move on:

Reporter 1: Mr. Secretary, you mentioned that the Marine Corps had asked for a partial exception. The Marine Corps made a very vigorous and detailed case for keeping some combat positions open to men only. In what ways did you find their argument unpersuasive?

Secretary Carter: I did review the Marine Corps data, surveys, studies, and also the recommendation of the commandant of the Marine Corps at the time, of course, who was General Dunford, now our chairman, that certain Marine Corps specialties remain closed to women. I reviewed that information and I looked at it carefully. I also heard from other leaders of other services who had studied similar issues in their own force, the recommendations of the other service secretaries and service chiefs, and I came to a different conclusion in respect of those specialties in the Marine Corps.

Reporter 1: You said—sorry—just a quick follow-up. You said you came to a different conclusion, obviously. I was asking what about the argument you found lacking?

Secretary Carter: Because I believe that we could in implementation address the issues that were raised.

Carter made no attempt to explain what that "implementation" would entail or how it would remediate the damage to combat readiness. The next reporter asked Carter about a recent terrorist attack and why General Dunford was not present.. Carter responded to the first part of the question and ignored the second part. The reporter persisted:

Reporter 2: And why is General Dunford not here, sir?
Secretary Carter: I'm sorry. Why is—is—
Reporter 2: [inaudible]
Secretary Carter: —well, this—I'm announcing my decision. I was the one who took this decision. I'm announcing my decision. I—you know, I should say, about General

Dunford, you're going to have an opportunity to talk to—to General Dunford. I've talked to him extensively about this subject. He's very knowledgeable about it. He will be with me as we proceed with implementation. I have taken parts of his—the conclusions he drew. Others drew different conclusions, including myself. And that's the decision I've taken, and that's the direction we're going to go.[25]

Many of the "others" who "drew different conclusions" cited the success of the first integrated class at Ranger School as proof.[26]

"It Was Doomed from the Get-Go"

Ray Mabus showed no interest in the Marines' careful study and assessment of the issue. He refused to visit the training center while the study was being conducted, and in May 2015, before the study was even complete, he tweeted that he was "personally committed to opening all operational billets to women. #PeopleMatter."[27] Anyone familiar with the evidence that the Marine Corps laid out in opposition to that policy would find Mabus's hashtag chilling. If "people matter," then the military's priority should be maximizing their chances of survival in battle, not fulfilling the dreams of progressive ideologues at the expense of a service member's life.

When I asked Major X about Mabus's lack of interest in the Marine Corps study—a study to which he had dedicated nearly a year of his life—he replied, "I mean, I hate to say that it was doomed from the get-go, but it really was. I mean, nobody wanted to hear it," though he added that "we did the right thing." One of Mabus's top deputies, Juan M. Garcia, the assistant secretary of the Navy for operations, did visit Twentynine Palms to conduct a site inspection of the Marines' study and came away with the opposite view from Mabus's. Garcia is a former Navy fighter pilot who served in the Persian Gulf. He told Major X that "the people in Washington, to include my boss and the decision makers, need to come see what you're doing right now." Major X described Garcia as "a great man" who was "very much into what we were doing." Unfortunately, Garcia was not the ultimate decision-maker.

When the report was completed, Mabus refused to read it in its entirety, denouncing it as the product of bias. He told National Public Radio that the study "started out with a fairly large component of men thinking 'this is not a good idea.' When you start out with that mindset, you're almost presupposing the outcome."[28] Mabus also implied that the Marines had stacked the deck in its study by choosing female Marines who were underqualified.[29] In February 2016, five months after the study's completion, Mabus, apparently innocent of the irony, tweeted, "Every single decision I make is in support of maximizing @USMC combat effectiveness."[30]

An approving article in *Time* magazine about the policy change leaves little doubt about what happened: "The defense secretary, who never served in uniform, relied on the advice of former Navy officer and current Navy Secretary Ray Mabus—who is the Marines' civilian overseer—for cover in steamrolling the Marines' recommendation against women serving in such combat assignments."[31] In other words, Ashton Carter followed the advice of a career politician and activist over the painstaking, meticulous study conducted by the US Marine Corps and its former commandant, General Dunford. Mabus's only "argument" in favor of the policy change was that a "commitment to diversity will ensure the Navy and Marine Corps team remains the world's greatest and most preeminent expeditionary fighting force."[32]

To the Marines who spent months on a rigorous study—especially the female Marines in the experimental company whom Mabus implied were substandard—Mabus's dismissal of their efforts was a "slap in the face."[33] "Mr. Mabus didn't even let the report get cold and was already bashing it and hadn't even read it. And he admitted he only browsed over the conclusions," X said. Other Marines who participated in the study, both male and female, complained that Mabus "threw us under the bus."[34] "All the work that the task force did, the rounds that we shot, didn't mean anything if he had already made up his mind," one sergeant said.[35] Sergeant Major Justin Lehew, the senior enlisted Marine at the USMC Training and Education Command (and a recipient of the Navy Cross to boot), lashed out at Mabus's comments in a rare public display of frustration by Corps leadership. Mabus's dismissal of the study and the Marines who participated in it, he said, was "counter to the interests of national security and unfair to the women who participated in this study."[36] One of the participants in the study told me that Mabus's remarks were "demeaning." Senator John McCain shared the Marines' frustration, asking the chief civilian of the Navy, "Why would you even have a study if you're going to disregard the results of it?"[37]

"They came back with absolutely hard data," a now-retired general from the Obama era said, but "it sort of didn't gain any traction. And I think after all that was said and done...the military said, 'It looks like this is going to happen regardless...so we better get our act together and make sure that we maintain a viable fighting force with women integrated into the combat arms.'" Another general who served in the Pentagon expressed his frustration that the Marines played everything by the book and "actually put a battalion out on the ground and were running around and got some actual results out of it, but [the results] never saw the light of day, really."

For the Marines I interviewed (and frankly, every other member of the military I have ever met), the fundamental question that must be asked of any proposed policy change is "Will this make us more lethal in combat?" And the answer to that question dictates everything. General John Kelly, who served forty-five years in the Marine Corps before becoming director of national security and then White House chief of staff under President Trump, told PBS, "If the answer to that is no, clearly don't do it. If the answer to that is, it shouldn't hurt, I would suggest that we shouldn't do it, because it might hurt."[38] Kelly's point is that combat is a zero-sum game. Anything that does not make your forces more lethal against the enemy, and thus safer, makes them less effective and therefore more vulnerable.

General Kelly's outlook was emphatically endorsed by James Mattis in 2016. Mattis "vociferously support[ed] the standard for determining military policies outlined by [General Kelly]: every change to established practice should be judged on whether it increases battlefield lethality." Mattis added that "Americans ought to fear more than we do the consequences of our prevalent lassitude about warfare."[39] It is easy to discuss these issues in the abstract and consider the implications only on a theoretical level, but the reality of warfare is that decisions made in the abstract inevitably affect the fate of an eighteen-year-old carrying a weapon and facing an enemy in a foreign land. We owe it to that soldier or Marine to ask if our political class's decisions make him or her safer or less safe.

Many experienced female Marines echoed Kelly's concerns. In July 2013, a focus group of female Marines of all ranks and ages delivered a similar message to Chuck Hagel, Carter's predecessor as defense secretary. The vast majority of the female Marines objected to integrated infantry units, and many of them cited firsthand experience to support their positions.[40] "I haven't met a female Marine or a female in general who is standing up and shouting, 'I want to be infantry,'" a female Marine captain told Hagel.[41]

At a CNN military town hall with President Obama in late September 2016, Marine Captain Lauren Serrano, a veteran of Afghanistan who earned a Bronze Star, asked the president why he had ignored the professional advice of the military. The question, respectful but direct, deserves to be reprinted in full:

Good afternoon, Mr. President. A study by the Marine Corps revealed that mixed-gender combat units performed notably worse and that women suffered staggeringly higher rates of injury. Just one of those statistics showed that mixed-gender units took up to 159 percent longer to evacuate a casualty than all-male units. As the wife of a Marine who deploys to combat often, that added time can mean the difference between my husband living or dying. Why were these tangible negative consequences disregarded and how does the integration of women positively enhance the infantry mission and make me and my husband safer?[42]

The commander in chief responded with an extended word salad promising that no decisions would be made on an ideological basis or out of political correctness and insisting that a reevaluation of existing policies was necessary to expand the recruiting talent pool. Obama also told Captain Serrano, "I don't think any studies are going to be disregarded." As I have shown in some detail, that statement was simply not true.

A Sex-Neutral Navy and Marine Corps

Mabus's insistence on changing the makeup of ground combat units was part of his broader, ideologically driven quest for a "genderless" Navy and Marine Corps. He directed senior naval commanders to "ensure [that job titles] are gender-integrated...removing 'man' from their titles."[43] Traditional naval and Marine Corps job titles such as "yeoman" and "rifleman"—titles that date to the founding of our republic—apparently needed to be changed to reflect a "gender-integrated" force. (After substantial outcry from both active-duty and retired sailors and Marines, Mabus relented, and the traditional terms remained in place.)

Uniforms were to be changed as well. Mabus tweeted, "We are trending towards uniforms that don't divide us male and female, but unite us as #sailors & #marines."[44] Mabus might have been surprised to discover that many of the fiercest opponents of "gender-neutral" uniforms were women. The *Navy Times* quoted one female helicopter pilot who said women in the Navy did not appreciate "the fact that they're changing the uniforms to make us all look like men."[45]

The absurd uniform changes demonstrate the senselessness of a "genderless" military. Male and female uniforms are shaped differently for the same reason many other military policies differentiate between males and females—the male and female physiques are different in important ways. Indeed, while Mabus was trying to eliminate the differences between men's and women's uniforms, Democrats on Capitol Hill, complaining that standard-issue body armor unfairly burdened the female physique, were pushing for distinct male and female versions.[46] The Pentagon told the press that eight new body armor sizes would be designed for women, "tak[ing] into consideration their anatomy, which leads to a redesign of the way the gear would fit."

In other words, senior Defense Department political appointees were telling Americans to ignore anatomical differences between men and women when evaluating the combat effectiveness of infantry units—and to ignore anatomical reality when determining which physical fitness standards transgender service members should serve under—but stressing the differences between male and female anatomy when designing the body armor male and female troops would wear downrange at the same time. The contradiction was apparently lost on (or ignored by) the politicians and political appointees in charge of the military.

Equality of Opportunity Is Never Enough

"Equality of opportunity" is never enough. As soon as the Marine Corps had been subjugated, progressives began to demand numerical parity. The only way to achieve that in a meritocracy is to establish quotas, and so Ray Mabus demanded in March 2015 that 25 percent of Navy and Marine Corps recruits be women.[47] Mabus's apparent inability to understand the issue was perfectly encapsulated in a tweet he made in October 2016: "Diversity gives us strength and ensures UsNavy & USMC are reflective & representative of nation they defend."[48]

These words of a political hack reveal how out of his depth Ray Mabus was. After a moment's reflection, one realizes that the military is not and never was intended to be "reflective" of the nation it defends. Nearly 75 percent of the population is ineligible to enlist for one reason or another.[49] If America's military perfectly mimicked the society it defended, for instance, then it would be 33 percent obese.[50] Congress, not the military, represents the country. In a fighting force, quotas are not the source of strength. *Standards* are.

The Marines did everything the politically minded appointees in the Pentagon and the White House demanded of them. They evaluated the question as instructed. They spent months conducting a study on their own, meticulously documenting and analyzing every scrap of data. The Marines also asked multiple teams of independent researchers to conduct parallel studies to double-check their conclusions. And after all of that, they returned to the Obama administration with mountains of evidence to support the position that *creating sex-neutral infantry units was detrimental to their effectiveness and would result in higher casualties to the force.*

The Obama administration simply didn't listen or didn't care.

CHAPTER

6

CONCLUSIONS FIRST, EVIDENCE SECOND

"This was done without the consent of the leadership."
—*Retired Army general who served while the review of the Army's policy on gender-neutral infantry units was ongoing during the Obama era*

"Research indicates that combat arms units are character-ized by a culture that emphasizes hyper-masculine traits such as dominance, aggressiveness, hiding fear, pursuit of physically demanding/potentially dangerous activities, and competitiveness.... The Army faces the challenge of changing combat arms culture. A balance is required to retain high morale while removing the culture's less-desir-able aspects. This will take time and require patience."
—*Army "Gender Integration Study," March 2015*

The debate about whether the military should adjust its policies to allow "women in combat" was contentious, politicized, and com-pletely off point. In reality, the debate was never about whether women were capable of being "in combat." The phrase "women in combat" is a triumph of Orwellian phrasing by left-wing partisans. No one seriously disputes the idea that women are capable of being shot at and returning fire. In fact, women regularly saw combat long before Ash Carter announced the integration of female service members into infantry and special forces units on December 3, 2015. That tradition dates at least back to "Molly Pitcher" of Carlisle, Pennsylvania (real name Mary Hays McCauley[1]), who manned a Continental Army cannon during the 1778 Battle of Monmouth in the Revolutionary War.[2]

Female Apache pilots in the post–9/11 era, for example, have flown close air support missions against enemy combatants and killed jihadis with 30mm chain guns synced to their pilot helmets. Army Specialist Monica Lin Brown became the first female soldier to be awarded the Silver Star in Afghanistan in 2008 for her courage under fire during a Taliban ambush.[3] I cannot think of anyone from my time in the military who labored under the belief that women were somehow constitutionally incapable of participating in combat operations. (And if anyone did hold that belief, the bravery of the all-female units of the Kurdish Peshmerga who fought countless battles against the Islamic State during its reign of terror ought to have disabused them of that notion.)

The discussion was framed by the media and many on the left as a debate between dinosaurs from a prior era who believed women were just too delicate to see battle and those who understood that a vast number of women were already "in combat" and merely wanted that fact to be officially recognized as a matter of policy. In reality, the issue was very narrow: Should female soldiers and Marines be integrated into the small subset of ground units who walk up to fifteen miles a day, carry eighty pounds of equipment, and often sleep and tend to bodily functions in austere environments with little to no privacy? (The narrowness of that question is reinforced by the fact that the Marines, after analyzing almost every possible metric, actually recommended that two of the three combat arms units that were previously all-male—tank and field artillery units—be fully opened to female Marines.)

Neither the dismissal of the Marines' Twentynine Palms study nor the events at Ranger School occurred in a vacuum. Each was the product of a long, sustained push by political forces who harbored different beliefs about the role of the military than many of the men and women who served in it. Why is this issue so critical, and why is it different from changes made in previous eras? Because, as James Mattis noted when he began his tenure as secretary of defense in early 2017 and began a holistic review of the policies left behind by the Obama Defense Department, ninety percent of all casualties occur in ground combat units.[4] Lethality and combat superiority at the squad and platoon level are the bedrock of military readiness.

Leon Panetta's news conference with General Martin Dempsey, the then-chairman of the Joint Chiefs, announcing the military's intent to open some, if not all, positions (supposedly after internal reviews) was the conclusion of that effort, not the beginning of it. The sea change in America's combat arms policy occurred in 2013 at a press conference convened four days after Barack Obama's second inauguration. When reporters asked Panetta about Obama's role in the decision-making process, he responded evasively:

> [General Dempsey] and I have the opportunity to meet with the president, you know, usually every week, depending on his schedule, but meet individually with him to go over issues. And I think, over the past year, I've regularly briefed the president on what was going on with regards to this issue, that we were—that we had opened up the additional positions, that we were looking at providing even more opportunities to women, and he was very supportive of that.[5]

Panetta immediately displayed his ignorance of the finer points of the discussion by comparing the potential integration of Army and Marine infantry units to the integration of female sailors into submarine crews. The Navy, he said, "re-jiggered the submarines to be able to adapt to that kind of situation.... The Marines and the Army, obviously, are going to move in the same direction."[6] A Navy submarine captain who was still on active duty while this book was being written and served as the commander of the Navy's submarine course dismissed the comparison out of hand. "Being a submariner is a highly technical and cerebral job. It doesn't have nearly the same physical requirements that come with being an infantryman," he told me. The contrast between the comparative lack of opposition from the brass to opening submarine positions to female sailors and the fierce, methodical resistance from Army and Marine Corps leaders to opening infantry units to female soldiers and Marines suggests that the latter was not simply the reflexive resistance to change from old dinosaurs who grew up in a previous era.

The most telling moment occurred when a reporter asked Panetta for examples of how the change would make infantry forces stronger. Before Panetta opened his mouth, General Dempsey intervened with a filibuster that began with saying that the discussion should not be purely military and talked about what a success opening West Point to women had been. He added:

> We've had this ongoing issue with sexual harassment, sexual assault. I believe it's because we've had separate classes of military personnel, at some level. Now, you know, it's far more complicated than that, but when you have one part of the population that is designated as warriors and another part that's designated as something else, I think that disparity begins to establish a psychology that in some cases led to that environment. I have to believe, the more we can treat people equally, the more likely they are to treat each other equally.[7]

Dempsey did not address the policy's effect on core infantry competencies like moving twelve miles on foot over terrain while carrying a heavy load, nor did he speak to any of the other tactical realities confronted by infantry units. I am not suggesting that Dempsey was being deceitful. He simply had the unenviable task of defending a policy change that was indefensible, at the tactical level, for the units it would affect the most. Fittingly, Dempsey's non-answer dovetailed with President Obama's non-answer to Captain Serrano when she asked him the same question at the CNN town hall. The repeated questions from military stakeholders about the practical consequences of the policy and the consistent dodges by the Obama administration's civilian leaders brings us to the heart of the issue: What was the administration's purported rationale for the change, and what did the military's key leaders think of it?

Senior Leaders' Reactions

"What problem are we trying to solve?"

"If you take a step back and look at this from our perspective, what's the readiness problem we're solving here by doing this?"

"How does [this policy] actually make us stronger and more capable of winning wars?"

During my conversations with senior military leaders, including many generals, about the Obama-era policy change, a common theme arose: Why are we doing this? Why now, during wartime? What problem are we trying to solve by implementing this policy? Officers serving in combat-arms units could see no combat-specific reasons for the changes—because there were none—and seemed genuinely mystified by the administration's decisions. Officers serving in positions closer to Capitol Hill were not confused at all; instead, they were angry. "Is there a shortage of infantrymen? No, there never has been," one exasperated general remarked. "It's not about a shortage of people to do the job.... It was purely about opening up a part of the military service [to make infantry units sex-neutral]. Which, okay, if we're going to do that, let's understand why we're doing it and what the long-term effects are going to be." The same general told me that his peers across the Army and Marine Corps "said 'we probably shouldn't do this,' 'this isn't a wise policy change.'" But, he added, "they were just overruled, *and it was done without the consent of the leadership.*... It was all people outside [the military] that were making these demands."

Other former generals echoed his assessment. One told me that the mindset of many military leaders simply became "this is going to happen, and we've got to figure out a way to make sure that it doesn't affect the force." He said they "just knew it was going to happen, and in fact it did." Another added, "I mean, this is so fraught with problems that nobody has talked about, nobody has thought about."

Eventually, several officers told me, they came to the reluctant conclusion that the administration had no interest in military readiness or lethality. Instead, it was waging an ideologically driven campaign with an end goal of creating an equal number of male and female generals and the first female chair of the joint chiefs. This belief did not emerge out of nowhere. Senior military positions generally go to members who have served in combat arms, and progressives have long complained that this is a major barrier to women achieving equal representation in the general officer corps. Indeed, a 2016 article in the *Atlantic* hailed the integration of Ranger School as a key step towards the goal of appointing the first female chair of the joint chiefs.[8] Consider this paragraph from a *Time* magazine profile of how the policy changes affecting combat arms came to be:

> A month before Panetta left office in 2013, he and Dempsey went to the press briefing room to announce a list of combat positions for which women could begin to compete and serve. After the briefing, [Panetta's chief of staff Jeremy Bash] joined Panetta and Dempsey to reflect on the moment. "That worked out very well. It was a very powerful message. One day, sir, there's going to be a female Secretary of Defense, and one day there'll be a female chair of the joint chiefs."[9]

No one I know or have spoken to from the military, active or retired, is opposed to female generals serving on the joint chiefs or a female secretary of defense. That is simply not the issue and never has been. The issue is making sweeping, deleterious changes to ground combat units, making them less effective and more prone to casualties solely for the purpose of achieving an ideological goal of equal outcomes on paper. Moreover, if the underlying purpose is to create greater parity among the military's senior leadership, that desired outcome should simply be stated upfront and the way promotions are evaluated and granted can be reexamined if need be. But achieving that goal by changing infantry units and pretending that the changes will have no consequences simply damages trust between the military's civilian leadership and its uniformed members all the way down the chain of command. As one officer told me: "Okay, if the goal here is to have gender equality across the general officer corps, you need to explain why that goal is more important than actual combat readiness. Because it seems that there is a trade-off here. And it was weird to hear these people who have no experience whatsoever in this regard tell me that that's a false choice."

The Army's "Feasibility Study" about Opening Combat-Arms Units

Like the Marine Corps, the Army conducted a study to determine how it could integrate infantry units and what the effect would be on their combat readiness. Unlike the Marines' study, however, the Army's evaluation of the issue was neither scientific nor objective. For all intents and purposes, the Army's study was the Ranger School test class. It was no coincidence that the Pentagon formally opened infantry billets to female soldiers four months after the first female candidates graduated from Ranger School. In fact, the purpose of the Ranger School experiment was to provide supporters of the policy change with "proof" that they could use to defend it. Army Secretary John McHugh marked the female candidates' graduation by releasing a statement that claimed that this "course has proven that every soldier, regardless of gender, can achieve his or her full potential."[10] A September 2015 *Washington Post* story noted that the "Pentagon face[d] increasing pressure to fully integrate women, following the historic Aug. 21 graduation of two female officers from the Army's Ranger School."[11]

An Army officer mailed me a hard copy of an Army "Gender Integration Study." Marked "Limited Distribution" at the time the source printed it a few years ago, he had kept a hard copy because he found its contents egregious and thought they needed to be made public someday. In August 2015, in response to Freedom of Information Act requests, the Army released a heavily redacted, eight-page "executive summary" of the fifty-four-page study.[12] (At some point after Ash Carter's Defense Department denied the Marines' request for a limited exemption, officially announced whole-scale changes to its existing policy on gender-integrated infantry units, and considered the matter officially settled, the document became publicly available with only the names of the study's authors redacted.[13])

The study itself was conducted by a combination of civilian academics and Army staff officers (though more of the former than the latter), and it is jam-packed with the types of social-justice platitudes that you would expect from a gender studies dissertation. The document explicitly begins with a conclusion in mind, saying the Defense Department has "required the Army to *plan for the expansion of opportunities for women by opening all remaining closed areas of concentration, MOSs, units, and positions as expeditiously as possible.*"[14]

The "Problem Statement" the document aimed to solve was this: "the Army must identify the institutional and cultural factors associated with gender integration, and where possible, identify risk mitigation controls to enable the successful integration of women into previously closed [units and occupational specialties]." So what were those "institutional and cultural factors," and how should the Army "mitigate" them? Here are some key passages from the study:

> Research indicates that combat arms units are characterized by a culture that emphasizes hyper-masculine traits such as dominance, aggressiveness, hiding fear, pursuit of physically demanding/potentially dangerous activities, and competitiveness. Part of unit culture relates to ways in which many male soldiers communicate with one another using crude language and behavior. Additionally, it includes how they respond to stress, and express emotion.[15] ... The Army faces the challenge of changing combat arms culture. A balance is required to retain high morale while removing the culture's less-desirable aspects. This will take time and require patience.[16]

Paternalism and traditional views on the "chivalrous duty" of men to watch over women... is primarily the result of male soldier upbringing prior to their entrance in the Army.[17]... [M]any male Soldiers hold traditional views on the "chivalrous duty" of men to watch over women. Many male Soldiers believe this paternalistic instinct to protect women is both genetic and culturally reinforced. As a result, these Soldiers indicate concern that having women in combat will detract them from their mission, citing their instinct to protect women.[18]... [T]here is a prevalent belief that these stereotypes are true and that Army and national leadership are exaggerating the benefits of integration and are in denial of the costs. As a result, many male Soldiers believe that unqualified women will enter combat arms specialties only to serve as tokens of an ill-conceived policy decision. To successfully integrate, the Army must confront these broad cultural stereotypes about men and women, while simultaneously communicating the rationale and importance of integration.[19]

The study never asks the question of whether the policy change it advocates helps troops on the battlefield. The contrast between the way war-fighters and progressive bureaucrats view this issue is stark. When a Virginia Military Institute cadet asked James Mattis about the wisdom of the policy, Mattis replied:

This is an issue right now that we have Army, Navy, Marines all looking at as we speak. And that is the close-quarters fight being what it is, you know, is it a strength or a weakness to have women in that circumstance?...[Infantrymen are] cocky, they're rambunctious. They're necessarily macho. And it's the most primitive, I would say even evil, environment—you can't even explain it.... This is an area we are going to have to resolve as a nation. And the military has got to have officers who look at this with a great deal of objectivity, and at the same time remember our natural inclination to have this open to all. But we cannot do something that militarily doesn't make sense, and I've got this being looked at right now by the chief of staff of the Army, commandant of the Marine Corps...this is a policy that I inherited.[20]

The legendary Marine got to the root of the issue, asking his audience, "In the event of trouble, you're sleeping at night, in your family home, and you're the dad, mom, whatever, and you hear glass break downstairs, who grabs the baseball bat and gets between the kids' door and whoever broke in and who reaches for the phone to call 911?" The answer to the question, Mattis asserted, depended on one's answer to a more fundamental question: "What kind of society do we want?"[21] Activist groups predictably criticized Mattis's comments, but he refused to disclaim them and pointedly declined to say that he supported the Obama-era policy.[22]

The vast majority of the authors of the Army's study were civilians with no military experience. One could argue that they had no business recommending military personnel policies or analyzing their effects on combat readiness when they had no firsthand experience of serving in the infantry. Yet their perspective apparently prevailed within the Obama administration over the objections of members of the joint chiefs and General Mattis and other officers who had spent the previous decade and a half immersed in the country's ongoing wars. Many junior combat arms officers I interviewed thought the real problem for the military was not the existing combat arms culture but the social engineers' desire to "mitigate" it. An Army captain who served in Afghanistan thought that trying to remove male chivalry, whatever its merits or demerits, was a practical impossibility: "So I'm supposed to essentially deprogram how many millions of years of evolutionary biology in these, like, eighteen, nineteen, and twenty-year-old kids? Like, are you kidding?" A Marine infantry officer on active duty put it this way: "If you're a red-blooded

American male," protecting women is "exactly what you do. And that's the problem—they want us to culturally shift."

The Army's gender study concluded that if its recommended "mitigation" measures were implemented, then opening infantry units to women would pose only a "moderate risk" to military readiness. The recommended "mitigation controls" included leveraging "best practices from currently integrated units," seeking "new materiel solutions for the differing field conditions of dismounted and mechanized operations (e.g., portable shower screens for use in differing settings to afford minimal levels of privacy during hygiene)," and assigning "men and women together to heighten awareness in order to mitigate the effect of some of these stereotypes."[23]

The final paragraph of the "Gender Integration Study" is worth reprinting in full:

> Finally, this study is not a traditional Army operations research analysis—it connects elements of sociology, psychology, economics, and law via the use of multimethod research design to merge quantitative and qualitative data. The combination of operations research and social science provides a powerful synergy. This coupling potentially points to the future of Army analysis where social science perspectives will complement traditional methods. As outlined in the recent Army Operating Concept, the first-order capabilities to succeed are not materiel solutions as in the past, but rather optimization of Soldier performance in the future. Examinations of the human dimension similar to this study will provide the necessary analysis for senior leaders to posture the Army to win in a complex world.

Think about this for a moment: a study commissioned by the United States Army concluded that a proposed policy change would impose a "moderate risk" of putting American soldiers in greater danger, *and then recommended that the policy be adapted anyway*. It's no wonder the study's authors congratulated themselves on eschewing "traditional" military research analysis.

The "Dempsey Rule"

Many senior officers worried that opening infantry units to women would inevitably lead not only to lowering physical standards but to abolishing them, so that the numbers of men and women would be more equal. In January 2016, Marine Corps General John Kelly expressed precisely this concern during an interview with PBS. "They're saying we are not going to change any standards," Kelly said. "[But] there will be great pressure, whether it's 12 months from now, four years from now, because the question will be asked whether we've let women into these other roles, why aren't they staying in those other roles? Why aren't they advancing as infantry people?"[24]

A lieutenant general from the Obama era echoed that concern to me, saying that as "the folks that are pushing these agendas generally have a tendency to do, they'll start looking at numbers.... What I'm concerned about is over the long term, I think we will see a push to balance the numbers. . . . There will be questioning about why there isn't a larger percentage of women who are infantry officers."

Another Army general dismissed the Army's public statements that standards will not change, telling me that the Army was already "in the process of changing all the physical standards. And they're doing it by MOS. So, every MOS is going to have its own set of physical requirements. And of course, those are going to be geared toward a mixed-gender force. So, of course they're going to change the standard. They were in the middle of changing the standards when they said that they would never, never lower the standard."

When General Dempsey accompanied Leon Panetta at the Pentagon press conference announcing the Defense Department's intent to explore opening combat positions to servicewomen, Dempsey said the following: "Importantly, though, if we do decide that a particular standard is so high that a woman couldn't make it, the burden is now on the service to come back and explain to the secretary, why is it that high? Does it really have to be that high?"[25] Dempsey's comments did not go unnoticed within the force.

Ellen Haring, a retired Army colonel and vocal proponent of gender-neutral infantry units, penned an op-ed in the *Marine Corps Times* in 2016 arguing that the Marines' standards for infantry officers were simply too high and "unrealistic." Haring wrote that even though eight female candidates at the Marine Infantry Officers Course had passed the Marine Corps' Combat Endurance Test, all eight "were later eliminated during hikes when loads began to exceed 100 pounds."[26] Apparently, the lesson one should take from this fact was that requiring Marine officers to carry one hundred pounds during certain exercises is discriminatory.

Of course, to the social engineers, success in the Marine Corps Infantry Officer Course is far from the only problem. Female enlisted recruits in Army Advanced Individual Training for the infantry had a 50 percent attrition rate (far exceeding the historical rates for male recruits), and this was even while having much lower physical fitness standards set for them.[27]

Even when standards are not lowered on paper, they inevitably become lowered in practice. Officers know that in a politically correct military, promotion can be dependent on meeting politically correct goals, or at least toeing the politically correct line. U.S. Naval Postgraduate School professor Anna Simons wrote in early 2015 about meeting with "a roomful of field grade officers" (majors, lieutenant colonels, and colonels) to discuss the policy changes proposed by the Obama Department of Defense. Simons reported that it was basically impossible to get them to speak frankly.[28] "Officers who balk at the idea of women serving in ground infantry units or on Special Forces Operational Detachments Alpha (ODAs) won't publicly say so, let alone publicly explain why," she wrote. The officers, she continued, worry "about retaliation that could hurt their careers. In contrast, those who have no reservations—usually because they won't be the ones who have to deal with the fallout from integration at the small unit level—slough off the challenge as just another minor problem or 'ankle biter.'"[29]

The "Foreign Militaries Do It" Myth

The Obama administration and the media often pointed to the example of Western European nations that had integrated women into ground combat forces as a lead that American should follow. But such policies are neither as widespread nor as successful as their champions in America would have you believe.

In the aftermath of the Iraq war, the United Kingdom conducted a full-scale evaluation of its combat capabilities, producing a document widely referred to as the "Iraq Inquiry."[30] Among other things, the commission investigated the effects of integrating female service members into ground combat units. Unsurprisingly, the commission reached the same conclusion as the Marines—that "survivability & lethality, deployability, and morbidity" simply "cannot be mitigated by changes to structure or training" and that "if the steps necessary to mitigate the risks are grossly disproportionate in terms of time, resources and cost, lawful exclusion may have to remain in place."[31] The commission also took the trouble to define "ground combat" and "combat effectiveness."

"Ground Combat" was defined as "those roles that are primarily intended and designed with the purpose of requiring individuals on the ground to close with and kill the enemy."[32] "Combat Effectiveness" was defined as the ability of a ground combat team "to carry out its assigned mission, role or function," and it underlined that the "cohesion," of a ground combat team "is a vital factor" in its combat effectiveness.[33] The commission concluded that, "Despite the differences [between the sexes], there will be some women, amongst the physical elite, who will achieve the entry tests for [ground combat] roles. But these women will be more susceptible to acute short term injury than men: in the Army's current predominantly single sex initial military training, women have a twofold higher risk of musculoskeletal (MSK) injury. The roles that require individuals to carry weight for prolonged periods are likely to be the most damaging."

Despite these conclusions, the forces of political correctness pressed forward. By 2016, the Ministry of Defence had begun integrating its ground combat units and had already begun to lower the physical fitness standards for those units because they considered them discriminatory against women.[34] A Ministry of Defence document stated that the British Army's physical tests were "optimized for male physiology." One of the infantry tasks under review was "completing an eight-mile march in less than two hours while carrying 25kg. The army's research suggests less than 5 per cent of 7,000 female recruits would currently pass the physical tests."

The UK government made everything gender neutral. "Infantrymen" became "infanteers."[35] Military training manuals that used "gender-specific language" were ordered revised. The British military built new barracks to accommodate "gender-neutral" combat arms units. And not a single female soldier asked to transfer to them. The *Daily Mail* reported in December 2018 that zero of the 9,000 female service members in the UK military volunteered to become infanteers. The article quoted an officer who said, "We've paid for adverts, built new barrack blocks and even changed how we are supposed to speak and what we read. But the truth is that at officer level and among women already serving, they're simply not interested in joining the infantry."[36]

As in the United States, military leaders and veterans protested loudly but were overruled. "No one pretends that [the policy change] enhances the army's capabilities," one senior officer told the *Independent*. A British government official responded by saying it would make the Army "more operationally effective," in part because it would make the military more reflective of society.[37]

The Australian military also provides a cautionary tale. The Aussies, too, integrated their ground combat units—and the experiment has been branded a "complete failure" by Australian defense observers.[38] Only one in ten female recruits managed to get through infantry training. Of the small percentage who did pass, a quarter were so injured they were classified as non-deployable. Accepting these facts, however, requires admitting that men and women are biologically different, and because the progressive left can't do that and because it apparently owns this policy debate, the Aussies doubled down on failure.

The Australian Defence Force lowered admissions standards for female recruits and created a seven-week "pre-conditioning course" to prepare female recruits for basic training.[39] All that was required to gain entrance to the course was four pushups and twenty sit-ups. Furthermore, the *Daily Telegraph* reported that recruiters were instructed to shun male recruits and only recruit females for available combat arms positions.[40] Recruiters were told they would be re-located if they disregarded the instructions. Thirty-five of fifty current vacancies were designated "female only." The policy was reportedly part of Australian Chief of Army Lieutenant General Angus Campbell's goal to make the Australian Army 25 percent female by 2025. (If that goal sounds familiar, it is because former Secretary of the Navy Ray Mabus announced a similar objective for the United States Navy.)

Perhaps the most commonly cited alleged success story is that of the Israeli Defense Force. Israel has indeed created three combat battalions in which women can serve, but these battalions are assigned to relatively peaceful areas, and the IDF has steadfastly refused to open up the rest of its combat battalions—the ones most likely to go into action—to women. With its survival at stake, Israel cannot afford political correctness.

The Bottom Line

The Obama ideologues—and their foreign counterparts—like to talk about "expanding the talent pool." But it was never really about that. If these new recruits require lower standards and special treatment and suffer higher rates of injury that does not *expand the talent pool*, it lowers the quality of the force. But the bureaucrats never cared about making the military more effective in combat. They simply have an ideological dedication to "equality" and forced their policies through, regardless of the consequences.

SOCIAL JUSTICE WARFARE

*"If micro-inequities are not managed,
morale can decrease."*
—*A 2013 Army Equal Opportunity Newsletter
at Fort Lee, Virginia*

"The Army is ordering its hardened combat veterans to wear fake breasts and empathy bellies so they can better understand how pregnant soldiers feel during physical training," a February 16, 2012, article in *Stars and Stripes* reported.[1] (Somehow, the article was not satire—this really happened.) "I didn't want to do it," Sergeant Michael Braden, 29, of Everett, Washington, told the newspaper, before adding that "he was ordered to attend the training even though he doesn't have any female soldiers in his unit."[2]

Who can blame him? What do fake breasts and empathy bellies have to do with fighting wars?

In 2015, Army ROTC cadets at multiple universities participated in "Walk a Mile in Her Shoes" events on campuses. The events—"designed to raise awareness about sexual violence against women"[3]—had male Army cadets replace their combat boots with bright red high-heeled shoes.

Cadets at Arizona State reported that their participation in the "volunteer" event was required. "Attendance is mandatory and if we miss it we get a negative counseling and a 'does not support the battalion sharp/EO mission' on our [cadet evaluation] for getting the branch we want [upon commissioning]," one cadet wrote on a message board. "So I just spent $16 on a pair of high heels that I have to spray paint red later on only to throw them in the trash after about 300 of us embarrass the U.S. Army tomorrow."[4] The spectacle of soldiers tottering around college campuses in their duty uniforms and high heels certainly humiliated the cadets, but apparently it did not embarrass those who were eager to change the Army's culture, including Obama administration progressives focused on building a "kinder, gentler military"[5] during wartime and while the military's ability to fight was being seriously degraded. An article on the Army's website dutifully highlighted a handful of units' participation in the marches,[6] but the ROTC cadets who were forced to participate were understandably demoralized: walking across college campuses in bright red high heels has nothing to do with military service—and in fact, it makes a mockery of it. But the Obama administration never seemed to understand what the military is all about.

Any combat-arms officer who has deployed in a leadership role (especially a leadership role at the company or platoon level) will tell you that one of the first thoughts that enters your mind after you step off the plane and onto the tarmac of a warzone airfield is "Did we do enough to prepare? Are my soldiers ready for this?" It was those inevitable questions that led me to resent the endless, politically correct lectures my men were required to attend as we prepared to deploy, lectures that were irrelevant, at best, to their preparation for war. A senior leader in the Navy described the fixation on social justice training as "a distraction to a young sailor on the deck, like, because they're looking at this like 'how is this going to make me do my job better?'" The mandatory training was "a distraction to their commanders, and for the department heads, and the company commanders," he added. The company commander of an Army Air Defense Artillery Commander echoed that assessment, recounting an episode after a mandatory training session while the unit was in the Middle East in which he vented his frustration to his First Sergeant, telling him "I thought our job was to fight wars."

Buzzwords like "diversity" and "inclusion," as used by progressive bureaucrats, were often merely covers for what is better described as "identity politics"—something that has no place in a military that is apolitical and that is focused *not* on individual wants or grievances, but on a group mission. In the Army, we often told soldiers, *"Don't be an individual."* In war, you focus on the goals of the unit, and you do things the military way. The Marines call those who don't conform "OFP Marines." OFP stands for "Own Fucking Program." In the military, everyone must be on the same program, or things don't work and lives get lost.

The military is a great equalizer. Your race is unimportant. Politics are not discussed. The kid from Harlem and the kid from Beverly Hills are paid equally as privates, airmen, or seamen. The job is what matters; you need to pull your weight. Troops respect those who do and look down upon those who don't. Identity politics and intersectionality, which label and divide people into categories and sub-categories of privileged victims, is completely incompatible with an effective military culture.

Transforming a Warfighting Institution into a Clogged Bureaucracy

The Obama era was transformational for the military. Political correctness moved front and center, which becomes evident upon looking at the list of Army Directives and publications issued from 2009 to 2016, as the number of directives that focused explicitly on social-justice issues increased sharply.[7] And that steady drumbeat of progressive identity politics filters down: over the past several years, several brigade or air wing newsletters have featured articles about curbing micro-aggressions or micro-inequalities. A February 2013 Equal Opportunity News Bulletin at Fort Lee, Virginia, contained an article titled *The Power of Micro-Inequities*, for example. The article listed "gestures like rolling eyes, change in voice pitch or volume, change in body posture, [and] fake or forced smiles" as examples of micro-inequalities and warned that if "micro-inequities are not managed, morale can decrease."[8] A summer 2017 article from the Equal Opportunity Office at Fort Riley, Kansas, told soldiers that they shouldn't "just stand by and watch micro-inequities occur and do nothing."[9] A newsletter for the 187th Fighter Wing of the Air Force similarly contained an article about "unmasking microaggression."[10]

Institutional and cultural changes of these types were made in every branch of the military. In 2015, the Army instituted a new "Breastfeeding and Lactation Support Policy."[11] Compliance with the policy would be monitored by a division of the Army Surgeon General's office run by a civilian doctor.[12] "Investing in the workplace Breastfeeding and Lactation Support program can yield substantial dividends for the Army—lower turnover rates, additional healthcare savings and productivity and loyalty," an article on the Army's website stated.[13] "These policies will help ensure commanders and Soldiers are informed on the benefits, services and support available for Soldiers breastfeeding in the workplace," it continued. The required changes under the policy included a force-wide mandate requiring breastfeeding rooms at commands with more than fifty female service members.

In an ordinary workplace, this would be a laudable initiative, but the Army is not an ordinary workplace. It is not staffed by ordinary workers. And it does not have an ordinary corporate mission. An Army major general who was serving in a command position when the directive came down explained what this policy may look like in practice:

> It also used to be that, okay, while you're pregnant—the nine months that you're carrying the child—plus about another three after the child is delivered, then you're on either light duty or basically not performing the function that the Army recruited you to do. Which is understandable, okay? . . . No problem.
>
> Then the Army two years ago put out a policy that was concerning lactating mothers. So for the first year of the child's life, it's the unit's responsibility to provide a location for the mother to express breast milk, even in the field, and to keep that milk refrigerated. But what's not mentioned in the new

policy change about lactating mothers and refrigerating the milk is the fact that now I also have to transport that milk to the child or the child to the milk. So you've got all these logistical issues now to the point where it doesn't even make sense to deploy the female soldier/mother to the field on a training exercise. You might as well just leave them back at garrison. So it really becomes [up to] two full years per child [that a breastfeeding mother under this policy is potentially unable to fully participate in unit field training or deployment]...That's just another indicator of how radical the change has been, with no consideration to how that affects the readiness of the units these soldiers belong to.[14]

The Obama administration apparently didn't bother to consult with military commanders about whether the policy was needed, desirable, or even possible. It appears that progressive bureaucrats didn't want military concerns to get in the way of social and cultural "progress."

"Anti-Hate" Training, Informed by a Hateful Group

Establishing guardrails to ensure that every service member is treated with human dignity and to prevent the poison of prejudice from infecting units is no doubt laudable. It is necessary both as a moral matter and a readiness matter. The cancer of racial prejudice, antisemitism, or hate of any other form is antithetical to the ideals upon which the military—and the country it protects—were founded. Further, cohesive units are more effective units; morale is a force multiplier. Toxic attitudes or beliefs, left unaddressed, can metastasize and destroy morale and cohesiveness, bringing the entire unit's effectiveness down with it.

But stamping out prejudice and fostering identity politics are very different things. The former is essential to the mission, while the latter detracts from it. How, then, are identity politics introduced to an institution that should be concerned primarily with merit and dedicated towards successful outcomes on the battlefield? The answer is through a relentless but subtle push from advocacy groups, working in tandem with political appointees and politically-minded bureaucrats.

In 2013, a small wave of disturbing stories emerged about the contents of briefings given to both active and reserve units. Troops at Camp Shelby, Mississippi, were told that mainstream evangelical groups like the American Family Association were "domestic hate groups" similar to the Ku Klux Klan or neo-Nazis.[15] Soldiers at Fort Hood reported that they were warned that supporting evangelical groups or the Tea Party could result in UCMJ discipline.[16] And a "briefing with an Army Reserve unit based in Pennsylvania" listed "Catholicism" and "Evangelical Christianity" as forms of religious extremism alongside the KKK, al-Qaeda, and the Nation of Islam.[17] The last incident was so egregious that thirty-four members of Congress wrote a letter to the Pentagon expressing grave concern.[18]

An Army spokesman apologized for the brief and blamed it on a presenter who "produced the material after conducting internet research."[19] The Army likewise blamed other incidents on "soldiers who included information found during an internet search."[20] Even if that were the case, however, those statements do not explain how all of those independent EO briefers arrived at the same conclusions about evangelicals and also thought the material was appropriate. The answer can be found in the Student Guide used by the Defense Equal Opportunity Management Institute (DEOMI). The DEOMI is a "three-month…course taught at Patrick Air Force Base in Florida" that trains the Equal Opportunity Officers and NCOs who lead unit EO briefings across the military. The Equal Opportunity Student Advisor Guide is a 637-page textbook given to officers and NCOs who attend the DEOMI.[21] And the version created during the Obama era was stocked with far-left, intersectional dogma.

One statement in the manual, for example, tells students that "Simply put, a healthy white, heterosexual, Christian male receives many unearned advantages of social privilege, whereas a black, homosexual, atheist female in poor health receives many unearned disadvantages of social privilege."[22] This, according to the student guide, is because "the unfair economic advantages and disadvantages created long ago by institutions for whites, males, Christians, etc. still affect socioeconomic privilege today."[23] The topic is addressed in a twenty-page section titled "Power and Privilege," which tells students that "White males represent the haves as compared to the have-nots."[24]

Perhaps most notable is the manual's listing of the Southern Poverty Law Center (SPLC) as a resource that EO briefers could use to obtain more information about hate groups and extremism. The SPLC was founded in 1971 with the laudatory purpose of exposing racist hate groups in the Deep South during the civil rights era and filing civil-rights lawsuits against the Klan in federal court. It has long since morphed into a smear merchant for the extreme fringes of the far left that indiscriminately label groups with opposing views as hateful and publishes "hate maps" that list mainstream conservative religious groups alongside neo-Nazis and the KKK. Despite the group's evolution of purpose and tactics—which was obvious to any neutral observer who cared to pay attention—it managed to maintain its credibility with major media outlets in the process. (The SPLC only lost some of that credibility recently, after reports exposed widespread allegations by current and former employees that the organization had a culture of sexual harassment, gender discrimination, and racism at its headquarters, prompting President Richard Cohen to resign and its founder Morris Dees to be fired.[25] The organization also was recently forced to pay a $3.375 million settlement to Maajid Nawaz, a Muslim who founded a group called the Quilliam Foundation to counter Islamic radicalism, because the SPLC included Nawaz on its bogus list of "Anti-Muslim Extremists."[26])

The result was an organization falsely labeling mainstream Christian and family advocacy organizations as "hate" groups and "extremists" because they merely espoused the beliefs of their faith, and media outlets and some public officials credulously repeating the lies. Those lies were not without consequence. In August 2012, Floyd Corkins entered the lobby of the Family Research Council's headquarters in Washington D.C. and opened fire, wounding a security guard. Corkins later told police that he wanted to attack hate groups and chose the FRC because it was listed on the SPLC's website as a hate group.[27] The FRC, however, is not a hate group by any stretch of the imagination—it merely advocates for policies that align with traditional Judeo-Christian values, which are supported by a substantial percentage of the country. For the SPLC, however, the FRC's sincerely held beliefs conflicted with far-left ideology and therefore it was a hate group.

With the DEOMI student manual's endorsement of the SPLC's labels, it's no coincidence that very similar and very problematic EO briefs occurred in units in all branches of the military. Some Marine and Air Force units, too, cited information from the SPLC in their EO briefs. A previously unreported lesson plan for a lecture titled "Extremism and Extremists" given to unit Equal Opportunity Representatives for the I Marine Expeditionary Force, for example, stated that "Christian Conservatism is closely tied to many of the extremist groups and organizations" in society.[28] A paragraph titled "White Supremacy Ideology" says, "The Christian Conservative 'Identity' explanation of the diverse races of mankind is grounded in Biblical interpretation." (When a Pentagon official I spoke to learned about the SPLC's involvement, he went straight to the colonel in charge of the Corps to explain who the SPLC was and inform the colonel that the group's materials were included in Marine EO briefings. The colonel "about had a heart attack" when he learned that his EO officers and NCOs were using the SPLC as a resource based on a recommendation from the DoD, the source said.) Despite pushback from legislators and religious organizations, the Obama DoD refused to stop relying on the SPLC, telling media outlets that while it "[did] not have a formal relationship" with the group, it would continue to use the SPLC's resources to "inform [its] training."[29] The DoD finally "severed all ties to the . . . SPLC" some time in 2017 after the change in administration.[30]

The problem with the Obama DoD's reliance on the SPLC and similar activist groups—and the teaching manual and EO briefs subsequently produced—is not that soldiers and Marines are likely to suddenly believe that Catholics, evangelical Christians, and conservatives within the ranks or otherwise are odious extremists. Rather, the episode speaks to the attitudes and ideology of the activists setting policies that affect servicemen and women.

Fighting the Phantom Enemy of Implicit Bias

Implicit bias theory, also referred to as unconscious bias, assumes that human beings often have prejudicial beliefs about sex and race that are buried in their subconscious and that those influence their interactions and decisions. As David French at *National Review* noted, "There is no way to show that you're immune to implicit bias, because you are by definition unaware of your subconscious."[31] The theory emerged in academic circles in 1998 when several researchers unveiled the Implicit Association Test (IAT) which, as French explained,

> asks you to make snap decisions on the basis of images or words flashing across the screen. You'll tap certain keys to indicate white or black faces—or Arab or other names—and then associate faces or names with good or bad items or characteristics. For example, the test allegedly shows that people are likelier to associate black faces with weapons and white faces with more-harmless objects. Or they might associate Arab names with "bad" words and non-Arab names with "good" words.

The IAT purports to prove the existence of implicit or unconscious bias, and the concept became one of the progressive left's pet issues during the Obama era.[32] If implicit bias is real and has the damaging impact the left believes it does, then it's reasonable for our institutions to conduct implicit bias training to teach people about subconscious prejudice and help them overcome it. This, in a nutshell, is progressives' justification for implicit bias training.

There's just one problem: the theory is bunk (and has been debunked). For years, the existence of implicit bias (and the need for retraining) was accepted as gospel in academic circles. It was dismissed out of hand by a few others, but almost no one actually subjected the IAT to rigorous analysis or analyzed the supposed link between IAT results showing "implicit bias" and the test subjects' actual behavior. Until recently. In 2017, the *Chronicle of Higher Education* reported that "[r]esearchers from the University of Wisconsin at Madison, Harvard, and the University of Virginia examined 499 studies over 20 years involving 80,859 participants that used the IAT and other, similar measures."[33] The result? "They discovered two things: One is that the correlation between implicit bias and discriminatory behavior appears weaker than previously thought. They also conclude that there is very little evidence that changes in implicit bias have anything to do with changes in a person's behavior."[34] One of the co-authors of the paper told the *Chronicle* that the changes "should be stunning" for those who have long believed in implicit bias theory. The bottom line: implicit bias is junk science and focusing on implicit bias training is worthless at best and counterproductive at worst.

But that didn't stop the Obama administration from pushing it on the military.

In his last major act as secretary of the Army, Eric Fanning signed Army Directive 2017-06, which required Army commanders to develop plans for force-wide "unconscious or implicit bias training" by March 1, 2017, with the training to begin no later than March 1, 2018. (Fanning said his directive was required by an executive order from President Obama mandating implicit bias training across government agencies.[35] The training was scrapped by the Trump-era Defense Department and was not implemented.) Retired Army Colonel Ron Crews called the policy a prime example of how the Obama administration's political appointees elevated progressive identity politics above combat readiness. In a letter to the Department of the Army shortly after the Trump administration took office, Crews and other retired brass urged the Army to rescind Fanning's order. "We believe [the military's] decline [in readiness] is in direct proportion to the social engineering forced on our armed forces during the previous administration," the authors wrote. The authors included a significant number of former generals and other national security professionals.[36]

Fanning dismissed their concerns. "Everybody in the Army should believe there is a path forward for them. Readiness is getting the most out of the force," he told *Stars and Stripes*. "I don't think opportunity and equality are political agendas. I think they're important American values."[37] The *Stars and Stripes* article (published two months after Trump took office) cited a "former senior official familiar with the directive's creation" who said that the Army evaluated its diversity policies by studying the policies of "private sector companies and outside organizations like Uber, Google, and the National Football League." "Recognizing unconscious bias is how private sector companies get the best people to work for them," the former Obama official said.[38] Therefore, the official apparently assumed, the military needs to do it, too, even though companies in the private sector compete for the best employees on the basis of salary, benefits, and working conditions while the military relies primarily (although certainly not exclusively) on patriotism.

Unconscious or implicit bias training proliferated throughout the rest of the services as well. The entire Marine Corps received unconscious bias training in 2016 after the Defense Department's civilian leadership ordered the Marines to begin integrating females into infantry combat units. The Marine Corps press release about the force-wide training stated that unconscious bias lessons "[p]rovide an understanding of the concept of cognitive bias, awareness of one's own cognitive bias via a performance-based exam, and cognitive bias mitigation techniques."[39] The goal of the training was to "begin to facilitate cultural change" within the Corps.[40] The effort to change Navy and Marine Corps culture occurred on nearly all fronts. The Navy's Fiscal Year 2015 report on Diversity and Equal Opportunity reported that, "in FY14, a majority of

DON [Department of the Navy] Commands addressed attitudinal barriers through training to educate supervisors and managers on DON reasonable accommodation procedures... [and] unconscious and hidden bias."[41]

The Air Force also implemented unconscious bias training at both the unit and command levels.[42] According to a 2016 fact sheet titled "Diversity & Inclusion Initiatives," every airman had to complete the training.[43] Lesson plans used by the Air Force Judge Advocate General (JAG) school included a section on "Diversity & Implicit Bias."[44] Additional instruction was required for members of promotion boards before they selected candidates for promotion: a memo from Secretary of the Air Force Deborah Lee James directed that, to "the fullest extent possible, unconscious bias training will be given immediately prior to promotion boards, prior to DT [Development Team] meetings on school assignments, prior to civilian hiring panels, and prior to annual performance evaluations."[45]

The Air Force's institutional commitment to root out alleged biases (one that airmen weren't even aware they possessed) was a direct result of a 2013 policy entitled the "Air Force Diversity Strategic Roadmap." The roadmap was full of corporate bureaucratic boilerplate and unexamined assumptions, beginning with this: "Diversity is a military necessity. Air Force decision-making and operational capabilities are enhanced by diversity among its Airmen, uniformed and civilian, helping make the Air Force more agile, innovative and effective." The Air Force's diversity roadmap was designed to fulfil President Obama's 2011 executive order to promote "diversity" and inclusion across "the federal workforce."[46] The roadmap called for the service to "develop and maintain comprehensive diversity initiatives," including to:

- Educate and train all personnel on the importance of diversity, including mutual respect, thus promoting an Air Force culture that values inclusion of all personnel in the total force and views diversity and inclusion as a force multiplier in accomplishing the Air Force mission;

- Ensure all personnel in the total force understand they are valued and have the opportunity to achieve their full potential while contributing to the mission;
- Establish effective diversity training, mentoring, and professional development that provide the tools for personnel to navigate personal career progression;
- Provide awareness training in cross-cultural competencies to enhance organizational capabilities;
- Ensure adequate resources (manpower and financial) are allocated to sustain effective diversity outreach/recruiting programs.[47]

The policy also created something called the Air Force Diversity Committee to "oversee and monitor key diversity and inclusion initiatives."[48] One of the roadmap's inevitable goals was making the Air Force an "employer of choice" for potential recruits.[49] The idea that potential recruits would choose the Air Force over other employers because of the Air Force's superior implicit bias training would be amusing if it weren't so sad. All that time, all that money, and all these new progressive Air Force bureaucrats come at the expense of an Air Force focused on winning the nation's wars.

The roadmap was clear that the Air Force's diversity policies would be set by the civilian secretary of the Air Force and be strictly enforced. To ensure that military leaders complied with the effort, the Air Force would develop "a framework to monitor/gauge senior leader commitment to, and support of, diversity and inclusion."[50]

The Coast Guard hopped on the implicit bias train as well, with Dr. Aram deKoven, the Coast Guard Academy's Chief Diversity Officer, praising the use of implicit bias training at the academy, saying that cadets "will take with them a sense of consciousness, a level of awareness, which many others don't have, about the value of inclusivity, diversity, and implicit bias, and they will lead equitably."[51]

Misplaced Priorities Impose Opportunity Costs in Addition to Cultural Costs

A casual observer might assume that this emphasis on implicit bias, equal opportunity training, and other progressive fixations amounts to a minor annoyance. They are anything but. These misplaced priorities take a serious toll on training and readiness. Hours spent teaching soldiers and sailors about their subconscious biases or instructing them about the respectful use of pronouns are hours that cannot be dedicated to preparing them for their essential tasks—jobs that our nation, which is sending that unit into harm's way, expects and relies on them to accomplish. A now-retired Army general told me:

> You should never waste one minute of your training time, of your preparation time, on something that does not contribute to readiness in the military.... Go back to January 2016 when two patrol boats were taken off the coast of Iran, and the crews were held. The guy that was in charge was a 2011 Naval Academy graduate. Now go further back to [the 1960s in the Vietnam War] when Jeremiah Denton, a Naval Academy graduate, was tortured for six months to get him to go on camera, and he blinked—with Morse code he blinked the word *torture*. He got a Navy Cross for it. What courage. What incredible courage. And now you go to 2016, and that Naval Academy graduate looked into the cameras and said this is all our fault and we want to apologize to the Iranians, and we want to thank them for their hospitality.
>
> You ask yourself what happened between Jeremiah Denton and 2016, when you've got another Naval Academy graduate in charge and he takes a totally—first of all— wrong approach,

and a total capitulation. And reflect on—did he get the code of conduct training, or did his people get code of conduct training? And the answer is, it's not real clear whether they did or not, but one thing is for sure: They didn't focus a lot of attention on it. They didn't drill their people on it before they put them into harm's way. But you know what they did go through? They went through all of the diversity training....

[The Iranian Navy debacle] is where it hurts you. That's how it destroys you. And if you're in a National Guard unit and you only get eleven drills a year plus your two weeks of active duty, and you waste even one of those drill weekends sitting in a classroom—which they do, and even members of Congress that are in the National Guard will tell you [they] spend an entire weekend sitting in a classroom taking these classes that contribute nothing to their readiness—that's why this whole social experiment is so foolish. Because it's not helping us to win wars.

Hours spent training young soldiers, sailors, airmen, and Marines about alleged unconscious biases, in other words, are hours that cannot be spent ensuring that every member of an infantry company is proficient at calling in a medevac or comfortable with all of the unit's weapons system (in case they are called upon to fill another soldier's role), or that sailors are cross-trained on different platforms. But the Obama administration was far more committed to ideological indoctrination than it was to prioritizing military training.

Diversity Metrics Became a Goal for Their Own Sake

Before he resigned from his position as undersecretary of defense, Brad Carson started implementing sweeping, controversial changes to the military's promotion and personnel systems as part of his "Force of the Future" program. Members of the Senate Armed Services Committee blasted Carson for meeting with federal labor unions, the media, and think tanks in Washington, D.C., as he developed these controversial changes but never once consulting them. Worse, senior military leaders told the committee that Carson had essentially cut them out of the decision-making process and that "they did not feel like they were properly consulted."[52]

The problematic changes sought by Carson, Fanning, and their colleagues were all part of an eight-year Obama administration priority to transform the military along the principles of progressive identity politics. For example, a former Navy rear admiral gave me a copy of a 2010 memo sent to senior naval officers. The memo, which contains the subject line "Diversity Accountability," directs commanders to identify diverse officers within their commands and provide the Navy with "the plan for their career progression."

The memo reads, in part:

> A change in focus of this year's diversity brief is the desire to identify our key performers (by name) and provide insight on each of them. [The Chief of Naval Operations] is interested in who are the diverse officers with high potential and what is the plan for their career progression. He may ask what is being done within to ensure they are considered for key follow on billets within the Navy. This list must be held very closely but will provide ready reference to ensure we are carefully monitoring and supporting the careers of the best and the brightest the Navy has to offer.
>
> [...] Your insight into the diverse composition of your command will assist in my discussion with [the Chief of Naval Operations].... This reporting requirement will not be put into [the Navy's internal task tracking system] due to the sensitive nature of the by name list.
>
> Note: "CNO" = Chief of Naval Operations; "N1" = Chief of Naval Personnel; "TV4" = the Navy's Internal Task Tracking System; TWMS = "Total Workforce Management System" (i.e. a human resources database.)

Why is that memo problematic? Because it explicitly uses identity politics as a proxy for merit. The American military should be—and long has been—a meritocracy.

Secretary of the Air Force Deborah Lee James sent a similar memorandum to Air Force leaders in 2016. The memo required Air Force leaders to "establish diverse slates [of candidates for promotion] for Key Military Developmental Positions."[53] Under James's policy, every candidate list was required to include "at least one qualified, diverse candidate."[54] The policy also required the head of every Command Selection Board (the promotion board that selects senior leaders for positions such as squadron commander) to "assess the diversity of both the selectees and those not selected for command following the board's decision."[55] The 2016 memo signed by James directed an assistant secretary of the Air Force to "conduct a one-year accountability review to track progress on the entire slate of Diversity & Inclusion initiatives."[56]

James said, in defending another diversity initiative, "A fundamental question I ask is: Are we spending as much time and resources and energy thinking about the next generation of our people, the next generation of our airmen, as we are thinking about the next generation of aircraft?"[57] The *Air Force Times* reported that "her proposals were met with suspicion from some current and former troops, who think the emphasis on diversity will inevitably lead to less-qualified airmen being selected for promotions or other jobs." The article quoted Terry Stevens, a recently retired Air Force colonel with 35 years of experience, who slammed the policy, saying, "Diversity don't win wars. Warriors win wars."

A common refrain of the Obama-era Defense Department was that diversity is a "strategic imperative."[58] (For example, the Navy Diversity and Inclusion Roadmap issued by Undersecretary of the Navy Franklin R. Parker, a Yale Law School graduate who worked in Silicon Valley before joining the Obama administration in 2009, emphasized repeatedly that diversity was "a strategic imperative."[59]) The Military Leadership Diversity Commission (MLDC) report, titled *From Representation to Inclusion*, likewise recommended that "diversity leadership must become a core competency" of military branches.[60] (The MLDC was created by Congressional fiat in 2009 when Democrats held a supermajority in Congress.) For comparison's sake, the Defense Department currently recognizes nine core competencies necessary for battlefield success, including "Command and Control," "Force Application," "Battlespace Awareness," and "Logistics."[61] To this list of operational capabilities, the MLDC wished to add "Diversity Leadership."

Eric Fanning likewise believed that "diversity" and "inclusion" were necessary to maintain a battle-ready force. Fanning tweeted that "Those who say military is no place for social experimentation *may* be right— but equality & inclusivity are not experiments—they're Amer [sic] values."[62] (Notice that Fanning apparently could not even bring himself to unequivocally affirm that "the military is no place for social experimentation," saying only that it "may" be the case.) Fanning framed the issue in similar terms during public appearances discussing the changes he was implementing.[63] But if buzzwords like "equality" and "inclusivity" in the context in which Fanning uses them are merely euphemisms for reduced standards or introducing corrosive identity politics to the force, then no, they're not necessary values. The Obama administration consistently ignored—and never seemed to care about—the real-world consequences of their progressive goals.

"Give Me Eleven Pushups" Is Asking One Pushup Too Many

The emphasis on "diversity" and "inclusion" went hand in hand with new restrictions on using exercise as a punishment, or "corrective action," for mistakes or misconduct. Revised Army regulations published in October 2012 drastically limited the use of physical exercise as a "corrective action" for mistakes or misconduct. Under the new rules, officers and non-commissioned officers can only require their subordinates to perform one of eight exercises and only for a maximum of ten repetitions.[64] (Ten reps wouldn't test the physical limits of a middle school athlete.) This policy was further integrated into regulations for the Army's Training and

Doctrine Command (TRADOC), which oversees basic training. TRA-DOC created the following chart of "acceptable" basic training punishments (Table 2-2 in Army Training Regulation 350-6):

Notice the text that says corrective PT should not "give the impression" that it is "punitive." This type of instruction implies that soldiers are somehow so fragile that they cannot be given the impression that they're being punished.

The Air Force also adopted significant changes to its code of conduct. In December 2013, Air Education and Training Command Instruction 36-2902, which governs Air Force basic training and all other training programs, was amended to prevent "hazing" and "maltraining." The Instruction notes that Chapter 3 of the publication "is new and establishes command-wide prohibitions and responsibilities regarding trainee abuse and hazing." Certainly, preventing hazing and the abuse of trainees is important—treating service members with dignity is one of the hallmarks of the American military that sets it apart from countries like Russia, which has an institutionalized epidemic of brutal hazing that destroys morale and often causes serious injuries.[65] But the changes adopted by the Air Force and the other services prohibit far more than hazing and abuse. They strip Non-Commissioned Officers and Drill Instructors of many of the time-honored instructional and disciplinary tools they have used to build personal and collective accountability, mental and physical stamina, and unit cohesion and camaraderie.

According to Instruction 36-2902, "Examples of maltraining include, but are not limited to: using abusive or excessive physical exercise; unnecessarily rearranging the property of a trainee to correct infractions; and misapplication of motivational training tools. Any practice for the purpose of inducing a trainee, cadet, or student to self-eliminate is considered maltraining. Other examples include... assigning remedial training to an entire group based on the deficiencies of an individual or a few individuals."[66]

Anyone who has attended basic training or boot camp (or in some cases even participated in high school sports) will recognize the absurdity

Table 2-2
Corrective action

Exercise	Phase I WK 1-3	Phase II WK 4-6	Phase III WK 7-9	Phase IV WK 10-13	Phase V WK 14-20	Phase V+ WK 21-Completion
	basic combat training			advanced individual training		
	one station unit training					
	repetitions/time					
Rower	5	5	5	5-10	5-10	5-10
Squat Bender	5	5	5	5-10	5-10	5-10
Windmill	5	5	5	5-10	5-10	5-10
Prone Row	5	5	5	5-10	5-10	5-10
Bent-leg Body Twist	5	5	5	5-10	5-10	5-10
Push-up	5	5	5	5-10	5-10	5-10
V-up	5	5	5	5-10	5-10	5-10
Leg Tuck & Twist	5	5	5	5-10	5-10	5-10
Supine Bicycle	5	5	5	5-10	5-10	5-10
Swimmer	5	5	5	5-10	5-10	5-10
8-ct Push-up	5	5	5	5-10	5-10	5-10
Push-up (Timed)	30 Sec	45 Sec	60 Sec	60 Sec	60 Sec	60 Sec
Sit-up (Timed)	30 Sec	45 Sec	60 Sec	60 Sec	60 Sec	60 Sec
High Jumper	N/A	N/A	5	5-10	5-10	5-10
Mountain Climber	N/A	N/A	5	5-10	5-10	5-10
Power Jump	N/A	N/A	5	5-10	5-10	5-10

b. Leaders must exercise good judgment in the administration of corrective action. Corrective action may be applied to entire units if appropriate (correcting an entire platoon failing to show teamwork during Red Phase in a given training event by having them do five repetitions of the pushup, for example), but will be focused at the individual level whenever possible. Improper use can lead to unauthorized mass punishment or hazing. Do not refer to this type of administrative corrective measure as "smoking" or "smoke sessions;" such references give the impression that these measures are punitive or oppressive.

of these regulations. No longer, if these rules are followed, can an instructor force an entire basic training platoon to do pushups because a trainee arrived late to formation (teaching collective accountability). No longer can a Drill Instructor overturn the entire contents of an improperly organized foot locker (reminding recruits to pay attention to detail).

Whether these new regulations are strictly followed or enforced varies based on each individual unit, to be sure. They are, however, far more likely to be followed closely in TRADOC units (units that fall under Training and Doctrine Command, such as basic training units), which are closely scrutinized and forced to hew tightly to official regulations and policies. I knew plenty of NCOs who ignored them as ridiculous, but I also witnessed some NCOs correcting their peers who imposed more than the allowable number of reps as a corrective. Regardless, merely having these limitations on the books as institutional policies is absurd. And unfortunately, the longer they remain in effect, the more likely they are to become the norm.

Some might say—and certainly the Obama administration apparently believed—that it doesn't matter that airmen and soldiers are no longer required to do disciplinary pushups or low crawls until muscle failure. But the military's traditional disciplinary approaches have a purpose, which is to save lives in high-pressure environments like combat. A kinder, gentler military should not be the goal. A current company commander in the 82nd Airborne Division framed the problem in blunt terms: "We have ceased to institutionally even acknowledge that our job is to kill America's enemies. The word 'kill' is now considered inappropriate in [marching] cadences, even though—like it or not—when it comes down to it, that's our job."[67]

Indeed, the new approach to disciplinary problems or poor performance in Army units is to "put it on paper." If a soldier is late to morning formation, is insubordinate, or commits any other similar infraction, then he or she receives a written "counseling statement" warning about the wrongfulness of his or her actions and perhaps requiring some form of non-physical corrective action (an essay about the importance of punctuality, for example). In essence, soldiers often bear no immediate, practical consequences for misbehavior and instead merely receive written warnings, a "first strike," so to speak. If the misbehavior persists, leaders conduct additional administrative "counseling sessions" with the offending service member and create a "paper trail" of their performance issues that can be used to justify punishments like temporary reductions in pay or eventually some form of administrative separation from the service.

The process is lengthy, paperwork-intensive, and bureaucratic. In some ways, it resembles a watered-down version of the civil service protections for poor performing employees that have plagued the Department of Veterans Affairs and other governmental institutions. It applies a civilian "human resources" approach to military discipline, which is ineffective and a major burden on officers and NCOs.

On one of my first days in the Army, I heard a veteran master sergeant who'd served multiple tours of combat and won a Purple Heart tell a private, "Words don't hurt. Bullets hurt. So, I don't give a shit about your stupid fucking feelings." He was right, but these days taking that type of blunt approach to "disrespectful language" could get an NCO in trouble, because the Army has also amended its Command Policy regulations to prohibit "bullying." The regulation defines bullying as "any conduct whereby a Servicemember or members, regardless of service, rank, or position, intends to exclude or reject another Servicemember through... behavior, which results in diminishing the other Servicemember's dignity, position, or status."[68] The regulation further explains that "bullying can occur in all settings but it most often appears as excessive correction of, or punishment for, perceived performance deficiencies." If you have followed the rapid development of the notion of "dignitary harm" as a form of legal injury (as in hate speech laws), then you know where these types of regulation can lead. "Affirmation" is the remedy for dignitary harm. In the future, will refusing to use a soldier's preferred pronouns be "bullying"? Consider the fact that the progressive ideology that has driven many of the changes discussed in this book is the same ideology behind, for example, the law that now makes it a crime for California state health care workers to "willfully and repeatedly" fail to use the preferred pronouns of transgender senior citizens in state facilities.[69] To be sure, no decent person should promote or defend actual bullying. But we're not talking about real bullying or hazing here; we're talking about eliminating or circumscribing traditional and necessary disciplines and methods of training. The range of prohibited behavior in this regulation is simply incompatible with traditional military life—and that, really, is the point. All these changes were meant to alter the military's culture to fit progressive designs. "Old school" NCOs and officers can revert to the real-life lessons of combat and their original training, but the new generation of leaders is being held to a different, bureaucratic, politically correct—and from a military perspective, self-defeating—standard that will inevitably result in a less combat-ready military. That needs to change.

CHAPTER
8

CLIMATE WARRIORS

"Every one of us—military, civilian, adult, and child—
needs to think of the mission, the environment and the
consequences to the community. When we think in this
way, it's really easy to say 'no' to Styrofoam."
—A speaker addressing troops and Department of the Army
civilians at a ribbon-cutting ceremony for a Net Zero Waste
Center at Fort Polk, Louisiana

On December 1, 2015, at a press conference in Paris, President Obama declared that the danger to Americans posed by climate change was "akin to the problem of terrorism and [the Islamic State]."[1] On December 2, 2015, Syed Farook and Tashfeen Malik pledged their allegiance to the Islamic State, walked into a conference center in San Bernardino, and killed fourteen people.[2] The juxtaposition of those two events, separated by only twenty-four hours—and the clash between the Obama administration's national security policies and reality that it highlights—is a perfect metaphor for the administration's insistent prioritization of green policies in the military, even when they had no rational relation to military readiness. In an interview with Jeffrey Goldberg of *The Atlantic*, President Obama went even further: "ISIS is not an existential threat to the United States. Climate change is a potential existential threat to the entire world if we don't do something about it."[3] Those statements were not slips of the tongue or the products of selective quotation by the president's political foes; they represent a worldview that was apparently pervasive across the administration. (Obama's Deputy National Security

Advisor Ben Rhodes, for instance, once pontificated about how "If you're consumed by the Middle East, you can't fix climate change."[4])

The Military's Job Is to Fight America's Enemies, Not Climate Change

Now, it's one thing for military planners to make contingency plans for developments that may occur due to changes to the climate, like potential changes to navigational channels in the Arctic; it's quite another to task the military with "mitigating" climate change, or fighting it as a declared enemy, which is what the Obama administration did.[5] (The Obama administration's mentality is widely shared on the activist left. Elizabeth Warren, for example, has published a plan promising to use the military to "lead the fight in combating climate change" if she is elected president in 2020.[6])

A 2012 Scientific American article caught the administration's direction with the headline "Military Forges Ahead with Plan to Combat Climate Change."[7] A similar article from an NPR-affiliate was titled "Marines on Front Line of Battle Against Climate Change in North Carolina."[8] The Army War College added Climate Change to its "Key Strategic Issues" list in 2011.[9] An Army infantry colonel who attended the War College during that period told me that climate change was the topic of his cumulative graded "threat assessment" exercise. "I was expecting to get a tactical scenario, and I got fucking climate change," he said. His experience was far from an anomaly.

The Great Green Waste

The environmental push began early in the Administration and never lessened. In 2009, Ray Mabus announced the creation of Task Force Climate Change, a working group that later evolved into the Department of the Navy for Energy, Environment and Climate Change. Even after the Trump administration took over, the Department's website still linked to a *Vice News* article headlined "The Pentagon Just Issued Marching Orders on Climate Change."[10] Shortly after he was confirmed by the Senate, Mabus announced that by 2020, he wanted half of all Navy buildings to obtain 50 percent of their energy from renewable sources, half of Navy buildings to use no more energy than they produced, and half of all fuel used by Navy ships, automobiles, and aircraft to come from alternative energy.[11] Refurbishing a Navy building that is safely ensconced within the borders of the territorial United States to make it a "green building" that derives its power from renewable sources has nothing to do with the Navy's ability to accomplish its mission of defending the country in the air and on the seas. It only saps money and effort away from other tasks that are related to that mission. Think of that directive as a very downscaled, Navy version of the Green New Deal's aspiration to refurbish every building in the United States within twelve years.)

Mabus's signature goal as Navy secretary was the creation of the "Great Green Fleet," with ships running on renewable sources of energy that included chicken grease and algae. In 2012, Congress discovered that the Navy—under Mabus's new initiative—was spending $26 per-gallon on the new biofuels instead of the $4 per-gallon cost of diesel fuel. Worse, although Mabus insisted that biofuel funding for a major exercise intended to prove the feasibility of his Great Green Fleet program had come from the Navy's Research and Development budget, a congressional investigation revealed that the resources for the exercise had actually been siphoned off from the Navy's Operations and Maintenance funds.[12]

Members of Congress were outraged and passed a law requiring biofuels purchased by the military to be obtained at a cost comparable to that of traditional fuels. (As a consequence of the law, the Navy used a blend of 90 percent diesel and 10 percent biofuels to power the Great Green Fleet when it finally set sail in 2016.) "This is more than just about saving gas," the Navy office of public affairs said in a press release touting the deployment of the fleet. "The Great Green Fleet is a mindset change across the board."[13] Indeed. An Obama-era two-star I spoke with had a decidedly different take: "[Navy crews were] out there, you know, on their ass, readiness-wise—and now we have ships running into each other like it's nobody's business—and he was worried about freaking *green fuel*."[14] A Vice Admiral who served during both of President Obamas terms echoed his peer's sentiments about Mabus: "Clearly, he was consumed by things along those lines—green energy, getting out of fossil fuels, and algae…he spent hundreds of millions of dollars on algae fuel and crap like that—hundreds of millions of dollars. Meanwhile, the ships that are supposed to be burning the green fuel are literally falling apart at the pier and can't deploy on time."[15] He also told me that, in his experience, Mabus rarely visited a ship except to talk about green energy.

In June 2010, Mabus tweeted from his official @SecNav twitter account, "shout out to [Naval Station] Norfolk for taking the bull by its horns and creating a 'green' roof to reduce runoff and pollutants."[16] The tweet linked to a Navy press release about the $613,000 project.[17] The text speaks for itself (emphasis added):

> Green roofs benefit the environment by filtering and retaining pollutants held in rainwater runoff thus improving the water quality that enters into sanitized sewer systems. Additionally, runoff is reduced resulting in reduced storm drainage system loads, while also reducing the phenomena of heat island effect, as well as filtering air pollutants that are deposited from the atmosphere and storing the carbon dioxide, which mitigates smog formation. *The result is the formation of a living environment that provides habitats for birds and other small animals, insulating the building thus reducing heating and cooling needs and offering an attractive alternative to traditional roofs.*[18]

Since leaving office, Mabus has leveled a steady stream of public criticism at the sitting commander in chief—however inappropriate that might be—protesting President Trump's decision to withdraw from the Paris Climate Accords[19] and warning about the "grave risks" that "inaction" on climate matters posed to America's military.[20] Mabus now runs a lobbying firm that employs his former chief of staff Thomas Oppel, who in 2016 defended Mabus's prioritization of environmentalist policies—while many of the Navy's most experienced Admirals were furiously waving a red flag about the near-decrepit state of the Navy's fleet and the exhausted and undermanned crews manning them, no less—by stating that the Navy's role is to "deter war by dealing with instability. Climate change = instability."[21] Mabus's firm also employs Tom Hicks, who served as an executive at the US Green Building Council and as Senior Program Manager at the Environmental Protection Agency before working with Mabus at the Department of the Navy.[22] When Hicks spoke in 2011 at the Clinton Global Initiative event, the Navy's official twitter account announced his speech as about the "Navy leading the way towards #Green security."[23]

The preoccupation with environmentalism was not limited to the civilian leadership of the Navy. Army Secretary John McHugh created the Army Office of Energy Initiatives in 2011, and the Army implemented its Net Zero Waste Initiative at nine installations across the country soon after. The Net Zero program aimed from Army posts' deposits of solid waste in landfills by 2020. According to the Defense Department's Fiscal Year 2017 Comptroller's Report, "Net Zero allows the Army to continue climate change adaptation and mitigation efforts and develop a strategy for all Army installations."[24]

To be clear, the program is not some large-scale expansion of government regulation, and sadly the tens of millions of dollars spent on it is comparatively minimal in the context of the mountain of wasteful spending in our defense budget, but it's just one small example of the many ways that the preoccupation with things outside the scope of basic military functions sap time and attention away from what the military needs to focus on. Like any program of its type, it comes with bureaucrats to ensure that people comply (and who create job security for themselves by doing exactly that). Environmental compliance officers—who perform the necessary task of enforcing the safe use and storage of biohazardous materials— now also inspect unit's compliance with the Net Zero regulations as well. In practice, that means environmental inspectors can dig through a unit's trash in search of plastic water bottles that were disposed improperly. A failed inspection creates headaches for a unit's leadership, which has to redirect their time and attention to dealing with the bureaucratic hassle that results and scheduling a re-inspection. (It can also come with an ass-chewing from an officer or a sergeant major up the chain of command who are, justifiably, annoyed that they have to waste their time hearing about it.) At Fort Hood, I saw more than one unit conclude that it was more time-efficient to post a guard outside their trash area during duty hours than it was to risk the administrative hassle of a failed inspection. The unlucky soldier on trash-guard duty was charged with ensuring that everything went in the right container and even with fishing plastic water bottles filled with dip spit out of the trash and rinsing out their contents before putting them in the recycling. It didn't exactly do wonders for their morale.

Some of the ways that the program wasted troops' time at least provide some comedic relief. At a ribbon-cutting ceremony for Fort Polk's new Net Zero Waste Center in November 2012 with the post commander in attendance, Fort Polk's "Qualified Recycling Program environmental contractor" told the assembled audience that "every one of us — military, civilian, adult and child needs to think of the mission, the environment and the consequences to the community. When we think in this way, it's really easy to say 'no' to Styrofoam because it's not just a single-use incident without long-term effects."[25] Fort Polk is the home of the Joint Readiness Training Center (JRTC), the final training stop for infantry brigades about to deploy. Of the hundreds of thousands of men and women who have passed through JRTC, preparing for dangerous missions in remote parts of the world, it is safe to say that precisely zero of them thought that "the mission" included saying no to Styrofoam.

The green waste (both of defense funds and, perhaps more importantly, the military's time and attention—neither of which are fungible
commodities) pervaded every branch of the Defense Department. Viewed
in context of the global emissions, the green projects on which the Obama
administration and its appointees in the DoD lavished money and attention
were essentially glorified neighborhood compost projects. But that did not
stop them from funneling taxpayer money that could have been allocated
for training or critical maintenance into those projects. The Defense
Department spent $20 million, for instance, on 500 rechargeable vehicles
for the military's non-tactical fleet (covering things like passenger vans),
which was more than double the cost of 500 conventional vehicles. If that
program were extended to replace the entire non-tactical fleet, it would
carry a price tag of more than $8 billion.[26] Similarly, the Air Force pursued
expensive biofuels to meet greenhouse gas standards set by executive
order.[27]And the Marine Corps' iconic Camp Pendleton became the "epi-
center of new green construction," according to the *San Diego Union-
Tribune*.[28] Pendleton was the focus of a $1.6 billion spending spree,
including a $9 million project to convert a barracks building (Camp Pend-
leton Building #41404) into a "green building." Defense dollars were also
used to replace the lawn in front of Building 41404 with "a pebble-strewn
rock garden, punctuated by a row of California native trees," which it was
presumed would require less water.[29] The *Union-Tribune* noted that similar "environmental projects are underway all over Camp Pendleton."[30]

All of this, of course, was in keeping with the vision of the commander in chief. Obama's National Security Advisor Susan Rice said in
a speech at the Brookings Institution that climate change was an integral
part of the administration's national security strategy. "We're making
smart decisions today that will pay off for generations," she told her
audience.[31] The President told graduates of the Coast Guard academy in
his 2015 that it would be a "dereliction of duty" for them to ignore the
threat posed by climate change.[32]

In 2016, Obama signed Department of Defense Directive 4715.21,
titled "Climate Change Adaptation and Resilience," requiring the

secretaries of the Army, Navy, Air Force, and Marines to integrate climate change considerations into their "policy guidance, plans, and operations."[33] The political appointees were only too happy to do so. The directive also required the under secretary of defense for personnel and readiness to integrate "climate change considerations" into Defense Department policy objectives. The president signed a similar directive to the nation's twenty national security agencies on September 21, 2016, in which he declared climate change to be a "national security threat."[34] For most serving military personnel, the more pressing threats were related to the battlefield and did, indeed, involve terrorism. The same month as the president's directive on the national security threat posed by climate change, the Islamic State used chainsaws to chop up Iraqi teenagers as punishment for allegedly collaborating with American forces.[35]

In 2016, defense spending on environmental compliance increased by more than $119 million. Many of these spending programs had no military purpose, and their actual environmental impact was often more political than real. For example, the website of the Department of the Navy for Energy Initiatives and Climate Change boasted in late 2016 that the Defense Department would reduce its greenhouse emissions by 34 percent by 2020.[36] But a quick look at the Defense Department's 2016 Sustainability Performance Plan reveals the key to that environmental "success." The report admits that the Department's actual greenhouse gas emissions rose by two percent in 2015, but its "net" emissions were reduced by 18 percent once *"credits are included."*[37] In other words, the Defense Department was attempting to improve its carbon footprint by spending defense funds on carbon credits to offset its greenhouse gas emissions.

The Obama administration often justified its environmentalist obsessions by presenting them as economical, and a sympathetic press frequently accepted that at face value. But the evidence for these assertions was speculative and optimistic at best and downright dishonest at worst. The Inspector General of the Department of Defense reviewed, for example, the Navy's claims about the cost-effectiveness of several of its renewable energy programs. After an exhaustive investigation, the

Inspector General concluded that "Navy personnel could not provide adequate documentation to support the assumptions and calculations in their assessments."[38] News stories about the Defense Department's rechargeable vehicle program acknowledged that the "military says it doesn't know how much all this will cost."[39]

A Government Accountability Office report of the Defense Department's renewable energy initiatives on military installations found that, of seventeen green projects surveyed, "only two of the projects were specifically designed to provide power to the installations in the event of a disruption of the commercial grid."[40] The remaining projects were essentially ventures that spent extra funds solely to avoid using fossil fuels. The report continued that, even though the vast majority of the projects do not contribute to the energy security of the base, Defense Department "officials told us that they believed all 17 of the projects in our sample provided an energy security benefit because the officials defined energy security broadly to encompass the diversification of fuel sources, among other things."[41] The report also found that the federal land used for the renewable energy projects had greater value than the projects themselves, and that it was land that could have been used for training.

The main point of highlighting these environmental programs is not to argue that renewable energy, reducing the use and reliance on fossil fuels, or anything else of that variety is somehow bad in and of itself. If pundits and politicians want to have debates about those issues in other contexts, that's great. But unless any of those programs enhance the military's ability to do its job, they shouldn't be consuming the military's time and resources. And many of the Obama administration's green programs failed to advance the military's mission.

Military Readiness Was Never the Purpose of the Obama Green-Energy Programs

National security and the best interests of the military were never the purpose behind the Obama green energy push at the Defense

Department. The green spending bonanza occurred while the military's readiness and training budgets were being slashed by the defense sequester-mandated congressional budget cuts. The Marines may have been cannibalizing old planes in their boneyard to find spare parts to repair their aircraft, and they may, as was reported in 2016, have been restoring retired aircraft to service because most of their F/A-18 strike fighters were "unable to fly on any given day,"[42] but hey—at least they had that pebble-strewn garden at Camp Pendleton.

When I was the executive officer of an infantry company during the height of the sequestration-driven budget cuts, I often had to wait six months or more to obtain minor—but important—equipment like the parts my soldiers needed to mount night vision devices on their helmets, because, we were told, funding simply wasn't available. During that fiscal year, however, the Pentagon increased its spending on green energy projects at stateside military installations by sixty percent.[43]

The Defense Department announced in 2016 that, per executive guidance, its directives, instructions, and manuals would be revised to "include the consideration of climate change."[44] That same year, the Department of the Navy enacted a policy requiring military contractors to calculate and report their companies' contributions to climate change as a precondition for obtaining military contracts. According to the Associated Press, "The move [sought] to leverage the Navy's $170 billion budget to encourage contractors to cut their overall output of climate-changing carbon."[45] Navy Secretary Mabus justified the decision by saying that the Navy has "skin in this game" when it comes to climate change.[46]

The Obama administration's fixation on environmentalism was not only wasteful and distracting, but it was also demoralizing for troops who had signed up to potentially fight for the country on foreign battlefields and for Pentagon officials who wanted to make decisions based on what was best for national security rather than what was preferred by environmental activists. I saw firsthand how some of the best young soldiers I had were discouraged at the suffocating progressive orthodoxy that had while cutting back on their military training and that made their chances of surviving on the battlefield an apparently secondary consideration to environmentalism.

In sum, the Obama administration's eight years of environmental activism disguised as "energy security" amounted to telling our soldiers, airmen, and Marines, "Yes, I know you are going to war soon. No, we still do not have enough money for you to train for that. But in the meantime, it is vitally important that you guard this dumpster and make sure no recyclables get past you. Thank you for your service."

CHAPTER
9

HOW TO FIX IT

"The Trump administration, its political allies, and all conservatives need to start viewing military policy as a moral matter. The Trump administration needs to have the moral courage to stop the Obama era social experi-ments and reverse them entirely. Conservatives don't back the military by throwing money at it. They back it by adhering to principles."
—A current Army major who has deployed to Iraq multiple times as an infantryman

Our military remains the finest fighting force the world has ever known. By virtue of its technological superiority alone, our armed forces far outclass their nearest rivals. Furthermore, the men and women who make up our military are some of the most capable and dedicated people you will ever meet. But they have to be given the tools and prepa-ration they need to succeed. The reality is that, because of our leaders' misplaced priorities over the past decade, we are not nearly as ready as we should be to fight a large-scale war against a geopolitical foe like Russia or China—or to fight a multi-theatre war—because of our lead-ers' misplaced priorities over the past decade. And any student of military history will readily acknowledge that technological superiority alone is not enough to win a nation's wars, at least not indefinitely.

The military's politically correct policies weaken our armed forces in many ways, but two obvious ones are lower standards and retention.

We are hurting our ability to retain talented officers and enlisted troops who entered the military for all the right reasons but find they spend their days acting as bureaucrats pushing counterproductive—and even immoral (in the sense that they put lives unnecessarily at risk)—policies rather than training for war. Many of the young soldiers I interacted with as a company-level officer were bitterly disappointed by what they saw as the neglect of the military's stated mission of fighting our nation's wars effectively in favor of an ideological mission of remaking the military into a progressive federal "workforce."

In 2013, an anonymous Marine lieutenant penned an op-ed in *Foreign Policy* magazine explaining his decision, and that of many talented junior officers, to leave active duty. Titled "We're Getting Out of the Marines Because We Wanted to Be Part of an Elite Force," the article said, "We joined because we wanted to be part of an elite organization dedicated to doing amazing things in defense of our nation. We wanted to make a contribution to something great, to be able to look back at a decisive chapter in American history and say 'yeah, I was part of that.'"[1] But the "implicit message" from current military culture is one of "low standards" and acceptance of "Mission Failure so long as all the boxes on the list are checked...so long as the PowerPoint slides are free of typos, no serialized gear is lost, and everyone attends the Sexual Harassment Prevention training."[2] The author was quick to add, "I don't want to be misunderstood. The most extraordinary and talented people I've ever met are still serving in the Corps," but his frustrations are widely shared by junior officers who feel they are judged as bureaucrats rather than as warfighters.

So, How Do We Fix It?

Okay, fine. Current policies are hurting the military. *But how do we fix the problem?* Repealing Obama-era policies, and keeping them repealed, will take political will, but it is certainly doable and must be done. This should not be a political issue—but nevertheless, it has become one— and conservatives need to focus on it. Too many conservatives blithely assume that all is well with the military or that progressive policies enacted by the Obama administration are minor annoyances rather than major degrading factors to our armed forces' combat effectiveness and morale.

As noted in the Preface, aside from the political issues, there are also enormous social issues that affect the military. The massive percentage of millennials who are ineligable for military service is but one of those issues.[3] For example, how do you attract recruits among a recruiting population of Millennials and Gen Z'ers, when more than 25 percent and 20 percent respectively say they are not "proud to be American" and of whom only 65 percent and 54 percent respectively say that America has a history to be proud of? (By comparison, 94 percent of Americans who came of age in the aftermath of World War II expressed American pride.)[4] And how do we prepare for combat a generation that experiences work-disrupting anxiety (in the normal workaday world) at twice the level of the workforce as a whole?[5]

In theory, the easier problems to fix are the political ones, though this requires of Congress a degree of seriousness and responsibility that it has regularly failed to demonstrate. For example, take the way defense spending is allocated. In 2016, our defense budget was $524 billion (not including another $58 billion in "overseas contingency funding" for the War on Terror). Our budget was more than twice the amount spent by second-place China and greater than the total defense budgets of China and the next five countries on the list combined.[6] (And those numbers were under the budget-caps imposed by the 2013 sequestration deal, which has been widely criticized as one of the main reasons for the training and maintenance crises in the military.) And yet, in spite of spending more than half a trillion dollars on defense in a single year, only one-third of the active duty Army's thirty-one brigade combat teams were ready to deploy in 2018—and *that* was a remarkable improvement over the combat readiness of the Obama era military.[7] Who's to blame for this wasteful allocation of resources? The answer is Congress. During sequestration, funding for Capitol Hill's pet projects (often pork barrel spending [8]) remained essentially unchanged,[9] but unglamorous readiness spending—money allocated for equipment repairs and training resources—was cut by 30 percent.[10]

In 2013, for example, when defense spending was cut by more than $30 billion due to sequestration, Republican Congressman Jim Jordan of Ohio (a member of the House Freedom Caucus, whose members are supposed to care about the budget deficit and curbing unnecessary spending) inserted a provision into the National Defense Authorization Act requiring the Army to spend hundreds of millions of dollars bulking up and refitting its fleet of Abrams tanks. Sounds like a good thing, right? It might have been, except for one problem: the Army already had more tanks than it needed (a surplus fleet of 2,000 Abrams tanks was parked unused in the California desert[11]), it had no strategic plan that required new tanks, and it was actually in the process of reducing the size of its tank corps to adapt to the operational needs of asymmetric warfare in the Middle East. Then-Army Chief of Staff General Raymond Ordierno told the Associated Press, "If we had our choice, we would use that money a different way."[12]

While Congress sets the budget and the president and the Congress set the priorities of the military, within the military itself, careerism compounds the problem of officers becoming politically correct bureaucrats. The military promotion system is timeline-based, inflexible, and unforgiving. It rewards compliance and discourages risk-taking. A poor Officer Evaluation Report can sink a brigade commander's chances for a star, a battalion commander's odds of getting a brigade, or an ambitious major's chances of getting tapped for battalion command. Because promotions occur on a relatively fixed timeline, senior officers have every incentive to remain quiet and go with the flow rather than risk their seventeen- or eighteen-year investments in their careers. Morally courageous policy changes require morally courageous leaders. And unfortunately, the current structure of the military's promotion system does not incentivize or reward morally courageous leaders.

Despite all of those external and institutional pressures, however, we can make several changes to our military policy to correct the problems discussed here. The rest of this chapter will address our broad institutional problems first and then focus on policy-based proposals that have the potential to undo some of the damage of the Obama era.

STEP ONE
Cultural Reform

It's Now or Never

The time to roll back the misguided Obama-era "reforms" to the military is now. As a Marine infantry captain who served multiple deployments in hotspots in southern Afghanistan and recently left active duty told me, "if we can't buck political correctness and refocus on war fighting with Donald Trump in the White House and Jim Mattis as SECDEF, when can we do it?"[13] Obviously, Mattis is no longer secretary of defense, but the officer's point remains. President Trump, as Washington pundits love to say, is a "disruptive" president, one willing to buck trends, reject conventional thinking, and make controversial changes. He campaigned as a pro-military leader whose political priorities included reforming the Veterans Administration, boosting defense spending, and rethinking American foreign deployments to ensure that they are worth American lives and are truly in America's interests. If there were ever an administration willing and able to absorb the predictable backlash from activist groups and progressive media personalities provoked by reprioritizing the military's warfighting culture and rejecting the militarily debilitating bureaucratic demands of political correctness, it would be this one. Truly rebuilding the military (as President Trump has repeatedly promised to do) requires more than a financial commitment (which he has made); it requires a restoration of the military's culture: the military exists to fight the nation's wars; it is not a laboratory for progressive social engineers to promote identity politics or green policies that serve no real military purpose and that actually undercut combat readiness and performance. As the commander in chief, the president's power over military personnel policy is sweeping and nearly incontestable—though entrenched "social justice" interests, a complicit media, activist courts making unprecedented decisions, reluctant bureaucrats, and an opposition party that deems itself "the resistance" have contested the President Trump's authority every step of the way, making change easier said than done. Still, President Trump has the constitutional authority to make profound changes in military policy (just as the Obama administration did); he should do so—but he'll also need strong allies in Congress and among the voting public who see military reform as a serious issue that deserves being made a priority.

The younger, company-level leaders I spoke to were optimistic about the prospect of meaningful reform. The general officers, however, thought that because of bureaucratic inertia, political cowardice, and a continuing leftward trend in our general culture, things would only get worse—until a catastrophe forced reform. Even then, a disturbing number of those generals assumed that even a serious military failure in a major conflict would fail to reverse the progressive tide. As one general told me, undoing the Obama administration's misguided policies, while technically easy, was unlikely, because "sometimes it's hard to put the toothpaste back in the tube."

Military Readiness Must Be Viewed as a Moral Issue

To make military reform more likely, it must be presented as a moral issue—because it is. In fact, it is a far more important moral issue than the progressives' emphasis on green energy and identity politics. The decisions we make as a society about our military can have life-and-death consequences for those we send into harm's way on our behalf. Our government has a moral responsibility to ensure that our military be as well-prepared as possible for the challenges of combat. Revolutionary War hero "Light-Horse Harry" Lee, said he could not "withhold my denunciation of the wickedness and folly" of a government that sent its soldiers "to the field uninformed and untaught." Such a government, he believed, was "the murderer of its citizens."[14] Now, the conditions of the Continental Army and of today's military are vastly different, to say the least, but the *principle* that Harry Lee articulated—that governments have a moral responsibility to ensure that the men and women they send to war have the greatest possible chance of survival and success—is no less true today than it was then. One of the admirals I spoke to described the previous administration's emphasis on politics over readiness, in a time of war no less, as "criminal."

Our elected officals know—and have known—what lies ahead for American men and women who raise their right hands and take the oath of office or enlistment in our era. In a commencement speech to the West Point Class of 2019, for example, Vice President Mike Pence told the assembled cadets, minutes away from becoming newly-minted Second Lieutenants, "It is a virtual certainty that you will fight on a battlefield for America at some point in your life. You will lead soldiers in combat. It will happen."[15] That "virtual certainty" must be foremost in the minds of our legislators, policymakers, and leaders when they make decisions affecting our service members. Our soldiers don't need more training in progressive ideology, and they don't need more instruction in the dangers of hurting people's feelings with microaggressions. They need to be able to focus on the profession the have chosen and upon which the rest of us depend. The people who join the military are volunteers who put their lives on the line to protect us all. We owe them the best equipment, training, and support we can provide. And we need to respect what they have signed on to do: to defend this country in armed conflicts. That is the military's purpose.

A Warfighting Force Must Be Staffed Only by Those Capable of Fighting Wars

To that end, we need soldiers who are fully deployable and can meet the demands of modern warfare because, for every soldier who cannot deploy overseas, another must take his place, and it is unjust to service members and their families to force them into additional deployments to make up for those who stay home because they are incapable of doing the job. The Obama administration did not think that way because it was not focused on war-fighting; instead, it was focused on remaking military culture in its own image. But thankfully Trump's first secretary of defense, James Mattis, did think that way. During his tenure, the Defense Department followed a policy of "deploy or get out"—and the results were excellent. In January 2018, eleven percent of the force was non-deployable. Eight months after Mattis instituted deploy-or-get-out, that number had fallen to six percent.[16] In raw numbers, that means that there were roughly 100,000 fewer non-deployable service members in the force. That's a lot of dead weight gone in a short period of time. (The Mattis policy rightfully made an exception for many soldiers who could not deploy because of wounds suffered during prior deployments. They've more than earned stateside billets.) Reducing the number of non-deployable service members is particularly important because military appropriations bills only authorize funding for a certain number of soldiers. So, removing 100,000 non-deployable soldiers allows the military to replace them with 100,000 soldiers who are actually able to go to war. Functionally, the policy increases our wartime force by 100,000 without spending an extra dime. And not only does it make our military stronger in the event of an all-out war, it reduces the strain on the rest of the military who must continue to meet the requirements of the Global War on Terror.

The Academies: True Reform Must Begin with Future Leaders

The military academies are where America's future military is made. "I really think starting out at [the academies] is a good first step," an officer and academy grad told me, because many trends in military culture filter down from what is taught at the academies. One reform that would have immediate benefits would be to amend the 1993 law that authorized the branch secretaries (who are political appointees) to hire more civilian professors for the academies. Congress should require branch secretaries to give hiring priority to serving military or to civilian professors who are veterans. Whenever possible, military experience should be a requirement for academy professors. It is more important for an English professor at West Point to have worn his or her country's uniform than it is for him or her to have the requisite number of peer-reviewed publications in academia's preferred journals.

In theory, there should be an abundance of candidates for teaching positions at the academies that not only have military experience, but have taught at the academies already. There are many military officers every year who receive orders to go to grad school and then teach at an academy for two or three years. Those assignments, in fact, are highly competitive and usually awarded only to officers who are some of the highest performers. After their two-three year rotations teaching at their respective academies, those officers return to the regular force to finish the remainder of their careers. If those officers were qualified to teach cadets at the midway point of their careers, there is no reason that they wouldn't also be qualified after completing twenty-plus year careers and retiring. To the extent the academies need to hire non-uniformed professors, they should give special priority to those veterans that served as academy professors while in uniform. All it would take is an amendment to the National Defense Appropriations Act.

Eliminating or reforming tenure and civil service protections for professors at the Naval Academy is another needed reform. No one has a "right" to instruct future military officers at our military academies any more than anyone has a "right" to be a United States naval officer. To be an instructor or a midshipman at the Naval Academy is—and must be treated as—a privilege earned by performance and service.

Make "Night Court" a Regular Event Across the DoD

Shortly after Mark Esper was sworn in as the new secretary of the Army in November 2017, he and Army Chief of Staff Mark Milley began holding "night court" sessions in the Pentagon. Esper wanted to know which weapons systems the Army was spending its money on and why.

So, officials were required to meet with Esper and Milley at the Pentagon after hours (hence the name "night court") and justify their programs' continued existence. Esper and Milley served as "judge, jury, and sometimes executioner" of the court.[17] They reviewed more than five hundred weapons programs, eventually identifying 186 for elimination or reduction.[18] In total, the cuts saved over $25 billion that will now be used to modernize the Army's capabilities, particularly in functions necessary to counter Chinese or Russian aggression.[19]

Esper said they went "program by program, activity by activity to look at each one and assess it and ask ourselves, 'is this more important than a Next-Generation Combat Vehicle? Is this more important than a squad automatic weapon? Is this more important than Long Range Precision Fires?'"[20] Night Court not only saves taxpayer money and invests the Army's resources more efficiently, it represents an outlook shift: decisions were made solely based on the answer to the following question: "will this help us win wars or not?" The Night Court model should be replicated in every branch of the DoD and held every few years.

Bring the VA Accountability Act to the Pentagon

One of the best laws passed by the Republican Congress in 2017 and signed by President Trump was the VA Accountability Act. It eliminated many of the roadblocks, thrown up by civil service laws, to removing low-performing officials. Essentially, it made firing people who weren't getting the job done at the Department of Veterans Affairs far easier. Congress should adopt a similar law for civilian employees at the Department of Defense. If they aren't effective at supporting our soldiers in the field, then they should find another line of work. Every time Congress can cut back on unnecessary bureaucracy, it can free up money for necessary combat readiness.

And make no mistake—the entrenched civilian bureaucracy at the Pentagon is a significant roadblock to implementing meaningful reforms and focusing on what should be the DoD's highest priorities. Several military officers in very high-level or otherwise influential positions in the Pentagon—during both the Obama and Trump eras—relayed anecdotes about bureaucratic resistance from the career civilian officials at DoD. A Navy Vice-Admiral who served among the highest levels of the Pentagon during Obama years told me, "I had senior government civilians tell me to my face that they were not going to do what I wanted because I'd be gone in two years and they wouldn't be. And I wish I'd had a tape recorder, because that would be a firing offense, but [without a recording,] they'll just say 'nah, he misunderstood me.'"[21] Likewise, a military official who served during the Trump era and interacted with then-Secretary Mattis on a daily basis told me that efforts to roll back some of the politically-correct changes of the Obama era were stifled and slow-walked by career DoD officials who enjoyed the full protection of civil service laws and disagreed with the new chain of command's proposals.

Congressional Inquiries Can Drive Military Priorities

Members of Congress who care about military readiness need to step up; their influence on military policy and priorities can be enormous. An Obama-era two-star general told me that "If you change the questions" from Congress, the military leaders "will change the answers" and the military will shift priorities. "The pressure from the Hill is always, 'What are you doing about your female promotion status?'" and similar progressive goals. "But nobody asks them about their aircraft readiness rates, asks them about their training time, asks them about flying hours. If you ask for that" you change what the military leaders will concentrate on. "But if all you ask them about is that social engineering stuff, then…that's what they talk about" and that's what they make a priority.[22] Our military is fully controlled by the politicians we elect. If congressional committees demanded accountability from military leaders about combat readiness, if they insisted on giving funding priority to military training, and if they ditched obsessing about vaguely defined "diversity" and "inclusion" initiatives, then we would have a military much more focused on doing its actual job of preparing for war. Getting

Congress to do its job is the responsibility of the voters. We need to elect, and hold accountable, representatives who care about our national defense.

Some Senior Military Leaders Need to Step Up

Solutions must also come from within the military itself. While all of the generals and admirals interviewed for this book forcefully advocated against various changes it discussed—one resigning, others getting forced out early, and all risking their professional careers as a result—they all had stories about their peers who seemingly chose promotions over principle. Their decisions were partly a result of moral cowardice, but they were also partly caused by aspects of the military's culture. "We have this cultural problem in the military—we sit there and, you know—and we just parrot what is told to us, despite it not reflecting reality. And that's [the case from the junior enlisted up to the general officer level]," an Admiral told me.[23]

A uniformed source in the Trump-era Pentagon told me that he was surprised to see some senior officers—who had vociferously opposed the Obama administration's policy changes on the grounds that they would make the military less effective in future wars—now repeating the party line about how those changes wouldn't have any effect, even though the policies hadn't been in place long enough to provide even anecdotal evidence of their success or failure. That cultural problem needs to change.

STEP TWO
Military Policy Changes That Should Be Implemented Now

Follow the Marine Corps' Study on Infantry Units

The Obama administration created sex-neutral infantry units, not because doing so increased these units' lethality, but because it was an "equal opportunity" goal; it is up to the Trump administration to reverse this policy entirely on the grounds of combat effectiveness. General

Mattis hinted that he was considering doing this before he resigned from the Trump administration, and carrying out this necessary policy will require a figure with broad credibility of the kind Mattis possessed.

If the Trump administration engages this political battle, as it should, the military's career-progression system will make this necessary reform much easier than most people might expect, even with a few hundred female servicemembers now serving in infantry units.[24] Both the Army and the Marines use a process called "branch detailing," a system in which some junior officers are officially assigned to a combat-support branch but are optioned to combat arms branches (such as infantry, armor, or field artillery) for the first four years of their careers. Once these new lieutenants are promoted to captain, they transition to the combat-support branch. The system is designed to accommodate the disparate manning needs of the Army and Marine Corps' various components — combat arms units need significantly greater numbers of junior officers than senior officers, but many of the specialty branches (like the signal corps and military intelligence, for example) have a much greater need for senior officers. (The career progression of the former resembles a pyramid, while the latter looks more like an inverted pyramid.)

All of these officers can easily be branch-detailed into other parts of the Army with no harm to their career prospects; in fact, the female officers can simply trade places with male officers slated for branch detail. As long as the military acts within the next few years, it can revert to the pre-Obama structure of infantry units without any disruption of the normal functioning or manpower levels of its officer corps. The career progression for enlisted soldiers is different from that of officers, and branch detailing is not an option. So for female soldiers who enlisted into infantry branches in the Army and Marine Corps, the only option is to re-class and attend training courses for their new Military Occupational Specialty. That transition is not nearly as burdensome as it may sound. It is not like switching careers in the civilian world. The core set of soldier skills are transferable, thousands of enlisted soldiers re-class every year, and so far, the number or women assigned to infantry units (and who would have to be reassigned) is very small.

Of course, that's the ideal-world solution, and we don't live in an ideal world. So, if the administration or its successors do not have the political will to weather the outcry a full reversal of the Obama policy would inevitably provoke, there are other steps it can take to mitigate its effects. Job-specific physical fitness standards that require the same physical fitness performance from male and female service members serving in the same positions are a good first step (and indeed, the Army and the Marines are both moving in that direction), but having objective, neutral standards on paper is meaningless if they are not enforced neutrally and objectively in practice. Recent history at Ranger School illustrates this perfectly. More important than job-specific standards is a culture that demands their enforcement without fear of repercussions.

Building on the idea of job-specific standards, James Mattis established a "lethality task force" in the Pentagon before he resigned,[25] which he tasked with examining potential changes to manpower policy at the platoon and squad levels within infantry units to make them more lethal. A source who worked under Mattis before he resigned told me that, in his view, the lethality task force was Mattis's way of ensuring that Army and Marine infantry units remained as effective as possible even if the Obama policy remained in place (an outcome Mattis pointedly refused to say he was ready to support). The task force's conclusions and recommendations should be watched closely.

Maintain the Trump-Amended Policy That Determines Eligibility Based on Biological Sex Instead of Gender Identity

The Trump administration is getting this policy right—and doing so with a far more nuanced approach than it has received credit for. The Trump policy is not a full return to the pre-Obama era policy; rather, it emphasizes physical fitness standards (which, yes, are derived from basic realities about human biology, but there are certain realities we can't ignore). Soldiers or sailors will not be discharged for openly discussing the fact that they identify as transgender, as they would have under the pre-Obama policy. Under the Trump policy, the chief criterion for service is whether soldiers and sailors are fit to be deployed. Their personal life is their own, as long as it does not interfere with their ability to deploy.

Focus on Fighting ISIS and America's Other Armed Enemies, Not Carbon Emissions

The Obama Administration's green programs are the easiest to rescind. The Army's wasteful and distracting Net Zero requirements can be removed by a simple stroke of a pen. Ditto with the Great Green Fleet. Any policy that was initiated by an Obama-era Defense Department political appointee can be rescinded by a Trump administration Defense Department political appointee. Other green spending programs can be discontinued, but doing so will generally require congressional cooperation—and unfortunately, such spending will have its boosters on Capitol Hill. Still, the Pentagon has it within its power to end many of these programs, and the Trump administration can make an issue of eliminating pork barrel green energy projects in favor of projects that actually serve combat readiness and supply the energy needs of the military in the most efficient, effective, and affordable way possible. The Trump administration has already been bold in advancing America's energy interests; it only needs to advance similar policies in regard to the energy needs of the military.

Remember That Military Installations Are Not College Campuses

The Trump administration is making progress in repealing some of the worst impositions of political correctness on the military. The unconscious bias training mandated by Eric Fanning in Army Directive 2017-06 has been canceled. The diversity quotas that the Obama administration instituted can be, and should be, simply replaced by formal directives from the Trump administration requiring that promotions be based entirely on merit rather than immutable characteristics. The reform of some military regulations, such as those involving discipline or "corrective action," is probably best left to the generals and admirals—as it should have been in the first place—with the admonition to do what is best to make their soldiers, sailors, airmen, and Marines the best fighting force possible.

Parting Thoughts

America's military belongs to the American people—and it should be regarded as one of our prized institutions, one that attracts our best, brightest, fittest, most dutiful, and most honorable citizens. If my book does nothing else, I hope it honors our military service members and reminds voters of the enormous responsibility they have when they go into the voting booth to elect a commander in chief, an administration, and congressional representatives who will set military priorities on our behalf. Our nation's military should not be a plaything of progressive ideologues, or of politically-motivated activists of any type for that matter, but an imposing and finely honed armed force for winning our nation's wars.

Douglas MacArthur wrote, "It is fatal to enter a war without the will to win it."[26] In an era in which our armed forces are engaged indefinitely in armed conflicts around the world, adopting military policies that aren't specifically intended to make our troops more effective in combat violates MacArthur's warning and risks the consequences he predicted. Our nation and our military deserve better.

ACKNOWLEDGMENTS

To the many people who made this book possible who cannot be named: you know who you are. Thank you. I am indebted to Elaine, Travis, B. M., G. C., and the almost countless others whose advice and insights I relied upon heavily throughout this project. I'd also like to express my deepest gratitude to Tom Spence and Harry Crocker at Regnery who gave me the chance to write this book; to Nicole Yeatman and the marketing staff; and to Kathleen Curran, who patiently humored my incessant edits and revisions. I'd be remiss if I did not also thank Captain Alan Keefer and SFC Tavaris Williams, from whom I learned a lot while in the Army, both overseas and stateside. I am also profoundly grateful to my family, who proofread endless drafts, put up with my late-night phone calls to "brainstorm" (i.e., subject them to my stream-of-conscious thoughts about a topic), and encouraged me throughout. Finally, and most importantly, I'd like to thank our Lord, with whom all things are possible.

NOTES

Preface

1. Thomas Spoehr and Bridget Handy, Heritage Foundation Report, *The Looming National Crisis: Young Americans Unable to Serve in the Military*, February 13, 2018, https:www.heritage.org/defense/report/the-looming-national-security-crisis-young-americans-unable-serve-the-military.
2. Thomas Spoehr, Director, Center for National Defense at the Heritage Foundation, *Why the U.S. Military Is in Serious Trouble*, November 19, 2018, https://www.heritage.org/defense/commentary/why-the-us-military-serious-trouble.
3. Spoehr, *Why the U.S. Military Is in Serious Trouble*.
4. Ibid.
5. Ibid.
6. James Mattis and Kori Schake, *Warriors & Citizens: American Views of Our Military* (Hoover Institution Press, 2016): 308–309, Kindle Version.
7. Mattis and Schake, *Warriors & Citizens: American Views of Our Military*.

Chapter 1: Fundamental Transformation

1. Statement of Valerie Jarrett, The White House, "Today Was a Victory for Equality," June 26, 2013, https://obamawhitehouse.archives.gov/blog/2013/06/26/today-was-victory-equality.
2. Tim Ryan, "In Context: What Obama Said About 'Fundamentally Transforming' the Nation," PolitiFact, February 6, 2014, https://www.politifact.com/truth-o-meter/article/2014/feb/06/what-barack-obama-has-said-about-fundamentally-tra/.
3. Peter Baker, "For Obama Steep Learning Curve as Chief in War," *New York Times*, August 28, 2010, https://www.nytimes.com/2010/08/29/world/29commander.html.
4. Rosa Brooks, "Obama vs. The Generals," *Politico*, November 2013.
5. Nedra Pickler, "Fact Check: Obama on Afghanistan," *Washington Post*, August 14, 2007.
6. Senator Barack Obama, Commencement Address at Wesleyan University in Middletown, Connecticut, May 25, 2008.

7. Karin McQuillin, "Obama's Strange Dependence on Valerie Jarrett," *The American Thinker*, August 14, 2012, https://www. americanthinker.com/articles/2012/08/obamas_strange_dependence_ on_valerie_jarrett.html#ixzz5WPldtfoa.

8. Barbara Starr, "Obama Advisor Mistakes 4-Star General for Waiter," CNN, February 6, 2011, http://www.cnn.com/2011/ POLITICS/02/05/army.general/index.html.

9. Fox Nation, "Obama Political Operatives Get Military Chauffeurs," May 11, 2010.

10. Susan Calloway Knowles, "President Obama and Valerie Jarrett Deserve a 'Dishonorable Discharge' For Failing to Respect the Chattanooga Victims," *The Blaze*, July 20, 2015.

11. Peter Applebome, "Mississippi Governor's Record at Issue," *New York Times*, September 16, 1991.

12. Applebome, "Mississippi Governor's Record at Issue.".

13. "Thomas Oppel," Mabus Group, https://www.mabusgroup.com/ bios/thomas-oppel.

14. Phillip Rucker, "Obama Taps Mabus for Navy Secretary," *Washington Post*, March 27, 2009, http://voices.washingtonpost. com/44/2009/03/27/obama_taps_mabus_for_navy_secr.html.

15. Jim Rutenberg, "Navy Secretary Nominee Drew Notice Over Divorce," *New York Times*, March 29, 2009.

16. Data on the various topics of Mabus's tweets was obtained by using Twitter's advanced search function to comb an archived version of the account Mabus used during his tenure (@SecNav) for any references to the terms in question.

17. The full biography provided by the White House to the press was published by the *Washington Post*. Phillip Rucker, "Obama Taps Mabus for Navy Secretary," *Washington Post*, March 27, 2009.

18. Center for a New American Security, "A Conversation with the Service Secretaries," transcript, October 24, 2016, https://www.cnas. org/events/a-conversation-with-the-service-secretaries.

19. Michael S. Schmidt, "Navy Secretary Ray Mabus Knows a Thing or 30 about First Pitches," *New York Times*, July 17, 2016, https://www. nytimes.com/2016/07/18/sports/baseball/navy-secretary-ray-mabus- first-pitches.html.

20. Robert Faturechi, Megan Rose, & T. Christian Miller, "Years of Warnings, Then Death and Disaster," *ProPublica*, February 7, 2019, https://features.propublica.org/navy-accidents/us-navy- crashes-japan-cause-mccain/?utm_content=bufferd6a34&utm_ medium=social&utm_source=twitter&utm_campaign=buffer.

21. Faturechi, Rose, and Miller, "Years of Warnings."
22. Ibid.
23. Ibid.
24. Ibid.
25. Ibid.
26. Ibid.
27. Ibid.
28. Ibid.
29. Ibid.
30. Ray Mabus (@SECNAV75), Twitter, March 13, 2019, 8:45 p.m. https://twitter.com/SECNAV75/status/1106023507945811970.
31. Brad Carson, "Vote Righteously!" *The New Republic*, 34, Nov. 22, 2004, available at http://www.uvm.edu/~dguber/POLS125/articles/carson.htm.
32. Brad Carson and Morgan Plummer, "Defense Reform in the Next Administration," War on the Rocks, September 12, 2016.
33. National Public Radio, Morning Edition, "Pentagon Makes Changes to Be More Family Friendly," February 15, 2016, https://www.npr.org/2016/02/15/466783831/pentagon-makes-changes-to-be-more-family-friendly.
34. "US Troops to Stay in Uganda until Rebel Chief Found," *Sydney Morning Herald*, November 21, 2011, https://www.smh.com.au/world/us-troops-set-to-stay-in-uganda-until-rebel-chief-found-20111120-1np86.html (reporting that pressure "prompt[ed] Mr. Obama last month to send 100 special operations forces there").
35. Karen De Young, "On the Hunt for Joseph Kony," *Washington Post*, March 23, 2014, https://www.washingtonpost.com/world/national-security/2014/03/23/aa468ca6-b2d0-11e3-8020-b2d790b3c9e1_story.html?utm_term=.9325eda00407.
36. De Young, "On the Hunt for Joseph Kony.".
37. Kate Otto, "Kony as a Catalyst," *Huffington Post*, March 12, 2012, https://www.huffingtonpost.com/kate-otto/kony2012_b_1337614.html.
38. "The Results: Unprecedented Awareness," Invisible Children, https://invisiblechildren.com/kony-2012/.
39. "Grant T. Harris," Obama White House website, https://obamawhitehouse.archives.gov/blog/author/grant-t-harris?page=3.
40. Lucy Westcott, "Obama Is Still Trying to Stop Kony, Send New Personnel and Aircraft to Uganda," *The Atlantic*, March 24, 2014, https://www.theatlantic.com/politics/archive/2014/03/obama-still-trying-stop-kony-sends-new-personnel-and-aircraft-uganda/359472/.

41. Camila Domonoske, "U.S., Uganda Call Off Search for Infamous Warlord Joseph Kony," NPR, April 21, 2017, https://www.npr.org/sections/thetwo-way/2017/04/21/525073251/u-s-uganda-call-off-search-for-infamous-warlord-joseph-kony.

42. "End of Joseph Kony Hunt Raises Fears Lord's Resistance Army Could Return," *The Guardian* (US Edition), https://www.theguardian.com/global-development/2017/may/01/end-joseph-kony-hunt-fears-lords-resistance-army-return.

43. Jay Price, "Reputation Remake: Tilt-Rotor Osprey Wins Fans in Afghanistan," *McClatchy*, May 9, 2013, https://www.mcclatchydc.com/news/nation-world/world/article24748960.html.

44. Military.com, Equipment Overview, CV-22 Osprey, https://www.military.com/equipment/cv-22-osprey.

45. Hope Hodge Seck, "Spare Parts Shortage Grounds Many Marine Corps Aircraft," Military.com, https://www.military.com/daily-news/2017/02/10/spare-parts-shortage-grounds-most-marine-corps-aircraft.html.

46. Robert Gates, *Duty: Memoirs of a Secretary at War* (New York: Vintage, 2015), 258.

47. Gates, *Duty: Memoirs of a Secretary at War*, 461.

48. Ibid.

49. Chris Johnson, "Soaring at the Air Force," *Washington Blade*, May 30, 2013.

50. John Riley, "Eric Fanning hints at lifting trans military ban in acceptance speech," *Metro Weekly*, June 2, 2016.

51. Chris Johnson, "Fanning: Trump Uninterested in Undoing LGBT Military Service," *Washington Blade*, December 9, 2016, https://www.washingtonblade.com/2016/12/09/fanning-trump-team-uninterested-in-undoing-lgbt-military-service/.

52. Stephen Losey, *Air Force Times*, "Deborah Lee James Vows: 'People First,'" September 21, 2015, https://www.airforcetimes.com/news/your-air-force/2015/09/21/secaf-deborah-lee-james-vows-people-first/.

53. Air Force Sergeants Association, *AFSA Magazine*, Interview With Deborah Lee James, Vol. 52, No. 4 (July/August 2014), https://members.hqafsa.org//AFSA_DOCS/Magazine/AFS-019_JulyAug14.pdf.

54. Author's interview with Chaplain Crews.

55. Author's interview with chaplain who wished to remain anonymous.

56. Travis J. Tritten, "Trump Withdraws Pentagon Nominee After Yearlong Delay," *Washington Examiner*, October 4, 2018, https://

www.washingtonexaminer.com/policy/defense-national-security/
trump-withdraws-pentagon-nominee-after-year-long-delay.

57. Nico Lang, "Trump's Secretary of Defense Pick Opposes LGBT
People, Women Serving in Military," *The Advocate*, December
2, 2016, https://www.advocate.com/politics/2016/12/02/trumps-
secretary-defense-pick-opposes-lgbt-people-women-serving-military.

58. Rebecca Kheel, "Mattis's Views on Women in Combat Takes Center
Stage," *The Hill*, January 12, 2017, https://thehill.com/policy/
defense/313871-mattis-to-face-questions-over-women-in-combat-and-
lgbt-troops-at-confirmation.

59. James Mattis & Kori Schake, *Warriors & Citizens: American Views
of Our Military* (Hoover Institution Press: 2016), 307.

60. Mattis and Schake, *Warriors & Citizens: American Views of our
Military*, 298.

61. US House of Representatives Joint Task Force on Central Command
Intelligence Analysis, Initial Findings, August 10, 2016, https://
intelligence.house.gov/uploadedfiles/house_jtf_on_centcom_
intelligence_initial_report.pdf.

62. US House of Representatives Joint Task Force on Central Command
Intelligence Analysis, Initial Findings.

63. Human Rights Campaign (@HRC), Twitter, July 30, 2017, 1:00 p.m.,
https://twitter.com/HRC/status/891750267883986944.

64. Pete Williams, Hans Nichols, & Marianna Sotomayor, NBCNews,
*Former Military Service Secretaries Join Lawsuit Opposing Trump
Transgender Ban*, August 31, 2017, https://www.nbcnews.com/
politics/politics-news/former-military-service-secretaries-join-lawsuit-
opposing-transgender-ban-n797851.

65. Screenshots of Fanning RTing these tweets from John Brennan:
https://twitter.com/JohnBrennan/status/1018885971104985093
and Joe Walsh https://twitter.com/WalshFreedom/
status/1018898310847975425.

66. Screenshot of Fanning RTing this tweet from John Dingle: https://
twitter.com/JohnDingell/status/895256013372362752.

67. Eric Fanning (@ericfanning), Twitter, July 31, 2017, 11:48 a.m.,
https://twitter.com/ericfanning/status/892094690543251457.

68. Screenshot of Mabus RTing this tweet: https://twitter.com/M_Breen/
status/1018888736577335296.

69. David Martin, CBS News, "New Warship 'Poster Child For How
You Don't Build a Ship,' Says ex-Navy Secretary," March 2, 2017,
https://www.cbsnews.com/news/uss-gerald-r-ford-poster-child-for-
how-you-dont-build-a-ship-says-former-navy-secretary/.

70. Associated Press, "Top Military Brass Resisting
Calls to Lift Transgender Ban," *New York Post*,
March 25, 2015, https://nypost.com/2015/03/25/
top-military-brass-resisting-calls-to-lift-transgender-ban/.

Chapter 2: The Academies

1. Melissa Leon, "Exclusive: Former West Point Professor's Letter
Exposes Corruption, Cheating and Failing Standards [full
Letter]," *American Military News*, October 11, 2017, https://
americanmilitarynews.com/2017/10/exclusive-former-west-point-
professors-letter-exposes-corruption-cheating-and-failing-standards-
full-letter/.

2. Jonah Bennett, "Communist West Point Graduate
Called Mattis an 'Evil, Vile F***,'" The Daily Caller,
September 27, 2017, https://dailycaller.com/2017/09/27/
communist-west-point-graduate-called-mattis-an-evil-vile-f/.

3. Kristina Wong, "Exclusive: West Point Professor Who Mentored
Antifa Soldier on Administrative Leave," Breitbart News, September
28, 2017, https://www.breitbart.com/politics/2017/09/28/exclusive-
west-point-professor-who-mentored-antifa-soldier-on-administrative-
leave/.

4. Melissa Leon, "Report: West Point Professor Rasheed Hosein Who
Mentored 'Socialist Organizer' Army Officer Placed on Admin.
Leave," *American Military News*, September 29, 2017, https://
americanmilitarynews.com/2017/09/report-west-point-professor-
rasheed-hosein-who-mentored-socialist-organizer-army-officer-
placed-on-admin-leave/.

5. Debra Heine, "West Point Commie May Have Been Radicalized by
His Mentor at the Military Academy," PJMedia.com, September 28,
2017, https://pjmedia.com/trending/2017/09/28/west-point-
communist-radical-investigation-military-academy-mentor/.

6. Wong, "Exclusive: West Point Professor Who Mentored Antifa
Soldier on Administrative Leave."

7. Ibid.

8. Recorded conversation with author.

9. Wong, "Exclusive: West Point Professor Who Mentored Antifa
Soldier on Administrative Leave."

10. Bradford Richardson, "Liberal Professors Outnumber Conservatives
Nearly 12 to 1, Study Finds," *Washington Times*, October 6,

2016, https://www.washingtontimes.com/news/2016/oct/6/
liberal-professors-outnumber-conservatives-12-1/.

11. Kirsten M. Keller, et. al, "The Mix of Military and Civilian Faculty
    at the United States Air Force Academy," Rand Corporation, 2013,
    https://www.rand.org/content/dam/rand/pubs/monographs/MG1200/
    MG1237/RAND_MG1237.pdf; Terry Babcock-Lumish, "The Magic
    of West Point," *New York Times*, December 4, 2013, https://atwar.
    blogs.nytimes.com/2013/12/04/the-magic-of-west-point/.

12. Franklin Powers, "Exclusive: Former Senior West Point Faculty
    Member Agrees With Criticism of Institution," The Daily Caller,
    October 13, 2017, https://dailycaller.com/2017/10/13/exclusive-
    former-senior-west-point-faculty-member-agrees-with-criticism-of-
    institution/.

13. Powers, "Exlusive: Former Senior West Point Faculty Member Agrees
    With Criticism."

14. Ibid.

15. Ender was the primary author of the article, but he was assisted by
    a few cadets under his tutelage, as many professors are when they
    publish academic articles.

16. Morton G. Ender et. al, "Dinner and a Conversation: Transgender
    Integration at West Point and Beyond," 6 *Soc. Sci.* 27, 3 (2017),
    https://www.mdpi.com/2076-0760/6/1/27.

17. Ender et al., "Dinner and a Conversation," 3.

18. Ibid., 8.

19. Ibid.

20. Ibid., 5.

21. U.S. Military Academy at West Point website, https://www.usma.edu/
    bsl/Shared%20Documents/PL377.pdf.

22. Ender et al., "Dinner and a Conversation," 14.

23. U.S. Military Academy at West Point website, https://www.usma.edu/
    bsl/Shared%20Documents/ARMY%20Sociology%20Newsletter
    %202016.pdf.

24. James Kirchick, "Politics on Parade: How Black Lives Matter Halted
    a Gay Pride Parade in Toronto," *LA Times*, July 6, 2016, https://
    www.latimes.com/opinion/op-ed/la-oe-kirchick-gay-pride-black-lives-
    matter-20160705-snap-story.html.

25. Babcock-Lumish, "The Magic of West Point."

26. "An Open Letter On Donald Trump's Vision of U.S. Foreign Policy,"
    The American Interest, https://www.the-american-interest.
    com/2016/07/19/an-open-letter-on-donald-trumps-vision-of-u-s-
    foreign-policy/.

27. Jeff Dyche, "The US Air Force: Elite Undergraduate College?" *AAUP Journal of Academic Freedom*, 2016, https://www.aaup.org/sites/default/files/Dyche.pdf.
28. Daniel Wiser, "The Nutty Professor," *Washington Free Beacon*, September 12, 2013, https://freebeacon.com/national-security/the-nutty-professor/.
29. Wiser, "The Nutty Professor."
30. Ibid.
31. Frank Bruni, "Tackling the Roots of Rape," *New York Times*, August 12, 2013, https://www.nytimes.com/2013/08/13/opinion/bruni-tackling-the-roots-of-rape.html.
32. Kirsten M. Keller et. al, "The Mix of Military and Civilian Faculty," 106.
33. Keller et al., "The Mix of Military and Civilian Faculty," iii.
34. 1993 Defense Authorization Act.
35. Maj. George Rhynedance, USA, U.S. Army War College Thesis, *More Civilians on the West Point Faculty: Good for the Army, or Not?* 1993, http://www.dtic.mil/dtic/tr/fulltext/u2/a272927.pdf, 4.
36. Keller et al., "The Mix of Military and Civilian Faculty," xvii.
37. Neela Banerjee, "Religion and Its Role Are in Dispute at the Service Academies," *New York Times*, June 25, 2008, https://www.nytimes.com/2008/06/25/us/25academies.html.
38. Ryan Pickrell, "Air Force Academy First Sergeant Reprimanded for Telling Cadets to Dress Properly," The Daily Caller, February 15, 2018, https://dailycaller.com/2018/02/15/air-force-michael-jordan/.
39. Pickrell, "Air Force Academy First Sergeant Reprimanded."
40. Ibid.
41. Stephen Losey, "Air Force Academy First Sergeant Admonished for 'Microaggression' Email," *Air Force Times*, February 16, 2018, https://www.airforcetimes.com/news/your-air-force/2018/02/16/air-force-academy-first-sergeant-admonished-for-microaggression-email/.
42. Pickrell, "Air Force Academy First Sergeant Reprimanded."
43. Mark J. Perry, American Enterprise Institute (AEI), Twitter, December 30, 2018, 8:28 p.m., https://mobile.twitter.com/Mark_J_Perry/status/1079564863435870208.
44. Emily Deruy, "The Tricky Pursuit of Diversity at the Air Force Academy," *The Atlantic*, May 16, 2016, https://www.theatlantic.com/education/archive/2016/05/why-the-air-force-academy-held-a-forum-on-ferguson/482895/.
45. Deruy, "The Tricky Pursuit of Diversity."

46. Audrey Hudson, "Lamborn Tells Air Force to Fix Religious Policy," *Colorado Observer*, April 17, 2014, https://thecoloradoobserver. com/2014/04/lamborn-tells-air-force-to-fix-religious-policy/.
47. Todd Starnes, "Air Force Drops 'So Help Me God' From Oaths," Fox News, November 19, 2013, https://www.foxnews.com/opinion/ air-force-drops-so-help-me-god-from-oaths.
48. Todd Starnes, "Air Force Academy Removes Bible Verse From Cadet's Whiteboard," Fox News, March 11, 2014, https://www.foxnews.com/opinion/ air-force-academy-removes-bible-verse-from-cadets-whiteboard.
49. Religion News Service, "Air Force Academy: Proselytizing and Religious Freedom Debate on School Campus," July 17, 2017, https:// www.huffingtonpost.com/2012/07/17/air-force-academy-religion- proselytism_n_1678092.html.
50. US Air Force Academy, Curriculum Handbook, 2018–2019, https:// www.usafa.edu/app/uploads/CHB.pdf.
51. "West Point Diversity & Inclusion Initiatives," *West Point Association of Graduates Magazine*, October 2018, https://www. westpointaog.org/file/westpointdiversityandinclusion.pdf..
52. U.S. Military Academy at West Point website, https://www.usma.edu/ bsl/Shared%20Documents/Army%20Sociology%20Newsletter%20 2017%20v5.pdf.

Chapter 3: The Transgender Mandate

1. Associated Press, "Top Military Brass Resisting Calls to Lift Transgender Ban," *New York Post*, March 25, 2015, http://nypost.com/2015/03/25/ top-military-brass-resisting-calls-to-lift-transgender-ban/.
2. Tom Vanden Brook, "Mattis Freezes Transgender Policy; Allows Troops to Continue Serving, Pending Study," *USA Today*, August 29, 2017, https://www.usatoday.com/story/news/politics/2017/08/29/ mattis-orders-pentagon-allow-transgender-troops-continue-serving- pending-study/614711001/.
3. Hank Berrien, "Navy Secretary Defies Trump: Transgender Toops 'Should Be Able to Serve,'" *Daily Wire*, https://www.dailywire.com/ news/19637/navy-secretary-defies-trump-transgender-troops-hank- berrien#exit-modal.
4. Lolita C. Baldor, "Military Chiefs Seek Transgender Enlistment Delay" Military.com, https://www.military.com/

daily-news/2017/06/23/military-chiefs-seek-delay-transgender-enlistment.html?ESRC=dod_170623.nl.

5. Baldor, "Military Chiefs Seek Transgender Enlistment Delay."
6. The Honorable James Mattis, Memorandum for the President, *Military Service by Transgender Individuals*, February 22, 2018, https://media.defense.gov/2018/Mar/23/2001894037/-1/-1/0/MILITARY-SERVICE-BY-TRANSGENDER-INDIVIDUALS.PDF.
7. Travis J. Tritten, "Jim Mattis, Kirsten Gillibrand Butt Heads Over Transgender Policy," *Washington Examiner*, April 26, 2018, https://www.washingtonexaminer.com/policy/defense-national-security/jim-mattis-kirsten-gillibrand-butt-heads-over-transgender-policy.
8. Tritten, "Jim Mattis, Kirsten Gillibrand Butt Heads."
9. Dan Lamothe, "Mattis Says the Pentagon Is Still Studying Transgender Military Service, Three Weeks after Trump Called for a Ban," *Washington Post*, August 24, 2017, https://www.washingtonpost.com/news/checkpoint/wp/2017/08/14/mattis-leaves-door-open-to-some-transgender-military-service-says-pentagon-is-still-studying-the-issue/?noredirect=on&utm_term=.37c298d7ec49.
10. Jennifer Rizzo & Zachary Cohen, "Pentagon Ends Transgender Ban," CNN, June 30, 2016, https://www.cnn.com/2016/06/30/politics/transgender-ban-lifted-us-military/index.html.
11. Brian Stone, "Is the Department of Defense Changing on Transgender Policy?" *Huffington Post*, July 16, 2013, http://www.huffingtonpost.com/brian-stone/is-the-department-of-defense-changing-on-transgender-policy_b_3592631.html.
12. Chris Johnson, "Soaring at the Air Force," *Washington Blade*, May 30, 2013, https://www.washingtonblade.com/2013/05/30/eric-fanning.
13. Helen Pow, "Pentagon Recognizes Transgender Service Members for First Time in 'Symbolic Move' for LGBT Community," *Daily Mail*, May 26, 2013, http://www.dailymail.co.uk/news/article-2325737/Autumn-Sandeen-Pentagon-recognizes-transgender-service-members-time-symbolic-LGBT-community.html.
14. Susan Page, "Air Force Secretary Supports Lifting Transgender Ban," *USA Today*, December 10, 2014, https://www.usatoday.com/story/news/politics/2014/12/10/usa-today-capital-download-air-force-secretary-deborah-lee-james/20165453/.
15. Page, "Air Force Secretary Supports Lifting Transgender Ban."
16. Helen Pow, "Pentagon Recognizes Transgender Service Members for First Time in 'Symbolic' Move for LGBT Community," *Daily Mail*, May 16, 2013, http://www.dailymail.co.uk/news/article-2325737/

Autumn-Sandeen-Pentagon-recognizes-transgender-service-members-
time-symbolic-LGBT-community.html.

17. Tom Vanden Brook, "Army Considers Easing Policy on
Transgender Soldiers," *USA Today*, February 16, 2015,
https://www.usatoday.com/story/news/nation/2015/02/16/
trangender-troops-chelsea-manning/23504073/.

18. German Lopez, "The Air Force Just Took a Big Step in Favor
of Transgender Rights," Vox, June 5, 2015, https://www.vox.
com/2015/6/5/8734685/transgender-air-force.

19. U.S. Department of Defense, transcript, *Remarks by Secretary
Carter at a Troop Event in Kandahar, Afghanistan*, February 22,
2015, https://dod.defense.gov/News/Transcripts/Transcript-View/
Article/607016/remarks-by-secretary-carter-at-a-troop-event-in-
kandahar-afghanistan/.

20. Landon Wilson, "Secretary of Defense, President Obama Back Open
Trans Military Service," National Center for Transgender Equality,
February 23, 2015, https://transequality.org/blog/secretary-of-
defense-president-obama-back-open-trans-military-service.

21. Sarah Wheaton, "Obama's LGBT Test: End Transgender
Military Ban," *Politico*, June 24, 2015, https://www.politico.com/
story/2015/06/obama-lgbt-transgender-military-serving-ban-119373.

22. Wheaton, "Obama's LGBT Test: End Transgender Military Ban."

23. Ibid.

24. Declaration of Deborah Lee James in Support of Plaintiffs' Motion
for Preliminary injunction, *Doe v. Trump*, Civil Action No.
17-cv-1597 (CKK), United States District Court for the District of
Columbia, https://www.glad.org/wp-content/uploads/2017/08/james-
declaration.pdf.

25. Declaration of Deborah Lee James.

26. Declaration of Brad R. Carson, *Karnoski v. Trump*, Case No.
2:17-cv-01297-MJP, United States District Court for the Western
District of Washington, available at https://www.courtlistener.com/
recap/gov.uscourts.wawd.249424.46.0.pdf.

27. Declaration of Margaret C. Wilmoth, *Doe 2 v. Trump*, No. 18-5257,
October 22, 2018 (D.C. Cir. 2018).

28. Transcript of Press Conference Held by Ash Carter, June 30, 2016,
available at https://www.defense.gov/News/Transcripts/Transcript-
View/Article/822347/department-of-defense-press-briefing-by-
secretary-carter-on-transgender-service/.

29. Declaration of Brad Carson, *Doe 2 v. Trump*, No. 18-5257, October
22, 2018 (D.C.Cir. 2018).

30. Dan Lamothe, "The Pentagon's Ban on Transgender Service Just Fell—But the Details are Complicated," *Washington Post*, June 30, 2016, https://www.washingtonpost.com/news/checkpoint/wp/2016/06/30/the-pentagons-ban-on-transgender-service-just-fell-but-the-details-are-complicated/?utm_term=.e81bdc3f2fab.

31. Carter Press Conference Transcript, *Supra*, https://www.defense.gov/News/Transcripts/Transcript-View/Article/822347/department-of-defense-press-briefing-by-secretary-carter-on-transgender-service/.

32. Joe Biden (@JoeBiden), Twitter, July 26, 2017, 7:31 a.m., https://twitter.com/JoeBiden/status/890218086909063169.

33. Oriana Pawlyk, "Transgender Airmen Can Now Seek Temporary Exemptions," Military.com, https://www.military.com/daily-news/2016/10/17/transgender-airmen-now-seek-temporary-exemptions.html.

34. Pawlyk, "Transgender Airmen Can Now Seek Temporary Exemptions."

35. U.S. Department of Defense, *Department of Defense Report and Recommendations on Military Service by Transgendered Persons*, February 2018, https://partner-mco-archive.s3.amazonaws.com/client_files/1521898539.pdf.

36. Julie Scelfo, "A University Recognizes a Third Gender: Neutral," *New York Times*, February 3, 2015, https://www.nytimes.com/2015/02/08/education/edlife/a-university-recognizes-a-third-gender-neutral.html.

37. New York City Commission on Human Rights, "Gender Identity Expression," https://www1.nyc.gov/assets/cchr/downloads/pdf/publications/GenderID_Card2015.pdf.

38. NBC News (via Reuters), "New York City Creates Gender-Neutral 'X' Option for Birth Certificates," October 10, 2018, https://www.nbcnews.com/feature/nbc-out/new-york-city-creates-gender-neutral-x-option-birth-certificates-n918506; See also Brigit Katz, "California becomes first state to introduce gender-neutral birth certificates," Smithsonian.com, https://www.smithsonianmag.com/smart-news/california-becomes-first-state-introduce-gender-neutral-birth-certificates-180965343/.

39. Kari Sonde, "These States Are Driving the Charge Toward Gender Inclusive Licenses," *Mother Jones*, June 22, 2018, https://www.motherjones.com/politics/2018/06/these-states-are-driving-the-charge-toward-gender-inclusive-licenses/(Licenses); Perry Stein, "No Longer Just Male or Female: D.C. Schools to Give Families a Third Option with 'Non-Binary,'" *Washington Post*, November 12, 2018, https://www.

washingtonpost.com/local/education/no-longer-just-male-or-female-
dc-schools-to-give-families-a-third-option-with-nonbinary/2018/11/12/
dc34d9e5-a70c-43a1-84b7-bcd6e3acd19b_story.html (School Districts).

40. Bre Payton, "Disabled Combat Veteran Speaks Out On Trump's
Transgender Military Ban," The Federalist, July 26, 2017, available
at https://thefederalist.com/2017/07/26/disabled-combat-veteran-
speaks-out-on-trumps-transgender-military-ban/.

41. Payton, "Disabled Combat Veteran Speaks Out."

42. Andrew M. Seaman, "Depression, Addiction Common
Among Young Transgender Women," Reuters,
March 21, 2016, https://www.reuters.com/article/
us-health-transgender-mental-idUSKCN0WN2AZ.

43. Katherine Schreiber, "Why Transgender People
Experience More Mental Health Issues," Psychology
Today, December 6, 2016, https://www.psychologytoday.
com/blog/the-truth-about-exercise-addiction/201612/
why-transgender-people-experience-more-mental-health.

44. An Air Force booklet for recruits preparing for basic training, for
example, informs them that "[d]ue to the nature and activities of
basic training, possession of over-the-counter and nonessential
medications (to include drugs for acne and sports supplements) is
prohibited," https://www.usafa.edu/app/uploads/2022_Appointee_
Booklet.pdf.

45. Ross R. Neto, et. al., Int. Braz. J. Urol. Jan–Feb; 38, no. 1: 97–107,
available at https://www.ncbi.nlm.nih.gov/pubmed/22397771.

46. Rowan Scarborough, "Pentagon Issues Sex Change Manual,
Allows Extended Time Off For Process," Washington Times, July
14, 2016, http://www.washingtontimes.com/news/2016/jul/14/
pentagon-issues-sex-change-manual-allows-extended-/.

47. MaryAnne Golon, "Tyler Becomes Taylor, A Transgender Coast
Guard Officer in Transition," Washington Post, July 28, 2017,
https://www.washingtonpost.com/news/in-sight/wp/2017/07/28/
tyler-becomes-taylor-a-transgender-coast-guard-officer-in-
transition/?utm_term=.7cef5c773294.

48. Andrea Long Chu, "My New Vagina Won't Make Me Happy,"
New York Times, November 24, 2018, https://www.nytimes.
com/2018/11/24/opinion/sunday/vaginoplasty-transgender-medicine.
html.

49. Military Personnel Drug Abuse Testing Program
"It is DoD and Army Policy that a urinalysis sample must be
collected by direct observation and that, absent an exception to

policy, the observer will be the same gender as the Soldier being observed (as reflected by the gender marker in DEERS).

Under DoD Instruction (DoDI) 1010.16, implementing the Military Personnel Drug Abuse Testing Program (MPDATP), "[s] pecimens are collected under the direct observation of a designated individual of the same sex as the Service member providing the specimen." Under DoDI 1300.28, implementing DoD's policy on in-service transition of transgender Service members, the Military Services "recognize a Service member's gender by the member's gender marker in the DEERS" and, "[c]oincident with that gender marker," apply all standards for MPDAPT participation, as well as "other military standards applied with consideration of the member's gender."

To the extent there was any apparent conflict or confusion between the DoDI 1010.16 requirement of "same sex" observers and the DoDI 1300.28 requirement that the Services apply the MPDAPT coincident with a Service member's gender marker in DEERS, the Office of the Under Secretary of Defense (Personnel and Readiness) (USD) (P&R) addressed this issue in a memorandum, dated 22 Sep 16, clarifying that "Service members providing a urinalysis specimen are observed by an individual with the same gender marker in DEERS." In other words, for the purposes of interpreting these two Instructions in conjunction with one another, "sex" in DoDI 1010.16 refers to the same thing as "gender" in DoDI 1300.28. This clarification is consistent with DoDI 1300.28 and Army Directive 2016-35, as well as the DoD Handbook and other guidance provided by OSD and Army, all of which state that MPDATP standards will be applied coincident with the gender marker in DEERS."

50. Associated Press, "Senator: West Point Case Shows Military Has 'Sexual Harassment Problem,'" *The Guardian*, May 23, 2013, https://www.theguardian.com/world/2013/may/23/us-military-usa.

51. Nicole Russell, "Twitter Permanently Bans Feminist For Writing that 'Men Aren't Women,'" The Federalist, November 25, 2018, https://thefederalist.com/2018/11/25/twitter-permanently-bans-feminist-writing-men-arent-women/.

52. Caroline Marcus, "The Politically Correct Purge On Our Language," *Daily Telegraph*, August 6, 2018, https://www.dailytelegraph. com.au/rendezview/the-politically-correct-purge-on-our-language/news-story/2758bd1908ce9c4e42ff9ef2fb0451e5..

53. Alex Green, "Military Chiefs Order Troops to Use Gender-Neutral Language at Training Base to Avoid Upsetting Women and Trans

Groups," *Daily Mail*, December 26, 2017, https://www.dailymail.
co.uk/news/article-5214117/Military-chiefs-order-troops-use-gender-
neutral-words.html.

54. United States Navy, Transgender and Gender Transition:
Commanding Officer's Toolkit, available at https://www.public.navy.
mil/bupers-npc/support/21st_Century_Sailor/lgbt/Documents/
CO%20Toolkit%20USN_Transgender%20and%20Transitioning
%20Command%20Officers%20Toolkit_V23.pdf.

55. Peter Hasson, "U.S. Military Instructed to be 'Sensitive' of Pronoun
Use, Warned Against Gender Assumptions," The Daily Caller,
October 3, 2016, http://dailycaller.com/2016/10/03/u-s-military-
instructed-to-be-sensitive-of-pronoun-use-warned-against-gender-
assumptions/?utm_source=akdart.

56. Elizabeth Harrington, "Naval Academy Hosting 'Transgender 101'
Training for Midshipmen," The Washington Free Beacon, December
7, 2016, http://freebeacon.com/issues/naval-academy-hosting-transgender-
101-training-midshipmen/?utm_source=akdart.

57. Marine Florin personal website, "About" Section, available at http://
www.marnieflorin.com/about-1/.

58. United States Navy, Transgender and Gender Transition:
Commanding Officer's Toolkit, https://www.public.navy.mil/
bupers-npc/support/21st_Century_Sailor/lgbt/Documents/CO%20
Toolkit%20USN_Transgender%20and%20Transitioning%20
Command%20Officers%20Toolkit_V23.pdf.

59. Dawn Ennis, "We Won! Trans Girl Can Now Use Girls'
Bathroom at Military School," NBC News website, October
22, 2016, https://www.nbcnews.com/feature/nbc-out/
we-won-trans-girl-can-now-use-girls-bathroom-military-n671196.

60. Tricare Policy Manual 6010.57-M, Chapter 7, September 6, 2016,
available at http://manuals.tricare.osd.mil/DisplayManualPdfFile/
TP08/175/ChangeOnly/tp08/c7s1_2.pdf.

61. The policy applies to children who have reached at least "Stage 2"
of puberty on the Tanner scale. The World Health Organization
definition of Tanner Stage 2 puberty occurs when children are
between eight and fifteen years old and before any significant genital
development takes place for males. See Antiretroviral Therapy for
HIV infection in Infants and Children: Towards Universal Access:
Recommendations for a Public Health Approach: 2010 Revision,
https://www.ncbi.nlm.nih.gov/books/NBK138588/.

62. Schaefer, et al., Rand Corp., *Assessing the Implications of Allowing Transgender Personnel to Serve Openly*, (2016), 86, 88 https://www. rand.org/pubs/research_reports/RR1530.html.

63. Kayla Williams, "Veterans Affairs Secretary Wilkie Should Expand Care to Transgender Veterans," *The Hill*, July 29, 2018, https:// thehill.com/opinion/healthcare/399268-veterans-affairs-secretary-wilkie-should-expand-care-to-transgender.

64. Rand Corporation, Press Release, *Impact of Transgender Personnel on Readiness and Health Care Costs in the U.S. Military Likely to be Small*, June 30, 2015, https://www.rand.org/news/press/2016/06/30. html.

65. Leon Shane III, "Poll: Active Duty Troops Worry About Military's Transgender Policies," Military Times, July 27, 2017, https:// www.militarytimes.com/news/pentagon-congress/2017/07/27/ poll-active-duty-troops-worry-about-militarys-transgender-policies/.

Chapter 4: The Real Ranger School Story

1. Scott Neuman, "First Female Soldiers Graduate From Army Ranger School," NPR, August 21, 2015, https:// www.npr.org/sections/thetwo-way/2015/08/21/433482186/ first-female-soldiers-graduate-from-army-ranger-school.

2. Brigadier General Malcom Frost, U.S. Army Press Release, Facebook, September 26, 2015, https://www.facebook.com/USarmy/photos/a.811 09118557.82903.44053938557/10153321189393558/?type=3&fref=nf.

3. Scott Faith, "Shots Fired: 'People Magazine' Journalists Calls Out Army General Over His Response to the Female Rangers Controversy," *Havok Journal*, September 28, 2015, https:// havokjournal.com/nation/ shots-fired-people-magazine-journalist-calls-out-army-general-over-his-response-to-the-female-rangers-controversy/2/.

4. Susan Keating, "First Female Ranger School Graduates: 'We Had Our Guards Up, But No Chips on Our Shoulders,'" *People*, August 20, 2015, https://people.com/celebrity/first-female-ranger-school-graduates-we-had-our-guards-up-but-no-chips-on-our-shoulders/.

5. Susan Keating, "First Female Soldiers Graduate Elite Army Ranger School: 'I Thought We Were Going to be Dropped,'" *People*, August 21, 2015, https://people.com/celebrity/ first-female-soldiers-graduate-elite-army-ranger-school/.

6. "Surviving The Cut: Ranger School," Discovery, August 18, 2010, https://www.discovery.com/tv-shows/surviving-the-cut/full-episodes/ranger-school.

7. All Army Activities (ALARACT) 222/2014 (II September 2014)]; *see also* Gary Sheftick, "Women Volunteers Needed for Ranger Course Assessment," Army.mil, September 12, 2014, https://www.army.mil/article/133641/women_volunteers_needed_for_ranger_course_assessment.

8. U.S. Army, Executive Report, "Ranger Assessment Study," August 10, 2015, https://dod.defense.gov/Portals/1/Documents/wisr-studies/Army%20-%20Ranger%20Assessment%20Study%20Executive%20Report2.pdf.

9. U.S. Army, Executive Report, "Ranger Assessment Study."

10. Susan Keating, "Was it Fixed? Army General Told Subordinates: 'A Woman Will Graduate Ranger School,' Sources Say," *People*, September 25, 2015, https://people.com/celebrity/female-rangers-were-given-special-treatment-sources-say/.

11. Jesse Byrnes, "GOP Lawmaker Questions Test Scores of Female Army Rangers," *The Hill*, September 22, 2015, https://thehill.com/policy/defense/254579-lawmaker-probing-whether-female-army-rangers-received-special-treatment.

12. U.S. Army, Executive Report, "Ranger Assessment Study."

13. Brigadier General Malcom Frost, USA, U.S. Army Press Release, Facebook.

14. U.S. Army, Executive Report, "Ranger Assessment Study."

15. Chuck Williams, "How May 29 Changed Ranger School Forever," *Columbus Ledger-Inquirer*, December 19, 2015, https://www.thestate.com/news/local/military/article50703900.html.

16. C. Todd Lopez, "Three Women Recycled Again in Ranger School," Army.mil, June 1, 2015, https://www.army.mil/article/149670/three_women_recycled_again_in_ranger_school.

17. Susan Keating, "Congressman Asks for Documents to Find Out Whether Women Got Special Treatment at Ranger School," *People*, September 22, 2015, https://people.com/celebrity/documents-requested-for-female-rangers/.

18. Keating, "Congressman Asks for Documents to Find Out Whether Women Got Special Treatment at Ranger School."

19. Chris Casteel, "U.S. Rep. Steve Russell Talks Leadership Turmoil, Female Rangers, and China," *The Oklahoman*, October 25, 2015, https://oklahoman.com/article/5455818/us-rep-steve-russell-talks-leadership-turmoil-female-rangers-and-china.

20. Susan Keating, "Some Documents Related to Females' Performance at Ranger School Shredded, Congressman Says in Letter to Army," *People*, October 13, 2015, https://people.com/celebrity/some-documents-related-to-females-performance-at-ranger-school-shredded/.

21. Chris Casteel, "U.S. Rep. Steve Russell Talks Leadership Turmoil, Female Rangers, and China," *The Oklahoman*, October 25, 2015, https://oklahoman.com/article/5455818/us-rep-steve-russell-talks-leadership-turmoil-female-rangers-and-china.

22. Chuck Williams, "Col. David Fivecoat Relinquishes Command of Airborne and Ranger Training Brigade," *Columbus Ledger-Inquirer*, June 30, 2016, https://www.ledger-enquirer.com/news/local/military/article86938517.html.

23. C. Todd Lopez, "Ranger School Hangs Out 'All Soldier Welcome' Sign," Army.Mil, September 2, 2015, https://www.army.mil/article/154897/ranger_school_hangs_out_all_soldiers_welcome_sign.

24. Susan Keating, "Female Rangers Were Given Special Treatment, Sources Say," *People*, September 25, 2015, https://people.com/celebrity/female-rangers-were-given-special-treatment-sources-say/.

25. Brigadier General Malcom Frost, USA, U.S. Army Press Release, Facebook.

26. Alexandra Hemmerly-Brown, "Training for Best Ranger: Guard Team Talks Extreme PT," Army.Mil, April 15, 2011, http://www.army.mil/article/55042/Training_for_Best_Ranger__Guard_team_talks_extreme_PT/.

Chapter 5: The Marines Overruled

1. Mark Thompson, "Women in Combat: Why the Pentagon Chief Overruled the Marines," *Time*, December 3, 2015, http://time.com/4135583/women-combat-marines-ash-carter/.

2. Paul Johnson and Jane Pinelis, *The Experiment of a Lifetime: Doing Science in the Wild for the United States Marine Corps* (2019), 155.

3. Johnson and Pinelis, *The Experiment of a Lifetime*, 73.

4. Ibid., 75.

5. Ibid., 31.

6. Ibid., 148.

7. Jude Eden, "Ashton Carter Betrays Military Women and Combat Effectiveness," *The Stream*, December 4, 2015, https://stream.org/ashton-carter-betrays-military-women-combat-effectiveness/.

8. Brig. Gen. George C. Smith, USMC, *Memorandum for the Commandant of the Marine Corps: United States Assessment of Women in Service Assignments*, August 15, 2015, http://cdn.sandiegouniontrib.com/news/documents/2015/09/24/USMC_WISR_Documents_Not_releasable.pdf (Marine Corps study).

9. Johnson and Pinelis, *The Experiment of a Lifetime*, 51.

10. Ibid.

11. Ibid., 52.

12. See, e.g., Transcript, CNN Town Hall with President Obama, aired September 28, 2016, available at http://transcripts.cnn.com/TRANSCRIPTS/1609/28/se.01.html.

13. Smith, *Memorandum for the Commandant of the Marine Corps.*

14. Hope Hodge Seck, "Mixed-Gender Teams Come Up Short in Marines' Infantry Experiment," *Marine Corps Times*, September 10, 2015, https://www.marinecorpstimes.com/news/your-marine-corps/2015/09/10/mixed-gender-teams-come-up-short-in-marines-infantry-experiment/.

15. Smith, *Memorandum for the Commandant of the Marine Corps.*

16. Ibid.

17. Col. Barbara E. Springer & Maj. Amy E. Ross, *Musculoskeletal Injuries in Military Women*, Borden Institute Monograph Series, 2011, https://www.cs.amedd.army.mil/FileDownloadpublic.aspx?docid=b42d1acd-0b32-4d26-8e22-4a518be998f7.

18. Epstein, Y, Fleischmann, C, Yanovich, R, and Heled, Y., Physiological and medical aspects that put women soldiers at increased risk for overuse injuries. J Strength Cond Res 29(11S): S107–S110, 2015—.

19. Julie Pulley & Hugh P. Scott, Los Angeles Times, *What Military Recruiters Aren't Telling Women: You'll Face Disproportionate Health Risks*, July 25, 2017, https://www.latimes.com/opinion/op-ed/la-oe-pulley-scott-are-recruiters-misleading-women-20170725-story.html.

20. Capt. Katie Petronio, "Get Over It! We Are Not All Created Equal," *Marine Corps Gazette* (July 2012), available at https://mca-marines.org/gazette/get-over-it-we-are-not-all-created-equal/.

21. Army Medical Command, "IET Injury Surveillance Entry-Level AIT at Forts Sill and Benning, Fiscal Years 2010-2013, May 12, 2015, http://cmrlink.org/data/sites/85/CMRDocuments/M-1IETInjurySurveillanceBates1-25-24JUL15.pdf.

22. Secretary of Defense Ash Carter, Department of Defense, *Department of Defense Press Briefing by Secretary Carter in*

Pentagon Briefing Room, December 3, 2015, https://dod.defense.gov/ News/Transcripts/Transcript-View/Article/632578/department-of-defense-press-briefing-by-secretary-carter-in-the-pentagon-briefi/.

23. Smith, *Memorandum for the Commandant of the Marine Corps*.
24. Gen. Joseph Dunford, USMC, *United States Marine Corps Assessment of Women in Service Assignments: Recommendations for the Secretary of the Navy*, 1.
25. Secretary of Defense Ash Carter, Department of Defense, *Department of Defense Press Briefing by Secretary Carter in Pentagon Briefing Room*, December 3, 2015, https://dod.defense.gov/ News/Transcripts/Transcript-View/Article/632578/department-of-defense-press-briefing-by-secretary-carter-in-the-pentagon-briefi/.
26. See, e.g., Jim Michaels, "First Female Soldiers to Graduate From Army Ranger School," *USA Today*, August 17, 2015, https://www.usatoday.com/story/news/world/2015/08/17/army-ranger-school-women-graduate/31887987/ (in which army Secretary John McHugh states that the success of the integrated class "has proven that every soldier, regardless of his or her gender, can achieve his or her full potential").
27. Ray Mabus (@SecNav), Twitter, May 13, 2015, 7:15 a.m., https://twitter.com/SECNAV/status/598491731651334144.
28. Thomas Gibbons-Neff, "Navy Secretary Threw Us 'Under the Bus,' Say Marines in Gender-Integrated Infantry Unit," *Washington Post*, September 14, 2015, https://www.washingtonpost.com/news/checkpoint/wp/2015/09/14/navy-secretary-threw-us-under-the-bus-say-marines-in-gender-integrated-infantry-unit/?utm_term=.7c4b9849ab62.
29. Gibbons-Neff, "Navy Secretary Threw Us 'Under the Bus,.'"
30. Ray Mabus (@SecNav), Twitter, February 2, 2016, 7:20 a.m., https://twitter.com/SECNAV/status/694540913675223040.
31. Thompson, "Women in Combat."
32. Ray Mabus, "Secretary of the Navy: Allowing Women to Serve in Every Combat Role Was Overdue," *Time*, December 3, 2015, http://time.com/4135649/women-in-combat/.
33. Gibbons-Neff, "Navy Secretary Threw Us 'Under the Bus.'"
34. Ibid.
35. Ibid.
36. Hope Hodge Seck, "Marine War Hero: SecNav 'Off Base' on Women in Combat," *Marine Corps Times*, September 14, 2015, https://

www.marinecorpstimes.com/news/your-marine-corps/2015/09/14/
marine-war-hero-secnav-off-base-on-women-in-combat/.

37. Jonah Bennett, "McCain to Mabus: Why Bother Having a Study
on Combat Gender Integration if You're Going to Ignore the
Results?" The Daily Caller, September 17, 2015, http://dailycaller.
com/2015/09/17/mccain-to-mabus-why-bother-having-a-study-on-
combat-gender-integration-if-youre-going-to-ignore-the-results/.

38. Lolita Baldor, "Debate Over Women in Combat Continues to Roil
Marine Corps," PBS, January 9, 2016, https://www.pbs.org/
newshour/nation/debate-over-women-in-combat-continues-to-roil-
marine-corps.

39. James Mattis & Kori Schake, Warriors & Citizens: American Views
of Our Military (Stanford: Hoover Institution Press, 2015), 309–10.

40. Thom Shanker, "Marines Share Frank Views With Hagel on Women
in Combat," New York Times, July 19, 2013, https://atwar.blogs.
nytimes.com/2013/07/19/marines-share-frank-views-with-hagel-on-
women-in-combat/?pagewanted=print&_r=1.

41. Shanker, "Marines Share Frank Views."

42. Transcript, CNN Town Hall with President Obama, aired September
28, 2016, http://transcripts.cnn.com/TRANSCRIPTS/1609/28/se.01.
html.

43. Mark D. Faram, "Navy Looks to Remove 'Man' From
All Job Titles," Navy Times, January 7, 2016, https://
www.navytimes.com/story/military/2016/01/07/
navy-looks-remove-man-all-job-titles/78415190/.

44. Ray Mabus, Twitter (@SecNav), May 13, 2015, 7:36 a.m., https://
twitter.com/SECNAV/status/598496935482413056.

45. Meghann Myers, "Women Officer Say Price Tag for
Navy's Uniform Push is Unfair," November 21, 2015,
https://www.navytimes.com/news/your-navy/2015/11/21/
women-officers-say-price-tag-for-navy-s-uniform-push-is-unfair/.

46. Scott Burton, "Military Addresses Need for Female Body Armor as
Women Are Approved for Combat Role," Body Armor News, March
18, 2016, https://www.bodyarmornews.com/female-body-armor/.

47. Derrick Perkins, "Mabus: 1 in 4 Marine Recruits Should Be
Women," Marine Corps Times, May 26, 2015, https://www.
marinecorpstimes.com/news/your-marine-corps/2015/05/26/
mabus-1-in-4-marine-recruits-should-be-women/.

48. Ray Mabus (@SecNav), Twitter, October 15, 2016, 3:14 p.m., https://twitter.com/SECNAV/status/787416319641677828.
49. Brig. Gen. George W. Smith, Jr. USMC, *Memorandum for the Commandant of the Marine Corps: United States Assessment of Women in Service Assignments*, August 15, 2015, http://cdn.sandiegouniontrib.com/news/documents/2015/09/24/USMC_WISR_Documents_Not_releasable.pdf (Marine Corps study).
50. Andrea King Collier, "Too Fat to Fight: Is the Obesity Crisis a National Security Risk?" NBC News, May 30, 2016, http://www.nbcnews.com/news/nbcblk/too-fat-fight-obesity-crisis-national-security-risk-n582331.

Chapter 6: Conclusions First, Evidence Second

1. Elizabeth Nix, "Who Was Molly Pitcher?" History.com, August 22, 2018, https://www.history.com/news/who-was-molly-pitcher.
2. Kristal L. M. Alfonso, *Femme Fatale: An Examination of the Role of Women in Combat and the Policy Implications for Future American Military Operations* (Air University Press, 2009), 1–6.
3. Associated Press, "Female Medic Earns Silver Star in Afghan War," NBC News, March 3, 2008, http://www.nbcnews.com/id/23547346/ns/us_news-military/t/female-medic-earns-silver-star-afghan-war/#.W2x6vdhKh8c.
4. Richard Sisk, "Pentagon's Lethality Task Force Needs More Funding: Mattis Aide," Military.com, October 9, 2018, https://www.military.com/dodbuzz/2018/10/09/pentagons-lethality-task-force-needs-more-funding-mattis-aide.html#.W70PTWrxlJM.twitter.
5. Leon Panetta and Martin Dempsey, Opening Statements and Press Q&A on the Direct Ground Combat Exclusion Rule re Women in Combat, January 24, 2013, http://www.americanrhetoric.com/speeches/leonpanettamartindempseywomenincombatpentagon.htm.
6. Panetta and Dempsey, Opening Statements.
7. Ibid., emphasis added.
8. Gayle Tzemach Lemmon, "When Women Lead Soldiers Into Battle," *The Atlantic*, September 9, 2016, https://www.theatlantic.com/international/archive/2016/09/women-combat-leaders/498800/.
9. Jay Newton-Small, "Inside the Decision to Open Up the Frontlines to Women," *Time*, January 5, 2016, http://time.com/4168433/military-women-frontlines-leon-panetta/.
10. Associated Press, "First 2 Women Set to Graduate From Army Ranger School," PBS News Hour, August 18, 2015, https://www.pbs.org/newshour/nation/first-2-women-set-graduate-army-ranger-school.

11. Dan Lamothe, "Marine Experiment Finds Women Get injured More Frequently, Shoot Less Accurately Than Men," *Washington Post*, September 10, 2015, https://www.washingtonpost.com/news/checkpoint/wp/2015/09/10/marine-experiment-finds-women-get-injured-more-frequently-shoot-less-accurately-than-men/?utm_term=.987575222d33.

12. "An 8-page, heavily-redacted draft document titled 'US Army Gender Integration Study Executive Report,' produced by Training & Doctrine Command (TRADOC), dated 5 May 2015" was obtained via FOIA requests filed by the Thomas More Law Center, http://cmrlink.org/data/sites/85/CMRDocuments/CMR%20Policy%20Analysis%20August2015.pdf.

13. Army Training and Doctrine Command Analysis Center, "Gender Integration Study," April 21, 2015, https://dod.defense.gov/Portals/1/Documents/wisr-studies/Army%20-%20Gender%20Integration%20Study3.pdf.

14. Army Training and Doctrine Command Analysis Center, "Gender Integration Study," 1.

15. Ibid., 31.

16. Ibid.

17. Ibid., 38.

18. Ibid., 47.

19. Ibid.

20. Tara Copp, "Here's Mattis' Full Response to VMI Cadets on Women in Infantry," Military.com, September 26, 2018, https://www.militarytimes.com/news/your-military/2018/09/26/heres-mattis-full-response-to-vmi-cadets-on-women-in-infantry/.

21. Copp, "Here's Mattis' Full Response to VMI Cadets."

22. Tara Copp, "Mattis Defends Remarks on Women in Infantry," Military.com, September 26, 2018, https://www.militarytimes.com/news/your-military/2018/09/26/mattis-defends-remarks-on-women-in-infantry/.

23. Army Feasibility Study, 32, 26.

24. Lolita Baldor, "Debate Over Women in Combat Continues to Roil Marine Corps," PBS, January 9, 2016, https://www.pbs.org/newshour/nation/debate-over-women-in-combat-continues-to-roil-marine-corps.

25. Panetta and Dempsey Press Conference, American Rhetoric website, http://www.americanrhetoric.com/speeches/leonpanettamartindempseywomenincombatpentagon.htm.

26. Ellen Haring, "Marines' Requirements for Infantry Officers are Unrealistic, Army Colonel Says," *Marine Corps Times*, October 15, 2016, https://www.marinecorpstimes.com/opinion/2016/10/15/marines-requirements-for-infantry-officers-are-unrealistic-army-colonel-says/.

27. "Nearly Half of Females Failed to Graduate Army Infantry Training, Standards Were Also Lowered," PopularMilitary.com, May 22, 2017, https://popularmilitary.com/nearly-half-females-failed-graduate-army-infantry-training-standards-also-lowered/.

28. Anna Simons, "Women in Ground Combat Units:Where's the Data?" Marine Corps Times, April 15, 2015, https://warontherocks.com/2015/04/women-in-ground-combat-units-wheres-the-data/.

29. Ibid.

30. United Kingdom Iraq Inquiry, Report of the Iraq Inquiry, July 6, 2016, http://webarchive.nationalarchives.gov.uk/20171123123237/http://www.iraqinquiry.org.uk/.

31. United Kingdom Iraq Inquiry, Report of the Iraq Inquiry, July 6, 2016, 5 #18d, http://webarchive.nationalarchives.gov.uk/201711231 23237/http://www.iraqinquiry.org.uk/.

32. Ibid., 2 #10.

33. Ibid.

34. Mark Hookham, "Fitness Test 'Relaxed' to Help Put Women on Front Line," *Times* (UK), April 3, 2016, https://www.thetimes.co.uk/article/fitness-test-relaxed-to-help-put-women-on-front-line-79d7bxp25.

35. Mark Nicole, "Don't Say Rifleman, it is 'Too Gender Specific': Army Officers Told to Refer to Combat Soldiers as 'Infanteers' Despite No Women Asking to Join Units," *Daily Mail* (UK), December 15, 2018, https://www.dailymail.co.uk/news/article-6500361/Army-officers-told-refer-combat-soldiers-infanteers.html.

36. Nicole, "Don't Say Rifleman."

37. Harriet Agerholm, "Former British Army Commander Says Having Women in the Army Will 'Cost Lives on the Battlefield,'" *Independent* (UK), July 10, 2016, https://www.independent.co.uk/news/uk/home-news/women-soliders-front-line-infantry-british-army-commander-tim-collins-no-place-for-woman-a7129271.html.

38. "ADF's 'Politically-Correct Plan' to Open Combat Roles to Women Branded a Complete Failure," 24 Australia, May 30, 2018, http://www.24australia.xyz/lifestyle/adfs-politically-correct-plan-to-open-combat-roles-to-women-branded-a-complete-failure/71875-news.

39. Rita Panahi, "Gender Quotas Make a Joke of Army's Female Fitness Test," *Herald Sun* (Australia), August 30, 2017, https://www.dailymail.co.uk/news/article-4779178/Australian-Army-turning-away-male-recruits-female.html.

40. Panahi, "Gender Quotas Make a Joke."

Chapter 7: Social Justice Warfare

1. Seth Robson, "Soldiers Don Fake Belly, Breasts, to Better Understand Pregnant Troops' Exercise Concerns," *Stars and Stripes*, February 26, 2012, https://www.stripes.com/news/army/soldiers-don-fake-belly-breasts-to-better-understand-pregnant-troops-exercise-concerns-1.168786.

2. Robson, "Soldiers Don Fake Belly."

3. Douglas Ernst, "Army ROTC Program Allegedly Pressured Cadets to Walk in High Heels for ASU Event," *Washington Times*, April 21, 2015, https://www.washingtontimes.com/news/2015/apr/21/army-rotc-program-allegedly-pushed-men-wear-high-h/.

4. Ernst, "Army ROTC Program Allegedly Pressured Cadets."

5. To borrow the title of Stephanie Gutmann's famous book, *The Kindler, Gentler Military* (Scribner, 2000).

6. SSG Patricia McMurphy, USA, "High Heels Event Elevates Awareness for Sexual Violence," Army.Mil, April 16, 2014, https://www.army.mil/article/124146/High_heels_event_elevates_awareness_for_sexual_violence/.

7. A linear analysis of the subjects of Army directives of time can be conducted by visiting the Army Publishing Directorate's website, which organizes Army directives by date. The list is available at http://www.apd.army.mil/ProductMaps/PubForm/ArmyDir.aspx.

8. Barbara C. Berryman, U.S. Army Garrison, Fort Lee, Equal Employment Opportunity (EEO) Office News Bulletin, February 2013, http://www.lee.army.mil/eeo/documents/nl0213.pdf.

9. David Rabb, "Understanding the Power of Micro-Inequities," *Fort Riley EEO Quarterly*, Summer 2017, http://www.riley.army.mil/Portals/0/Docs/Units/Garrison/EEO/Summer2017EEONews.pdf?ver=2017-06-01-101406-223.

10. Capt. Maranda Brown, USAF, 187th Fighter Wing In Formation, "Unmasking Microaggression in the Workplace," February 2012, https://www.187fw.ang.af.mil/Portals/1/documents/AFD-140220-013.pdf?ver=2016-12-27-123931-430.

11. Secretary of the Army, "Breastfeeding and Lactation Support Policy," Army Directive 2015-37, September 20, 2015, https://www.army.mil/e2/c/downloads/412349.pdf.
12. Andre Butler, "Breastfeeding and Lactation Support to Implement Phase 2," Army.Mil, January 17, 2017, https://www.army.mil/article/180777/breastfeeding_and_lactation_support_to_implement_phase_2.
13. Butler, "Breastfeeding and Lactation Support."
14. Interview with author.
15. Todd Starnes, "US Army Defines Christian Ministry as 'Domestic Hate Group,' Fox News, October 14, 2013, updated May 8, 2015, https://www.foxnews.com/opinion/us-army-defines-christian-ministry-as-ldomestic-hate-group.
16. Cheryl K. Chumley, "Fort Hood Soldiers Say Army Warned Them Off Tea Party, Christian Groups," *Washington Times*, October 24, 2013, https://www.washingtontimes.com/news/2013/oct/24/fort-hood-army-warned-them-tea-party-christians/.
17. Todd Starnes, "Military Labels Evangelicals, Catholics as 'Religious Extremism,'" Town Hall, April 5, 2013, https://townhall.com/columnists/toddstarnes/2013/04/05/military-labels-evangelicals-catholics-as-religious-extremism-n1559433.
18. Todd Starnes, "Exclusive: Army Halts Training Program That Labeled Christians as Extremists," Fox News, October 24, 2013, updated May 8, 2015, https://www.foxnews.com/opinion/exclusive-army-halts-training-program-that-labeled-christians-as-extremists.
19. Starnes, "Military Labels Evangelicals, Catholics, as 'Religious Extremism.'"
20. Starnes, "Exclusive: Army Halts Training Program."
21. Todd Starnes, "Pentagon Training Manual: White Males Have Unfair Advantages," Fox News, October 31, 2013, updated September 30, 2015, https://www.foxnews.com/opinion/pentagon-training-manual-white-males-have-unfair-advantages.
22. Todd Starnes, "Pentagon Training Manual."
23. Ibid.
24. Ibid.
25. "SPLC Chief Resigns to Give Turmoil-Hit Civil Rights Group 'Best Chance to Heal,'" *The Guardian*, March 23, 2019, https://www.theguardian.com/us-news/2019/mar/23/southern-poverty-law-center-richard-cohen.

26. Marc A. Thiessen, "The Southern Poverty Law Center Has Lost All Credibility," *Washington Post*, June 22, 2018, https://www.washingtonpost.com/opinions/the-southern-poverty-law-center-has-lost-all-credibility/2018/06/21/22ab7d60-756d-11e8-9780-b1dd6a09b549_story.html?utm_term=.6680e0af01bd.

27. Mark Hemingway, "The Media's Double Standard," *The Weekly Standard*, August 19, 2013, https://www.weeklystandard.com/mark-hemingway/the-medias-double-standard.

28. A 2013 Marine Corps lesson plan for a session training unit Equal Opportunity representatives, titled "Extremism and Extremist Organizations: Instructors Guide, Lesson Number 13," https://www.imef.marines.mil/Portals/68/Docs/IMEF/EOA/uLesson%20 13-IG%20Extremism%20and%20Extremists.doc.

29. Penny Starr, "DoD to Continue Using Liberal Southern Poverty Law Center as Training Resource," CNS News, February 24, 2014, https://www.cnsnews.com/news/article/penny-starr/dod-continue-using-liberal-southern-poverty-law-center-training-resource.

30. Jonah Bennett, "Exclusive: DoD Drops SPLC From Extremism Training Materials," The Daily Caller, October 2, 2017, https://dailycaller.com/2017/10/02/exclusive-dod-drops-splc-from-extremism-training-materials/.

31. David French, "Implicit Bias Gets an Explicit Debunking," *National Review*, January 10, 2017, https://www.nationalreview.com/2017/01/implicit-bias-debunked-study-disputes-effects-unconscious-prejudice/.

32. Former FBI director James Comey, for example, decried the "widespread existence of unconscious bias" and its connection to community policing in a 2015 speech at Georgetown University, likening the problem to the *Avenue Q* Broadway song "Everyone's a Little Bit Racist." During a town hall in the aftermath of the Dallas police shooting in which a gunman associated with the Black Lives Matter movement assassinated four Dallas police officers, President Obama discussed the role that implicit bias plays in police confrontations with African American males and how it contributes to animosity between the African American community and law enforcement. Hillary Clinton likewise blamed implicit bias for police shootings during the 2016 presidential campaign and doubled down on the claim when asked about it during her first debate with Donald Trump. Before leaving office, President Obama issued an executive order mandating implicit bias training in a wide range of federal agencies whose missions ranged from national security to conserving natural resources.

33. Tom Bartlett, "Can We Really Measure Implicit Bias? Maybe Not," *Chronicle of Higher Education*, January 5, 2017, https://www. chronicle.com/article/Can-We-Really-Measure-Implicit/238807

34. Bartlett, "Can We Really Measure Implicit Bias? Maybe Not."

35. President Barack Obama, Presidential Memorandum, *Promoting Diversity and Inclusion in the National Security Workforce*, October 5, 2016, https://obamawhitehouse.archives.gov/the-press-office/2016/10/05/presidential-memorandum-promoting-diversity-and-inclusion-national.

36. Chaplain Alliance for Religious Liberty, *Letter to Hon. Robert M. Speer, Acting Secretary of the Army*, February 24, 2017, http://chaplainalliance.org/site/wp-content/uploads/2017/03/SEC-Army-Letter-Feb-2017.pdf.

37. Alex Horton, "Chaplain Group: Army's Diversity Directive an 'Assault' on Religious Beliefs," *Stars and Stripes*, March 29, 2017, https://www.stripes.com/chaplain-group-army-s-diversity-directive-an-assault-on-religious-beliefs-1.461128.

38. Horton, "Chaplain Group: Army's Diversity Directive an 'Assault.'"

39. WITW Staff, "Marines to Undergo Sensitivity Training in Preparation for Female Integration," WomenintheWorld.com, March 25, 2016, https://womenintheworld.com/2016/03/25/marines-to-undergo-sensitivity-training-in-preparation-for-female-integration/.

40. Hope Hodge Seck, "All Marines to Get 'Unconscious Bias' Training as Women Join Infantry," Military.com, March 18, 2016, http://www.military.com/daily-news/2016/03/18/all-marines-unconscious-bias-training-women-join-infantry.html.

41. Department of the Navy, EEOO Program Status Report FY 2015, available at http://www.secnav.navy.mil/donhr/Site/EEO/Documents/DON%20FY15%20MD-715%20Report.pdf.

42. Stephen Losey, "Air Force Aims to Improve Diversity of Pilots, Other Key Positions," *Air Force Times*, September 30, 2016, https://www.airforcetimes.com/news/your-air-force/2016/09/30/air-force-aims-to-improve-diversity-of-pilots-other-key-positions/.

43. Air Force Fact Sheet: 2016 Diversity & Inclusion Initiatives, AF.Mil, http://www.af.mil/Portals/1/documents/diversity/Attach2_2016%20Diversity%20and%20Inclusion%20Initatives%20Fact%20Sheet.pdf?ver=2016-09-30-111307-623.

44. U.S. Air Force, The Judge Advocate General's School Lesson Plan Senior Officer Legal Orientation: Military Justice 101 Course Code/

Lesson No.: SLO 209, January 2017, https://dacipad.whs.mil/images/ Public/07-RFIs/Set_4/AF_RFI4_Q1_2_AF_SOLO_Lesson_Plans. pdf.

45. Secretary of the Air Force Deborah Lee James, Memorandum for All Commanders, Subject: 2016 Diversity & Inclusion (D & I) Initiatives, September 30, 2016, https://www.usafa.af.mil/Portals/21/documents/ Leadership/Culture,%20Climate%20and%20Diversity/Diversity_ Inclusion_2016.pdf?ver=2016-11-28-170619-897.

46. Air Force Global Diversity Division, *United States Air Force Diversity Strategic Roadmap*, March 12, 2013, https://www.af.mil/ Portals/1/documents/diversity/diversity-strategic-roadmap.pdf.

47. Air Force Global Diversity Division, *United States Air Force Diversity Strategic Roadmap*.

48. Ibid., 9.

49. Ibid., 11.

50. Ibid., 10.

51. Lt. J.G. Alexis Davis, "Eclipse 2017: Who You Are When No One is Looking," *Coast Guard All Hands Blog*, May 2, 2017, http://allhands.coastguard.dodlive.mil/2017/05/02/ eclipse-2017-who-you-are-when-no-one-is-looking/.

52. Brendan McGarry, "Senators Blast Pentagon Nominee Over Proposed Personnel Changes," Military.com, https://www.military. com/daily-news/2016/02/25/senators-blast-pentagon-nominee-over- proposed-personnel-changes.html.

53. SecAF Deborah Lee James, Memorandum for All Commanders, 2016 Diversity & Inclusion (D&I) Initiatives, September 30, 2016, https:// www.usafa.af.mil/Portals/21/documents/Leadership/Culture,%20 Climate%20and%20Diversity/Diversity_Inclusion_2016. pdf?ver=2016-11-28-170619-897..

54. U.S. Air Force Fact Sheet: 2016 Diversity & Inclusion initiatives, https://www.af.mil/Portals/1/documents/diversity/Attach2_2016%20 Diversity%20and%20Inclusion%20Initatives%20Fact%20Sheet. pdf?ver=2016-09-30-111307-623.

55. Ibid., 55.

56. SecAF Deborah Lee James, Memorandum for All Airmen, 2016 Diversity & Inclusion Initiatives, September 30, 2016, https:// www.af.mil/Portals/1/documents/diversity/Tri-Sig%202016%20 Diversity%20and%20Inclusion%20Initiatives%20-%2030%20 Sep%2016.pdf?ver=2016-09-30-111308-717.

57. Stephen Losey, "Air Force Secretary's Diversity Plan Will Mean Quotas, Critics Say," *Air Force Times*, March 9, 2015, https://www. airforcetimes.com/education-transition/jobs/2015/03/09/air-force-secretary-s-diversity-plan-will-mean-quotas-critics-say/; Center for New American Security Forum, "Women and leadership in National Security," Video at 22:30 mark, March 19, 2015, https://www. youtube.com/watch?v=XKybLMY_LHs.

58. Navy Office of Information, "Department of Navy Releases New Diversity and Inclusion Roadmap," Nav.Mil, January 27, 2017, https://www.navy.mil/submit/display.asp?story_id=98608.

59. Office of the Assistant Secretary of the Navy, Diversity and Inclusion Roadmap, Department of the Navy, January 2017, https://navyleader. org/CMC/docs/culture/Diversity.pdf.

60. Military Leadership Diversity Commission, *From Representation to Inclusion: Diversity Leadership for the 21st Century Military*, FINAL REPORT, March 15, 2011, https://diversity.defense.gov/ Portals/51/Documents/Special%20Feature/MLDC_Final_Report. pdf.

61. Department of Defense, Quadrennial Roles and Mission Review Report, January 2009, https://dod.defense.gov/Portals/1/features/ defenseReviews/QDR/QRMFinalReport_v26Jan.pdf, 6–7.

62. Eric Fanning (@SecArmy22), Twitter, July 15, 2016, 6:56 p.m., https://twitter.com/SecArmy22/status/754132459042680833 (emphasis added).

63. C. Todd Lopez, "Fanning, Equality, Inclusivity Are Not Experiments, but American Values," Army.mil, December 9, 2016, https://www. army.mil/article/179389/fanning_equality_inclusivity_are_not_ experiments_but_american_values.

64. Army Field Manual 7.22 5-15.

65. See, e.g., Jeremy Bender, "The Hazing Epidemic That's Holding Back Russia's Military," *Business Insider*, May 29, 2014, https://www. businessinsider.com/hazing-is-holding-back-russias-military-2014-5

66. Air Force Instruction 36-2902, 14.

67. Interview with author.

68. Army Regulation 600-20, Paragraph 4-19.

69. Brooke Singman, "New California Law Allows Jail Time for Using Wrong Gender Pronouns, Sponsor Denies That Would Happen," Fox News, October 9, 2017, https://www.foxnews.com/politics/new-california-law-allows-jail-time-for-using-wrong-gender-pronoun-sponsor-denies-that-would-happen.

Chapter 8: Climate Warriors

1. Timothy Cama, "Obama Equates Threats From Climate Change, ISIS," *The Hill*, Dec. 1, 2015, http://thehill.com/policy/energy-environment/261665-obama-equates-climate-change-islamic-state.

2. Missy Ryan, Adam Goldman, Abby Phillip, & Mark Berman, "Officials: San Bernardino Shooters Pledged Allegiance to the Islamic State," The Chicago Tribune, Dec. 8, 2015, https://www.chicagotribune.com/nation-world/ct-san-bernardino-shooting-20151208-story.html.

3. Jeffrey Goldberg, "The Obama Doctrine," *The Atlantic*, April 2016, https://www.theatlantic.com/magazine/archive/2016/04/the-obama-doctrine/471525/#9.

4. Michael Grunwald, "Ben Rhodes and the Tough Sell of Obama's Foreign Policy," Politico EU, May 11, 2016, ttps://www.politico.com/magazine/story/2016/05/ben-rhodes-nytimes-tough-sell-of-obamas-foreign-policy-213883.

5. Susan A. Resetar and Neil Berg, "An Initial Look at DoD's Activities Toward Climate Change Resiliency," Rand Project Air Force, February 2016, https://www.rand.org/content/dam/rand/pubs/working_papers/WR1100/WR1140/RAND_WR1140.pdf.

6. Team Warren, "Our Military Can Help Lead the Fight in Combating Climate Change," Medium.com, May 15, 2019, https://medium.com/@teamwarren/our-military-can-help-lead-the-fight-in-combating-climate-change-2955003555a3.

7. Joshua Zaffos, "U.S. Military Forges Ahead with Plans to Combat Climate Change," The Scientific American, April 2, 2012, https://www.scientificamerican.com/article/us-military-forges-ahead-with-plans-to-combat-climate-change/ (emphasis added).

8. Dave DeWitt, "Marines on Front Line of Battle Against Climate Change in North Carolina," WBUR.org, July 16, 2015, http://www.wbur.org/hereandnow/2015/07/16/camp-lejeune-climate-change.

9. US Army War College, Key Strategic Issues List, 2011–12, https://ssi.armywarcollege.edu/pdffiles/2011ksil.pdf.

10. Renee Cho, Earth Institute, Columbia University, What the U.S. Military is Doing About Climate Change, September 20, 2017, https://blogs.ei.columbia.edu/2017/09/20/what-the-u-s-military-is-doing-about-climate-change/.

11. Eric Wolff, "Energy: 'Green' Barracks Usher in Camp Pendleton's Future," *San Diego Tribune*, May 24, 2010, http://www.sandiegouniontribune.com/

sdut-energy-green-barracks-usher-in-camp-pendletons-2010may24-story.html.

12. Statement of Senator James Inhofe, Obama Sec. Mabus' Green Fleet Not Just R&D After All, July 27, 2012, https://www.inhofe.senate.gov/newsroom/inhofe-informant/obama-sec-mabus-green-fleet-not-just-r-and-d-after-all.

13. John C. Stennis Strike Group Public Affairs, "The Great Green Fleet Explained," Navy.Mil, June 27, 2016, https://www.navy.mil/submit/display.asp?story_id=95398.

14. Interview with author.

15. Interview with author.

16. Ray Mabus, @SECNAV, Twitter, June 11, 2010, 1:29 p.m., https://twitter.com/SECNAV/status/15947612728.

17. Naval Station Norfolk Public Affairs, Groundbreaking "Green" Roof Project Begins at NS Norfolk, June 9, 2010, http://www.navy.mil/submit/display.asp?story_id=53951.

18. Naval Station Norfolk Public Affairs, Groundbreaking "Green" Roof Project Begins at NS Norfolk, June 9, 2010, http://www.navy.mil/submit/display.asp?story_id=53951.

19. Ray Mabus, @SECNAV75, Twitter, Jun. 4, 2017, https://twitter.com/SECNAV75/status/871430405043363841.

20. Ray Mabus, @SECNAV75, Twitter, Apr. 4, 2017, https://twitter.com/SECNAV75/status/849353824510910465.

21. Thomas Oppel, Twitter, @tpoppel, February 7, 2016, 8:26 PM ET, https://twitter.com/tpoppel/status/696550637409017856. Thomas Oppel, Twitter, @tpoppel, August 8, 2017, https://twitter.com/tpoppel/status/895079221588090880 ; Thomas Oppel, Twitter, @tpoppel, August 8, 2017, 6:44 PM ET, available at https://twitter.com/tpoppel/status/895098341318643712

22. Mabus Group, Biography of Tom Hicks, (last accessed December 22, 2018,) available at https://mabusgroup.com/tom-hicks.

23. U.S. Navy, Twitter, @USNavy, September 20, 2011, https://twitter.com/USNavy/status/116171026399887360.

24. Office of the Under Secretary of Defense, Operation and Maintenace Overview, Fiscal Year 2017, Budget Estimates, https://comptroller.defense.gov/Portals/45/Documents/defbudget/fy2017/fy2017_OM_Overview.pdf.

25. Kelli Neiman, "Recycling Center Points Polk Towards Net Zero Waste 2020," Fort Polk Guardian, Nov. 29, 2012, https://www.army.mil/article/92108/Recycling_center_points_Polk_toward_Net_Zero_Waste_2020.

26. Annie Snider, "Pentagon Places Big Bet on Vehicle-to-Grid Technology," E&E News, February 5, 2013, https://www.eenews. net/stories/1059975837.

27. Susan Kraemer, "Successful F-22 Flight on 50% Camelina Biofuel as Military Obeys Executive Order to Reduce GHGs," Clean Technica, March 19, 2011, https://cleantechnica.com/2011/03/19/ military-f-22-50-percent-camelina/.

28. Eric Wolff, Energy: 'Green' Barracks Usher in Camp Pendleton's Future, *San Diego Tribune*, May 24, 2010, http://www. sandiegouniontribune.com/sdut-energy-green-barracks-usher-in-camp-pendletons-2010may24-story.html.

29. Wolff, "Energy: 'Green' Barracks Usher in Camp Pendleton's Future."

30. Ibid.

31. Susan Rice, Remarks by National Security Advisor Susan Rice on the 2015 National Security Strategy, Feb. 6, 2015, https:// obamawhitehouse.archives.gov/the-press-office/2015/02/06/.remarks-national-security-advisor-susan-rice-2015-national-security-stra.

32. Barack Obama, "Remarks by the President at the United States Coast Guard Academy Commencement," The White House, May 20, 2015, https://obamawhitehouse.archives.gov/the-press-office/2015/05/20/remarks-president-united-states-coast-guard-academy-commencement.

33. Office of the Under Secretary of Defense for Acquisition, Technology, and Logistics, DoD Directive 4715.21 "Climate Change Adaptation and Resilience," January 14, 2016, https://dod.defense.gov/Portals/1/ Documents/pubs/471521p.pdf.

34. National Intelligence Council, "Implications for U.S. National Security of Anticipated Climate Change," September 21, 2016, https://www.dni.gov/files/documents/Newsroom/Reports%20and% 20Pubs/Implications_for_US_National_Security_of_Anticipated_ Climate_Change.pdf.

35. Amir Abdallah, "ISIS Slices Nine Youths With Chainsaw in Mosul," Iraqi News, August 31, 2016, https://www.iraqinews.com/iraq-war/ isis-slices-nine-youth-with-chinsaw-mosul/.

36. James Hasson, "3 Wasteful Military Programs Congress Should Cut to Free Up Money for Upgrades," The Federalist, May 2, 2017, http://thefederalist.com/2017/05/02/3-wasteful-military-programs-congress-cut-free-money-upgrades/.

37. Hasson, "3 Wasteful Military Programs."

38. Department of Defense Inspector General Report No. DODIG-2016-130, The Navy Needs More Comprehensive Guidance for Evaluating and Supporting Cost-Effectiveness of Large-Scale Renewable Energy Projects, Aug. 25, 2016, http://www.dodig.mil/pubs/documents/DODIG-2016-130.pdf.

39. Annie Snider, "Pentagon Places Big Bet on Vehicle-Grid-Technology," E&E News, Feb. 5, 2013, https://www.eenews.net/stories/1059975837.

40. United States Government Accountability Office, Report to Congressional Committees, DOD Renewable Energy Projects, September 2016, https://tacpdf.com/gao-16-487-accessible-version-dod-renewable-energy.html (38).

41. United States Government Accountability Office, Report to Congressional Committees, DOD Renewable Energy Projects, September 2016, https://tacpdf.com/gao-16-487-accessible-version-dod-renewable-energy.html at 17.

42. Jeff Schogol, "Marines Pull Aircraft From 'Boneyard,' Get Used Navy Jets Amid Aviation Crisis," Marine Corps Times, June 23, 2016, https://www.marinecorpstimes.com/news/your-marine-corps/2016/06/23/marines-pull-aircraft-from-boneyard-get-used-navy-jets-amid-aviation-crisis/.

43. Government Accountability Office (GAO) Report 16-487, "DoD Renewable Energy Projects: Improved Guidance Needed for Analyzing and Documenting Costs and Benefits," September 2016, https://www.gao.gov/assets/680/679620.pdf.

44. Department of Defense, Strategic Sustainability Performance Plan FY 2016, Sep. 7, 2016, http://www.denix.osd.mil/sustainability/dod-sspp/unassigned/department-of-defense-strategic-sustainability-performance-plan-fy-2016/.

45. Ellen Knickmeyer, "Navy to Require Climate Change Reporting from Vendors," Associated Press, April 12, 2016, https://www.militarytimes.com/news/your-military/2016/04/12/navy-to-require-climate-change-reporting-from-vendors/.

46. Knickmeyer, "Navy to Require Climate Change Reporting."

Chapter 9: How to Fix It

1. Thomas E. Ricks, "We're Getting Out of the Marines Because We Wanted to Be Part of an Elite Force," Foreign Policy, January 4, 2013, https://foreignpolicy.com/2013/01/04/were-getting-out-of-the-marines-because-we-wanted-to-be-part-of-an-elite-force-2/.

2. Ricks, "We're Getting Out of the Marines."
3. Thomas Spoehr & Bridget Handy, Heritage Foundation Report, *The Looming National Crisis: Young Americans Unable to Serve in the Military*, February 13, 2018, https://www.heritage.org/defense/report/the-looming-national-security-crisis-young-americans-unable-serve-the-military.
4. YouGov, Patriotism Study, Prepared on Behalf of the Foundation for Liberty and American Greatness (FLAG), November 2018, https://www.flagusa.org/wp-content/uploads/2018/11/FLAG-Patriotism-Report-11.13.2018.pdf.
5. Lila MacLellan, "Millennials Experiencing Work-Disrupting Anxiety at Twice the US Average Rate," QZ.com, December 5, 2018, https://qz.com/work/1483697/millennials-experience-work-disrupting-anxiety-at-twice-the-us-average-rate/.
6. Niall McCarthy, "The Top 15 Countries for Military Expenditure in 2016 [Infographic]," *Forbes*, April 24, 2017, https://www.forbes.com/sites/niallmccarthy/2017/04/24/the-top-15-countries-for-military-expenditure-in-2016-infographic/#61e4e50e43f3.
7. Heritage Index of Military Strength, "An Assessment of U.S. Military Power: U.S. Army," The Heritage Foundation, October 4, 2018, https://www.heritage.org/military-strength/assessment-us-military-power/us-army.
8. Colin Clark, "Senator Slams Pentagon for Spending on Beef Jerky, Twitter Slang—and More," Breaking Defense, November 15, 2012, https://breakingdefense.com/2012/11senator-slams-pentagon-for-spending-on-beef-jerky-microbrewerie/.
9. Mandy Smithberger, "Pentagon's 2017 Budget is Mardi Gras for Contractors," Project on Government Oversight, February 10, 2016, https://www.pogo.org/analysis/2016/02/pentagons-2017-budget-is-mardi-gras-for-defense-contractors/.
10. Tara Copp, "Slew of Military Helicopter Deaths Raises Question of Whether Budget Cuts Endanger Troops," Stars and Stripes, January 25, 2016, https://www.stripes.com/news/slew-of-military-helicopter-deaths-raises-question-of-whether-budget-cuts-endanger-troops-1.390587#.WNqF1hLyvsG.
11. Drew Griffin & Kathleen Johnston, "Army to Congress: Thanks, But No Tanks," CNN Security Clearance Blogs, October 9, 2012, http://security.blogs.cnn.com/2012/10/09/army-to-congress-thanks-but-no-tanks/.

12. David Francis, "Congress Packs Defense Bills With Millions in Pork," The Fiscal Times, May 1, 2013, http://www.thefiscaltimes.com/ Articles/2013 /05/01/Congress-Packs-Defense-Bills-with-Millions-in-Pork.
13. Interview with author.
14. Journal of the Military Service Institution of the United States, Vol. 58, 361-62 (1916).
15. Associated Press, "Mike Pence Tells West Point Grads They Should Expect to See Combat," CBS News, May 25, 2019, https://www. cbsnews.com/news/mike-pence-west-point-graduation-vice-president-says-they-should-expect-to-see-combat-today-2019-05-25/.
16. Corey Dickstein, "Pentagon: Mattis' 'Deploy or Get Out' Policy is Working," Stars and Stripes, October 2, 2018, https://www.stripes.com/news/ pentagon-mattis-deploy-or-get-out-policy-is-working-1.550122.
17. Anthony Capaccio, "Army's Five-Year Plan Outlines a $25 Billion Shift in Weaponry," Bloomberg, Mar. 12, 2019, https://www. bloomberg.com/news/articles/2019-03-12/army-s-five-year-plan-outlines-a-25-billion-shift-in-weaponry
18. Anthony Capaccio, "Army's Five-Year Plan Outlines a $25 Billion Shift in Weaponry," Bloomberg, Mar. 12, 2019, https://www. bloomberg.com/news/articles/2019-03-12/ army-s-five-year-plan-outlines-a-25-billion-shift-in-weaponry.
19. Ibid.
20. Jen Judson, "Army's 'Night Court' Finds $25 Billion to Reinvest in Modernization Priorities," Defense News, October 8, 2018, https:// www.defensenews.com/digital-show-dailies/ausa/2018/10/08/ armys-night-court-finds-25-billion-to-reinvest-in-modernization-priorities.
21. Interview with author.
22. Interview with author.
23. Ibid.
24. Meghann Myers, "Almost 800 Women Are Serving in Previously-Closed Army Combat Jobs. This is How They're Faring," Army Times, October 9, 2018, https://www.armytimes.com/news/your-army/2018/10/09/almost-800-women-are-serving-in-previously-closed-army-combat-jobs-this-is-how-theyre-faring/.
25. Todd South, "A Look Inside the Work, Future of Jim Mattis' Task Force Focused on Infantry, Close Combat," MilitaryTimes.com,

January 29, 2019, https://www.militarytimes.com/news/your-army/2019/01/29/a-look-inside-the-work-future-of-jim-mattis-task-force-focused-on-infantry-close-combat/.

26. Bill Federer, "Douglas MacArthur 'It Is Fatal to Enter a War without the Will to Win It,'" News Maven, American Minute, February 9, 2019, https://newsmaven.io/americanminute/american-history/douglas-macarthur-it-is-fatal-to-enter-a-war-without-the-will-to-win-it-Mu8nrpWbpkCQgxBVC48ydA/.

INDEX